Great War Modernisms and
The New Age Magazine

Historicizing Modernism

Series Editor

Matthew Feldman, Lecturer in Twentieth Century History, University of Northampton, UK and Erik Tonning, Lecturer, University of Oxford, UK

Editorial Board

Professor Chris Ackerley, Department of English, University of Otago, New Zealand; Professor Ron Bush, St. John's College, University of Oxford, UK; Professor Roger Griffin, Department of History, Oxford Brookes University, UK; Professor Steven Matthews, Department of English, Oxford Brookes University, UK; Shane Weller, Department of Comparative Literature, The University of Kent, UK.

Historicizing Modernism challenges traditional literary interpretations by taking an empirical approach to modernist writing: a direct response to new documentary sources made available over the last decade.

Informed by archival research, and working beyond the usual European/American avant-garde 1900–45 parameters the series reassesses established images of modernist writers by developing fresh views of intellectual backgrounds and working methods.

Series Titles:

The Autobiographies of Mina Loy
   Sandeep Parmar
Katherine Mansfield and Literary Modernism
   Edited by Janet Wilson, Gerri Kimber and Susan Reid
Reframing Yeats
   Charles Ivan Armstrong
Samuel Beckett and Arnold Geulincx
   David Tucker
Samuel Beckett and Science
   Chris Ackerley
Samuel Beckett's 'More Pricks Than Kicks'
   John Pilling
Samuel Beckett's German Diaries 1936–1937
   Mark Nixon

Great War Modernisms and *The New Age* Magazine

Paul Jackson

continuum

Continuum International Publishing Group
A Bloomsbury company

50 Bedford Square	80 Maiden Lane
London	New York
WC1B 3DP	NY 10038

www.continuumbooks.com

British Library Cataloguing-in-Publication Data
A catalogue record for this book is available from the British Library.

ISBN: HB: 978-1-4411-8008-7

Library of Congress Cataloging-in-Publication Data
Jackson, Paul, 1978-
Great War modernisms and The new age magazine : historicizing modernism / Paul Jackson.
p. cm.
Includes bibliographical references and index.
ISBN 978-1-4411-8008-7 – ISBN 978-1-4411-2781-5   1. Little magazines–Great
Britain–History–20th century.   2. Periodicals–Publishing–Great Britain–History–
20th century.   3. Literature publishing–Great Britain–History–20th century.
4. New age (London, England)   5. World War, 1914-1918–Literature and the war.
6. Press and politics–Great Britain–History–20th century.   7. Modernism (Literature)–
Great Britain.   8. Great Britain–Intellectual life–History–20th century.   I. Title.

PN5124.L62J33 2012
050.941–dc23

2012011899

Typeset by Newgen Imaging Systems Pvt Ltd, Chennai, India

*Thank you to everyone who
has helped me get this far. You all know
who you are.*

Contents

Introduction

This book examines a selection of radical, political, cultural and artistic attitudes that developed in Britain before and during the First World War. Specifically, it is concerned with the view that a new epoch would, or at least should, emerge as a consequence the conflict. Though far from a comprehensive survey of British intellectuals of the era, it identifies a variegated set of views that coalesced around the argument that the war needed to be understood as more than merely a destructive event, and that the conflict should not be followed by a simple reversion to the prewar culture. Moreover, a central, underlying concern of the book is to explore the trope of war as creative destruction, war as renewal and even redemption. This proved to be an ideal found in a wide range of radical political, philosophical and artistic discourses.

Case-study analysis will begin by focusing attention on one of the key spaces for developing such forward-looking views in this period, the radical journal *The New Age*. By 1914, this Little Magazine had emerged as a rich venue for major and more minor intellectuals to debate the latest developments in political and cultural thought, and so here a range of voices became concerned with developing a wide variety of radical viewpoints in a highly eclectic intellectual forum. Within its pages, one finds not merely radical commentary on the war as a potentially revolutionary event, especially from its leading contributor and editor, A. R. Orage, but also a far wider discourse styling the war as a social-political watershed, at least if it was to have any real meaning. As a consequence, examination of *The New Age* takes the study's analysis into the fields of radical politics and economics, especially guild socialism and later Social Credit, alongside various interpretations of the war through a Nietzschean lens.

Aside from the eclectic writers publishing essays in *The New Age*, the closing chapters of the book develop in more depth two further case studies, each setting out idiosyncratic visions of the radically new. First it will examine Wyndham Lewis, an aesthetic modernist for whom the war period directly followed his major breakthrough as one of the most radical and original British-based artists and writers, elaborating on themes he culled from continental figures such as Nietzsche, Bergson and Picasso. Finally, in a very different manner, the example of H. G. Wells offers an opportunity to examine a clearly radical, yet far more mainstream, cultural figure who also read the war through the lens of creative destruction. Though his writing style remained firmly realistic, and aesthetically speaking we do not need to think of Wells as a modernist, in terms of developing a reading of the war as an event of major social and cultural change, he was highly significant. For example, one finds that Wells's wartime record included the promotion of a new religion for the postwar world. So although he was developing his ideas in a far more populist, and popular, register, many of the underlying tropes of war as renewal that were also being expressed by the clearly avant-garde figures such as Lewis, and those within *The New Age* circle, can also be found in Wells's wartime oeuvre. For Wells too, the war could be given meaning if it was somehow redemptive, and was framed hopefully, as an event ushering in a new more technocratic society – a peculiar kind of 'populist modernism'.

Via exploration of these diverse case studies, the book will also develop some of the current trends in 'modernist studies'. It will be interested in how cultures of modernism became manifest in various Little Magazines, as has been examined recently by Robert Scholes and Clifford Wulfman among others.[1] Moreover, it will develop the interpretive frameworks that have emerged from a new wave of historians who have examined cultures of modernism, such as Dan Stone and Roger Griffin, as well as Modris Eksteins's important, earlier exploration of the topic. Such cultural historians of modernism are consciously moving away from simply analysing the canonical writers commonly associated with Anglo-America literary modernism. Although such figures are clearly a central part of one of the 'stories' of modernism, the conceptual framework developed by this study examines the premise that cultures of modernism are essentially heterogeneous phenomena, and can be expressed through a wide range of opinions that attempt to radically confront a modernity that has been deemed decadent and out of control. In order to set out this methodological paradigm within the context of an analysis of the First World War, the opening chapter proposes a heuristic model for reconceptualizing cultures of modernism as fundamental clashes with a decadent modernity.

This modelling draws on the expansive framework for analysing modernisms recently proposed by Roger Griffin. Griffin's work on modernism and fascism has been notable for arguing that fascism has a clearly cultural dimension, and that key cultural modernists, such as Julius Evola and Ezra Pound, were not merely temporary sympathisers with a fascist politics, but rather were creative figures who saw revolutionary art, and revolutionary ideology, as part of the same continuum.[2] In other words, such fascists could be seen as political modernists. Moving beyond this focus on fascist modernism, Dan Stone is notable for developing Griffin's approach with regard to English-based case studies, especially in his monograph *Breeding Superman*. Importantly, this study develops Griffin's concept of cultural rebirth (palingenesis) as a central component to examining cultures of English modernism. As such, Stone emphasizes that British intellectuals were intimately connected with the ideas that made up Europe's numerous modernisms, and were often doing so in response to modernity's radically new tensions and possibilities. Stone also rightly stresses that, in order for intellectual history to reflect the polysemic nature of the cultural debates of the early twentieth century, cultural historians need to reject approaches that restrict an understanding of modernism to a reductive core canon of central protagonists. He too argues that, as a result of the omission of the role of 'contingent' figures in cultural-historical analysis, often modernism 'is still defined by two or three key players, while others, no less influential in facilitating and driving forwards "its" reception (as if modernism was a unitary beast), are overlooked'.[3] So Stone is also important as he epitomizes the call for historical analyses of modernism to develop an understanding of concurrent trends within the thinking of a period, and sets out the need to explore the variegated nature of debates and thought.

It is also important to underscore here the problematic issue of scope with this historical approach. Griffin and others propose a much broader conception of what modernism is than many literary and cultural critics currently would be comfortable with. Indeed, this reflects many debates among cultural historians, who have been trying to find more expansive ways to develop a working understanding of modernism, not merely as a critical term, or broad label for a set of writers, but as an underlying attitude within intellectual production developed as a consequence of the radically destabilizing conditions of modernity. Robert Wohl has offered further discussion on the ways in which modernism is being re-developed by cultural historians, who have traditionally been wary of the term.[4] Examination of the connection between the First World War and a diverse set of modernisms has been most fruitfully explored by Modris Eksteins, especially his monograph *Rites of Spring*.

In this landmark study of European culture before, during and after the war, Eksteins is sensitive in particular to the dialectic between modernizing impulses and the mood of *anomie* and rootlessness that modernity introduced, and which the war further radicalized. As a conceptual metaphor for the era, Eksteins presents Igor Stravinsky's modernist ballet of 1912, *Le sacre du printemps*, as a cultural event epitomizing this tension between modernity as *ennui* and decay, and for the crisis to be solved through an act of ritualistic renewal. Moreover, Eksteins's work shows how numerous figures within the European intelligentsia invested sustained intellectual effort into mythologizing the war itself as an event whereby 'the new' could be ushered in ritualistically, via a massive, apocalyptic experience. Indeed, many in Europe could even be duped into giving their own lives in order to be a part of this elemental sense of renewal. So Eksteins highlights that war was something that could be encoded via this spirit of revolt, often framed within a distinctly primordial register. This was a mood endemic in the political and artistic discourses generated by the continent's intellectuals before the war, and was even sustained by some who experienced the fighting first hand. Consequently, between 1914 and 1918 soldiers and intellectuals across Europe could become sensitive to liminal 'feelings of alienation, marginality, and, at the same time, novelty', alongside a belief that the

> world was in the throws of destruction, which now seemed irreversible, but was also in the process of renewal, which seemed inevitable. In this latter process lay a reality of astounding implications: the soldier represented a creative force. As an agent of both destruction and regeneration, of death and rebirth, the soldier inclined to see himself as a 'frontier' personality, as a paladin of change and new life.[5]

Regarding the study of modernisms, what is instructive in Eksteins's analysis is employment of the term itself as signifier for much more than an artistic trend. 'The notion of *modernism*', he stresses, can be used to subsume both avant-garde and the intellectual impulses behind the quest for liberation and the act of rebellion. Very few critics have ventured to extend these notions of the avant-garde and modernism to the social and political as well as artistic agents of revolt, and to the act of rebellion in general, in order to identify a broad wave of sentiment and endeavour.[6]

This formulation is important to stress when discussing Eksteins's work, and his expansive use of the term will be developed further here. However, one striking feature of Eksteins's analysis is its tendency to place Germany at the forefront of modernism, thus understood. Indeed, the book concludes by presenting Nazism's visionary, yet hyper-destructive politics as the epitome of the political form of modernist impulses to overthrow the old and introduce the new at all costs. Yet with a focus on Germany as the exemplar of the rebellious, modernist nation, one consequence of his analysis is to overstate the conservative nature of wartime Britain. Indeed, this relative conservatism in British cultural production is taken for granted by Eksteins, not regarded as worthy of closer scrutiny.[7] Though not wanting to overturn fully Eksteins's reading here, this position does need to be finessed more carefully: one of the aims of this study.

To develop further Griffin and Eksteins's core point that modernism was not merely an artistic trend, but rather was a radical tenor that can also be found in political and cultural, as well as artistic discourses, the opening chapter of this study will offer a cultural historical model for modernism that sets out some parameters for exploring these wider aspects of modernist cultures of rebellion. This discussion will offer a conceptual framework that sets out the underlying approach to modernism that animates subsequent chapters: that modernist impulses were a creation of the conditions of modernity in the late nineteenth and early twentieth centuries, drew on a wide range of intellectual roots, and were essentially framed as radical confrontations with a modernity somehow gone wrong, thus needing to be radically confronted through revolutionary forms of artistic representation, philosophical ideals or even programmatic political action. With this conceptual framework established, the subsequent case-study chapters will then allow us to examine a variety of such modernisms in wartime Britain, operating in political and philosophical as well as artistic registers. Indeed, pushing at the outer boundaries of such a viewpoint, Wells's new religion developed during the war can even be seen as a part of this new wave of rebellion against an 'actually existing' modernity, combined with the quest for elemental renewal.

1

Great War Modernisms

In his influential study *Modernisms: A Literary Guide*, Peter Nichols begins the chapter 'Modernity and the Men of 1914', by stressing that 'the problematic of time occupies a central place' in the understanding of modernist culture, and that 'a discontinuous cultural memory [is] conceived as the very matrix of the new modernism'. Exploring the nexus between, on the one hand, cultural production and political positions styled as fundamental breaks with a previous epoch, and, on the other, the radicalizing effects of war, will be central to the paradigm for interpreting modernism this opening chapter will unpack. Nichols's survey stresses that classic statements of high modernism, especially T. S. Eliot's 'The Waste Land' and Ezra Pound's 'Hugh Selwyn Mauberley' epitomized this trend in poetry, and exemplified the view that the war ushered in a fragmented relationship with what went before.[1] While cultural historians such as Jay Winter would suggest this was not necessarily the overall situation for wider society,[2] certainly there is broad consensus on the point that, among intellectuals, many sought to give the war artistic significance through this lens of radical rupture and renewal. We will return to this point towards the end of this chapter. Moreover, for Nichols the aesthetics of the various cultures of modernism he analyses do not form neat cultural interventions, and so 'modernisms' should not be viewed as a simple, coherent body of ideas with a singular common and definable set of intellectual roots. Rather, modernisms are presented as diverse creations, radical positions that bleed into political as well as cultural concerns, and inherently connected to the rise of the modern world.

So building on this core theme of modernity as a profoundly disruptive force, inspiring the radically new visions found in a variety of modernisms, this opening chapter sets out what is understood, ultimately, as a heuristically useful approach to mapping a wide range of such cultures, with a particular focus on the era of the First World War. Following the lead set by cultural historians of the Great War, especially Modris Eksteins discussed in the Introduction, this paradigm seeks to extend an understanding of modernisms beyond aesthetics, and into other realms of creative thought, including politics and philosophy. As such, cultures of modernism can be understood as complex discursive fields, sets of radical ideas combining a wide range of intellectual reference points, yet gravitating around revolutionary confrontations with modernity. In the case studies to follow in later chapters, we will see such modernist tendencies being developed in a highly variegated set of discourses, ranging from the contributors to *The New Age*, to the Nietzschean-influenced attitudes of Wyndham Lewis, and even in the radically innovative political visions, if not the aesthetic style, of

H. G. Wells's more 'populist modernism'. Yet, for any study that seeks to contextualize aspects of modernism in such an expansive manner, examining the wide range of ideas 'facilitating and driving' the modernist movement, it is vital to have a richer and fuller understanding of what is signified by the term, and especially how the phenomenon can be seen to relate to modernity.

In order to develop a coherent methodological framework for studying modernisms in this manner, what follows in this chapter will set out some important parameters in order to propose an ideal typical definition for studying modernisms. As will become clear, this approach also builds on more recent interventions by Peter Osborne, whose approach to modernism will be discussed later. In sum, what will be dubbed 'modernisms' by this ideal type will be cultural ideas marked by readings of modernity as decadent, and which seek a revolutionary confrontation with such decadence, either by somehow developing sustained diagnosis of modernity's crisis to give the condition a novel form of expression, or even by developing a new sense of the transcendent as a resolution to the perceived chaos of modernity.[3]

Sociology of modernity

To develop such a conceptual schema for interpreting modernism, it is useful to revisit some of the core sociological theories of modernity, in order to bring into sharp focus how its chaotic, destabilizing qualities have affected social and cultural thought. From this excursus, it will be possible to then explore further why modernism should be regarded as radical responses to chaotic, decadent interpretations of modernity in the later nineteenth and early twentieth centuries. So, to begin unpacking the paradigm of modernism as revolutionary confrontations with modernity perceived as decadence, it is helpful to begin with analysts of modernity itself. Clearly, all modernisms are responses to modernity, though far from all responses to modernity are modernist ones. Yet when we want to understand what modernity is, we find that there is no single authority to offer a singular, clear definition of modernity itself. Rather like modernism, the term is nebulous and slippery.

Picking a path through such a conceptual minefield, one fruitful place to kick off a discussion is the work of Anthony Giddens. In his *Modernity and Self-Identity*, Giddens essentially presents the main 'consequence of modernity' as one evoking sense-making crises for its inhabitants. How a modernizing world is to be understood is increasingly not a 'given', as in previous eras, but becomes inherently more problematic, at least for figures such as intellectuals who become highly self-reflexive about their wider positions and roles in the world. Indeed, we can see such existential reflections afflicting a wide range of figures across Europe in the late nineteenth and early twentieth centuries. Giddens also develops the theme of modernity as a destabilizing force by identifying what he calls modernity's 'disembedding mechanisms', innovations that appear to hollow out preconceived notions of the most elemental categories for interpreting one's place in the world, time and space. In sum, for Giddens the 'experience' of modernity is inherently one of a destabilizing social world, and offers no clear solutions to such problems.

The core assertion is that modernity erodes established norms and relatively stable, more localized cosmologies, and replaces these with more expansive, and potentially more alienating cultural paradigms.[4]

Moreover, although 'modernity' is a term riddled with variegated subtleties of meaning depending on different sociological methodologies, it is usually deployed to somehow signify the mentality of living during times of widespread social, material and psychological change: 'modernization'. Linkages between modernity, and the ways in which technological advancement and scientific enquiry create new realms of experience are well-worked themes of the literature on modernity. For example, in his often-cited exploration of this theme, *All That Is Solid Melts into Air*, Marshall Berman emphasizes that modernity is not primarily an objective historical category defined by clear temporal boundaries, but rather a much more nebulous, experiential phenomenon. He reminds us that '[t]o be modern is to find ourselves in an environment that promises us adventure, power, joy, growth, transformation of ourselves and of the world – and, at the same time, that threatens to destroy everything we have, everything we know, everything we are'. Berman also notes that modernity creates new unities of people that cut across established geographical, ethnic, national and even religious boundaries, adding that, as a consequence, modernity 'is a paradoxical unity, a unity of disunity: it pours us all into a maelstrom of perpetual disintegration and renewal, of struggle and contradiction, of ambiguity and anguish'.[5] Such understandings of radical change characterizing modernity may either be experienced positively, as an underlying sense of elemental change for the better, or negatively as fears of an established order falling away. For modernist intellectuals in particular, such variegated readings of the condition of modernity, both positive and negative, are equally important to emphasize, as they can create profound reasons for visionary optimism or deep-seated despair.

Touching on some similar themes, Zygmunt Bauman characterizes modernity as an ambivalent state generated by conflicting interpretations of the modernizing world regarded as either in a state of order, or in a state of chaos. Like Berman, in *Modernity and Ambivalence*, Bauman suggests the condition is something essentially experienced, and offers the following abstract description of the mentality of modernity: 'We can think of modernity as of a time when order – of the world, of the human habitat, of the human self, and of the connection between all three – is reflected upon; a matter of thought, of concern, of a practice that is aware of itself, conscious of being a conscious practice and wary of the void it would leave if it were to halt or merely relent'.[6] Bauman too stresses that modernity is a 'reflexive' state, and suggests that it is a condition where this heightened self-awareness has the potential to undermine myriad established cultural patterns and value systems. So, although modernity can corrode received knowledge, the probing, questioning, self-reflexive consciousness encouraged by modernity does not necessarily offer new certainties to fill existential voids thus created. Especially significant here is Bauman's sensitivity to ways in which modernity can inculcate a sense of the falling away of the most profound ontological truths, senses of order often created by religious paradigms, but also by established senses of political sovereignty, ostensible laws of physics, established aesthetic forms and so on. As with Giddens's 'disembedding mechanisms', we see emphasized the notion that deep-seated, established norms – an underlying sense of nomic order – becomes subject to erosion, especially through scientific enquiry and political changes that have characterized post-Enlightenment European history.

Modernity and 'crisis consciousness' in the early twentieth century

Summarizing these debates is revealing in the abstract, but such general observations need to be grounded in something more historically specific too. So putting some flesh on these hypothetical bones relevant to the time period under analysis here, we can see that the period immediately before the First World War was a time when these 'crises of modernity' were becoming acutely important to European intellectuals. Indeed, the work of cultural historian Stephen Kern emphasizes how the impact of modernity's forces of destabilization affected European society around the turn of the twentieth century. In his *The Culture of Time and Space, 1880–1918*, Kern draws out not only how a subjectively experienced increase in the 'pace' of life occurred at this time, but also elaborates on the theme that a new, increasingly globalized sense of temporality reflected the emergent, interconnected nature of a rapidly modernizing world. This development was epitomized by, but far from limited to, the creation of World Standard Time. Indeed, more generally, by the late nineteenth century advances in telecommunications and mass media had led to a substantial increase in the awareness of concurrent, global actions, creating increased realization of synchronicity between a sense of 'here and now' and related events in distant parts of the earth. Time and space were becoming increasingly destabilized and reordered via modernity. Simultaneously, Christianity's traditional cosmology, not to mention Newtonian conceptions of time and space, were being overturned, thus further fuelling revolutionary attitudes towards science and technology, as well as the arts.[7] Thus, from Kern's analysis, we can see clear examples of time and space losing their traditional significances, as the thrust of modernity's technological innovation created new, more globally connected and instantaneous forms of human interaction at the turn of the twentieth century.

Furthermore, the impact of modernity on a host of intellectual trends is central to understanding the structural forces at play within the cultures of modernism that responded to the emergent, modernizing world. Reflecting on such cultural dynamics within European modernity, in *The Condition of Postmodernity* David Harvey offers an important discussion on the materialization of the modernist movement in Europe, and its relationships with modernity and modernization. Harvey's reading also develops modernism broadly, and dates the movement as one emerging roughly from around the mid-nineteenth century onwards, becoming especially active from the 1890s. He highlights how influential figures such as Marx and later Nietzsche epitomized a rejection of the idea of steady progress that had been developed during the Enlightenment era, and embraced the destructive yet creative powers of modernity. Such modernist reactions were based on a chaotic interpretation of modernity's impact on the present, and invariably found unique ways to replace the visions of modernization of society as steady progress with ideas emphasizing change through the lens of rupture and renewal, creative destruction. For Harvey, the latter formed the underlying tenor of modernist thought, as it responded to modernity. By identifying what fundamental ideas and values needed to be destroyed, according to Harvey the modernists rejected piecemeal change and could also point towards what could be created in the wake of modernity's power to realize large-scale destruction.[8] Confronting the decadence of the old led to revolutionary visions for the future being developed in a number of registers, not merely aesthetics. Broadening out the term to include not merely artists but many radical thinkers, intellectuals as diverse as William Morris, Joseph Schumpeter and even Albert Speer become included in Harvey's embracing analysis of key 'modernist' figures. Indeed, such a viewpoint is entirely compatible with Eksteins's own identification of the Nazi state as the modernist project *par excellence*. Consequently, Harvey's sensitivity to the creative destructive paradox of what he identified as a widespread and highly variegated modernist movement (perhaps more accurately understood as a highly heterogeneous, 'rhyzomic tangle' of international movements) underscores how such cultural production and thought sought to capture modernity's dynamic of elemental change. It did so in a radicalized form, and, characteristically, attempted to articulate an identification of what needed to be destroyed and what needed to be renewed.

In sum, from such perspectives it seems to matter less whether modernist ideas were expressed in purely aesthetic terms, and more whether they were highly radical and innovative reactions to modernity. In other words, modernisms can be seen as revolutionary confrontations with a perception of modernity characterizing the present as falling into decadence. A sense of rupture and renewal underpinning modernist thinking can be seen as central to modernism, thus understood. Such rejections of liberal-bourgeois notions of steady progress, coupled with the radical embrace of creative destruction by modernists, suggest that modernisms can be viewed as phenomena predicated on a highly radicalized relationship between unstable temporalities and processes of change. So from the sociology on modernity we can already see that modernism and time are intertwined, but how can we best view this relationship for cultural historical inquiry?

Many commentators have identified that visions of rupture and renewal were central elements within the emerging intellectual climate at the end of the nineteenth century and into the early twentieth century: the era of modernism. We can develop a range of heuristic concepts to help capture such a dynamic. Like Kern, another cultural historian acutely sensitive to the revolutions in European thinking from the 1890s to the 1930s is H. Stuart Hughes. In his *Consciousness and Society*, Hughes coins the term 'the revolt against positivism' to describe a revolution in social thought and cultural production developing at this time. As with both Kern and Harvey's work, though not primarily concerned with modernist aesthetics, Hughes's thesis elaborates on the theme that influential pockets of European culture at this time were gripped by new ideas that regarded older, rationalist and mechanistic schema for conceptualizing the human condition as essentially out-dated. The label 'positivism' became a pejorative catchall term for the variety of intellectual and philosophical trends that were associated with the 'rational', ostensibly empirically based models that had characterized much of nineteenth-century social thought. 'Positivism' thus broadly and negatively defined extended beyond its normal boundaries as a signifier for scientific and logical thought in philosophy, and, as Hughes put it, came to signify a general tendency to 'discuss human behaviour in terms of analogies drawn from natural science'.[9] In the place of 'positivism' came many new variants of social awareness, articulated in numerous ways by influential academic and artistic figures. Indeed, Hughes notes the importance of artistic figures such as Proust in mapping the dynamics of the modernizing world, or George Sorel promoting the idea of revolution through the rediscovery of a mythology of violent action. Such ideas were not a total break with earlier traditions, and could draw on the styles and approaches of 'positivism', but also took far more seriously non-empirically measurable factors, such as emotion and intuition, within their methodologies.

To give some other examples of Hughes's key targets, Bergson's concept of the *élan vital* synthesized a poetic interpretation of the natural world with the scientific conceptions of evolution, proposing a higher realm that could be discovered where a non-rational sense of intuition would be restored, and the human experience could retreat from the shallow materialism proposed by modern science. Indeed, the Bergson cult was highly influential on the thinking of many intellectuals, including a key case study here, Wyndham Lewis. Meanwhile, Nietzsche, another key influence for many, notoriously called for a 'transvaluation of all values' in order to go beyond traditional notions of 'good' and 'evil'. The intellectual registers here are very different, but can be seen to fit together as part of the wider revolt against positivism. The turn of the twentieth century was also the era of renewed interest in Schopenhauer, the development of Durkheim's concept of *anomie* to diagnose the malaise of modernity, the theosophy movement, and the proliferation of scientistic, racial ideologies, as presented by intellectuals such as Houston Stuart Chamberlain and Joseph Arthur Comte de Gobineau that blurred identity politics and pseudo-science. These were the ideas that would later germinate into full-blown eugenics, and attempts to breed a superior form of human being – a sort of human alchemy. Again, such positions offer us far from a coherent body of thought, but did present numerous intellectual pathways to radically confront pre-existing bourgeois notions of acceptability, and consider radically new possibilities for the future. Such heady combinations synthesizing rhetorical tropes of positivism and a rejection of positivist certainties were epitomized by the thinking of Sigmund Freud. His new 'science' of human emotions, developed in an assiduously rational and scientific style of discourse – the presentation of research papers, the testing of hypotheses through case studies and so forth – again typified the radical shifts in thinking around social issues of this period. So Hughes identifies that at the turn of the twentieth century a variety of new schools of social thinking postulated sophisticated and persuasive arguments to demonstrate why humans were far more irrational beings than was previously believed, bundles of ideas and memories detached from a discernable higher purpose. Such ideas radically subverted the hegemonic Enlightenment concept of man as a sensible and rational being, again a troubling development for Europe's thinking classes.

So, Hughes's sensitivity to a revolt against the more rational approaches to thought reveals that such ideas were central to radical intellectual debates that developed from the late nineteenth century. In particular, their development could allow such figures to believe they were entering a new era, one where the progressive themes, and the certainties proposed by the Enlightenment, were no longer applicable. A more problematic, 'disembedded' understanding of time could become central to such intellectual developments. Indeed, as we have seen, the period immediately before the war was an era that Peter Nichols identifies as one of discontinuities for those we consider to be modernists. Here, Frank Kermode's renowned lecture series *The Sense of an Ending* offers further discussion on the issue of intellectuals of this period developing a new, less rational, more poetically apocalyptic, appreciations of the modern world's temporarily. He argues that a central characteristic of modernist intellectual output was the identification of a 'sense of an ending' in the cultural construction of time, revealed by apocalyptic representations of the present, alongside a growing embrace of cyclic conceptions of history.[10] Modernists, according to Kermode, often became figures highly critical of rational constructions of clock time, of human temporality characterized by an endlessly flowing state of rectilinear *chronos*, divided into equal units of seconds, minutes, hours, etc. Rather, such rational approaches could become counterpointed with ideas of time that sought to reconnect with a perceived 'higher' appreciation of temporality and existence. This new mood was expressed through elisions between senses of crisis and the notion of opportunity for creativity and fundamental renewal, a heightened sense of temporality, rich in possibility, that Kermode dubbed *kairos*. This desire for reconnection with a subjective and poetic 'higher' time, specifically conceived as an escape from the relentless 'tick' 'tock'[11] of a deadening clock time, could be found in myriad versions in modernist cultural production. Kermode's approach stresses an important theme: at the heart of modernist thought lay highly individualized attempts to reconnect with a 'higher' time, thereby offering, albeit temporary, senses of escape from the *chronos* of modernity's relentless narrative of progress, often caricatured as one of the core ideals of the conventional bourgeoisie.

The interpretation of cultures of modernism as a nexus of ideas charged with secularized, apocalyptic temporalities have been developed in the literature more recently too. Again epitomizing an approach that stresses the sensitivity of modernists to the impact of modernity's change in both material reality and also in the realm of perceptions, we can turn to issues developed by Ronald Schleifer in his *Modernism and Time*. Schleifer's thesis combines appreciation of both a material and an intellectual crises affecting European history during the 1890 to 1930 period. Regarding the material crisis, he highlights the massive increase in consumable production, the growing commodification of society, that he dates as really taking off from around the 1880s and the 'second industrial revolution'. In its wake, more complex associations between capitalist and worker began to develop, especially concerning the proletariat's growing disposable income. Meanwhile, regarding the intellectual crisis, echoing Hughes's pioneering work, Schleifer emphasizes how the professionalization of many new academic disciplines, such as sociology and psychology, alongside the rapid growth in the sciences, began to produce an abundance of new research, both technical and philosophical. This process not only created a wealth of new data, but also an exponential growth in the variety of systems of thought with which this information could be interpreted.

As a result of the growth in the production of both material goods and human knowledge, Schleifer argues that a new 'logic of abundance' developed in Europe from the last decades of the nineteenth century. In terms of predominant moods, he emphasizes that this 'second industrial revolution' was marked by increased senses of 'panic, free-floating anxiety, bewilderment, and a pervading sense of crisis'.[12] Further, attempting to illustrate the essence of this shift, Schleifer describes the transformation to the 'logic of abundance' in terms of a radical change in the construction of time for some. Echoing Kermode's analysis, the cultural models for understanding temporality that were developed from within this milieu tended to be not only far more openly subjective and intuitive, but the phenomenological properties of time, especially in intellectual circles, were marked by what he calls a 'ubiquitous and often unnoticed transformation' where 'the experience of time' was 'conditioned [by] the apocalyptic sense of the "new" – a "crisis consciousness"'.[13] Schleifer's thesis further argues that this 'crisis consciousness' became a hallmark of modernist thought, and was capable of both diagnosing the decadence of modernity, as well as potentially revealing radically new possibilities.

What we can take from Hughes, Kermode and Schleifer, then, is the theme that the period between the 1890s and the 1930s was particularly marked by a crisis in temporality for many European thinkers. Further, this was central to the intellectual climate in which modernisms flourished. The work of Peter Osborne also helps to clarify the approach being sketched out here. Osborne highlights in his books *The Politics of Time* and *Philosophy in Cultural Theory* that a nuanced appreciation of the impact of the radical new sense of temporality created by modernity is integral to understanding modernism. Osborne too opens out 'modernism' to include a much larger range of social thinkers than many literary critics would do. Again, examining changing patterns in the perception of time is central to Osborne's analysis. He makes the point that modernist thinkers were able to conceive of human temporality as an endless, potentially open-ended unfolding of the historical process, detached from a limiting religious cosmology, and so they became empowered to develop and play out innumerable schema that rationalized fundamental breaks with the past while also, potentially, promoting the creation of discrete new epochs. This characteristic, offering a clear focus on the relationship between radical approaches to temporality and social and cultural change, is again very useful for defining modernist forms of thought. Thus, Osborne presents modernisms as radically future orientated – what he calls *futural* – approaches to resolving the perceived crisis condition of modernity. The radically future-orientated, *futural* quality of modernism thus understood draws

> attention to the modernistic temporality of reaction *per se*, once the destruction of traditional forms of social authority have gone beyond a certain point. This point appears to have been reached in the leading European societies around the time of the First World War; hence the tremendous upsurge of revolutionary ideologies of both the 'reactionary' and the 'revolutionary' types.[14]

This is an important identification of the role of the First World War, a point that will be developed further later in this chapter. More generally though, by extending modernism into wider fields in this manner, including the political realm, for Osborne the political racialism of the far left and the far right can also be seen as offering *futural* forms of modernism.

Indeed, by the interwar period, both revolutionary Marxists and equally revolutionary fascists were trying to enforce new, utopian visions, and a new time, onto European societies, in order to transcend an allegedly decadent era of liberal democracy. For Osborne any such radically *futural* response to modernity is a definitional feature of modernism, even if, as with fascism, this *futural* vision is evoked through sustained recourse to themes also found represented in previous eras. Therefore, following this approach, modernisms can be seen to embrace politics and philosophy as well as aesthetic developments. To give some specific examples of such non-aesthetic, ideological modernisms, according to Osborne's analysis the *Communist Manifesto* can be regarded as a clear, early instance of a political modernist text.[15] Meanwhile, the 'conservative revolution' of fascism offers another instance of political modernism, though operating under a very different, utopian vision of the future to the Marxist idea of revolutionary change through the fundamental reorganization of class structures. Finally, social and cultural thought linked to the revolutionary left and right can be regarded as modernist too. Thus radical, early-twentieth-century philosophers such as Walter Benjamin and Martin Heidegger offer examples of philosophical modernism.

Modernism's palingenetic core

As a consequence of such expansive interpretations of modernism, when analysing the cultural production marked by sensitivity to modernity, it is useful to interpret how intellectuals perceived processes of historical change. Did they regard their contemporary history through a lens of evolution and innovation leading to progress for humanity, or rather did they view the transition from past to present to future through the lens of chaos and crisis, ultimately leading to renewal and regeneration? The former viewpoint is most clearly epitomized by the 'myth of progress', the teleological belief that the pursuit of rationalism and liberal ideals will inevitably lead humanity into brighter and better worlds. Though such 'progress' is clearly a response to modernity, it is not a modernist one. The latter viewpoint, however, is typified by intellectuals who regarded modernity as at least in part a regression, of the present being defined by pervasive sense of decline and fall, of the order of things coming under attack, of norms being subverted to the point of absurdity, in short, of the present manifesting, in some form, decadence.

It is this latter perspective, eschewing mainstream visions of progress and instead developing esoteric, radical new thinking to critique the modern world, where cultures of modernism can be found. In taking the latter approach, highly critical, modernist readings of modernity might dwell and even revel in the notion of a world in decline, perhaps using this as a muse for thought and art, even leading to some new innovation in creative expression. Meanwhile, they might opt for drawing on such a sensitivity to the alleged chaos of modernity to develop a programmatic solution to its crisis, and begin to construct a utopian vision of an 'alternate modernity' in order to escape the decadence perceived to define modernity.

In order to signify the distinct, radical nature of modernist forms of regeneration, conceived as an escape from a decadent world, and especially to signify its concern with developing renewed connections with a sense of the transcendent, we can use the term 'palingenesis'.[16] Already familiar to scholars of generic fascism,[17] this comparative term, broadly speaking synonymous with 'rebirth', can be used to signify a profound reconnection with a 'higher', mythic sense of existence, though in a modernized format. To take some of the wide-ranging examples of modernist palingenesis, we can see this radically regenerative thrust in: Baudelaire's desire to distil higher artistic expression from the dingy realities of the seamier side of mid-nineteenth-century Paris; Kandinsky's notion of the spiritual in art; Nietzsche's redemptive *Übermensch* figure; Marx's prophecy of class revolution wiping away bourgeois decadence; and even Hitler's attempt to inaugurate a new '1000-Year Reich' by launching an anthropological revolution in Europe after 1939. All these are instances of what this study will call palingenesis. Although each of these cases represents a highly idiosyncratic phenomenon, they are each also variegated articulations of a sense of escape from an 'actually-existing modernity' (to use Griffin's term) which is regarded as having fallen into profound decadence and decline, and promise at least a glimpse of something new, thereby seeking to resolve in a radical fashion allegedly chaotic aspects of modernity. It is this palingenetic thrust which marks out the modernists from their contemporary artists and thinkers.

An ideal type of modernist thought

From this somewhat lengthy excursus into the academic debates on modernity, modernism and cultural change, we are now in a position to develop what is presented as a 'heuristically useful', ideal typical characterization of modernism:

> Modernism represents a highly heterogeneous variety of revolutionary cultural and political trends that have emerged primarily as a result of the rapid modernisation of European material and mental realities from the French and industrial revolutions, and especially from around the 1890s. These diverse, often contrary and intellectually incompatible, instances of cultural production possessed the common denominator of interpreting the modern world as a realm characterised by an underlying sense of decline and fall. Modernists radically confronted this problem either by lamenting the loss of an earlier world or by finding ways to reinvest a seemingly decaying realm with renewed senses of transcendence. Counterpointing highly variegated, radical readings of modernity as the fragmentation of society, of civilisation in decline, of reality becoming decentred, and even morally bankrupt, in short, of modernity as decadence, modernists sought ways of developing thought and cultural production that offered solutions to the ideas promoted by forms of 'mainstream', hegemonic thought. Often, these ideas were based on senses of escape from the culturally dominant perceptions of social reality as progressive, which tended to be identified with a decadent mindset by modernists. This process could be achieved either by revealing to fellow intellectual groups the extent of the decadence of modernity, by developing a new sense of spirituality, or even by

presenting an alternate modernity based on a new world and a new shared culture. The latter would not only embrace technological aspects of modernity, but would also seek to re-root these traits through the development of renewed senses of the transcendent and the mythic.

The aim of such revitalised senses of reality was to transform the chaotic, anomic qualities of modernity into a new sense of higher order. This specifically futural desire for forms of cultural rebirth was the palingenetic dynamic at the core of modernist thought and cultural production. Often, this thrust was articulated in a mood of what might be called visionary pessimism, namely that only by demonstrating that one is fully aware of the sense of despair generated by modernity's decadence can one achieve thought that authentically offered a renovated poetic sense of higher 'kairos' emerging from the anomic 'chronos' of modernity. Cultural palingenesis, or rebirth, might have been articulated in the form of a new 'organic' ideology offering a novel mode of politics for the modern state, a fresh aesthetic style capable of transforming modernity's ills into renewed creativity, or simply through cultural production that offered a sense of temporary shelter, a fleeting sense of the transcendent, as an escape from modernity's contrary nature, potentially expressed through admixtures of mystical, religious and / or philosophical registers.

Far from merely forming a literary or artistic category, then, in its full scope modernism could be articulated in a range of cultural fields. One can apply adjectives in order to offer rough distinctions between particular dimensions of cultural production through which a modernist tone is being articulated. For example: political modernism located a sense of decadence within hegemonic political ideologies and offered a vision for a new political order emerging from a revolutionary moment; religious modernism offered a new sense of the sacred, often fusing aspects of established religions with novel methods for expressing a religious temperament, one specifically tuned to imbuing modernity with a renewed spiritual quality; philosophical modernism sought to diagnose a sense of crisis within western thought and present radical new modes of thinking that emphasised modernity's rupture with traditional ideas; and finally aesthetic modernism sought to revolutionise artistic styles in literature, poetry, the visual arts, and so forth, offering cultural production expressing the fragmentation of reality, the breakdown of received values, the lack of autonomy, and the powerlessness of the self in a dynamic society.

In sum, from such an expansive ideal type definition, cultures of modernism can be understood and examined as a generic phenomenon, the term signifying radical cultural and intellectual confrontations with an allegedly decadent modernity. Modernists do not view modernity as progress and do not believe in trouble-free continuities between past, present and future. Rather, unlike more moderate engagements with modernity, radical modernists emphasize discontinuity between past, present and future, highlight the sense of a deep-seated crisis of modernity in the present, and can even be seen to programmatically develop radical means to resolving this crisis in the future.

Great War modernisms

As touched on above when discussing both Peter Nichols and Peter Osborne, we should regard the Great War a central event in the modernist era, and so analysing its impact on existing modernist tendencies is highly revealing of the phenomenon more generally. So before embarking on case-study analysis of modernists operating in this period, it will be helpful to get a sense of how the war was causing Europeans to rethink their conceptions of the world, and how the model set out above can be useful in developing analysis of the variegated discourses of modernism that it opens up to us.

Before examining some of the key point made in the existing secondary literature here, it is worth briefly visiting a telling example of how the war was viewed as creative destruction through a new intellectual register of the era: psychoanalysis. We can turn to an essay titled 'War and Individual Psychology', by the Welsh, Freudian psychiatrist Ernest Jones. In June 1915, he concluded that: 'War furnishes perhaps the most potent stimulus to human activity in all its aspects, good and bad, that has yet been discovered.' And continued: 'It reveals all the latent potentialities of man and carries humanity to the uttermost confines of the attainable, to the loftiest heights as well as the lowest depths. It brings man a little closer to the realities of existence, destroying shams and remoulding values . . . It can make life as a whole greater, richer, fuller, stronger, and sometimes nobler.' The thesis of this fascinating essay, published in *Sociological Review*, essentially argued that the First World War was allowing Europeans to reconnect with their primeval, animalistic urges. For many, Jones claimed, the war offered escape from a widespread neurosis pervading European society, a world where social conventions prevented people from sufficiently sublimating their primal desires in healthy pursuits, such as adventurous sports and especially sex. Only through combat could men find the sense of escape from their unhealthy states of repression, resulting in a temporary embrace of the animalistic desires of the unconscious in more or less their raw form. For Jones, it was an open question 'whether the psychological benefits that regularly recurring warfare brings to a nation are not greater than the total amount of harm done, terrific as this may be'.

When we apply the modernist framework set out above to Jones's reading of the social function of war we can see that the essay presented the Great War as an escape from a crisis-ridden world, and so participation in conflict could offer a profound form of regeneration for individuals and, by extension, possibly even entire cultures. Here, based on the emergent 'science' of human emotion, war was seen as the site for secular human transcendence, and the discussion suggested that warfare offered people the potential for elemental renewal. Meanwhile, Jones's article also proposed that the First World War was purging Europe of a state of neurosis, not only allowing many of its inhabitants a moment of profound psychic intensity, but also offering the hope that a new social reality could be established after a period of destruction, creating a new world in which a healthy mentality would be allowed to grow.[18]

This sort of positive attitude to the Great War, regarding war as regeneration, has been very well documented by many historians of the early twentieth century. For example, James Joll stresses how, across national and class divisions, in 1914 there was a common 'willingness to risk or accept war as a solution to a whole range of problems, political, social, international, to say nothing of war as apparently the only way of resisting a direct physical threat'. Further, for Joll, it was 'these attitudes that made war possible; and it is still in an investigation of the mentalities of the rulers of Europe and their subjects that the explanation of the causes of the war will ultimately lie'.[19] Other, general studies of this period highlight that many artists and thinkers across Europe not only saw the First World War as a deeply disturbing event but also believed that, from its melting pot, would come a new order, a new reality. Strikingly, Eric Hobsbawm claims 'the peoples of Europe, for however brief a moment, went lightheartedly to slaughter and to be slaughtered'. Indeed, they were 'surprised by the moment, but no longer the fact of war, to which Europe had been accustomed, like people who see a thunderstorm coming'. Continuing with this metaphor, Hobsbawm claims that the war was often perceived at the time as:

[A] release and a relief, especially by the young of the middle classes . . . Like a thunderstorm it broke the heavy closeness of expectation and cleared the air. It meant an end to the superficialities and frivolities of bourgeois society, the boring gradualism of nineteenth-century improvement, the tranquillity and peaceful order which was the liberal utopia for the twentieth century and which Nietzsche had prophetically denounced . . . [I]t meant the opening of the curtain on a great and exciting historical drama in which the audience found itself to be the actors. It meant decision.[20]

In the more specialist literature here, Robert Wohl has come to similar conclusions, highlighting that, by the end of the nineteenth century, European cultural production 'began to split into two related but mutually antagonistic camps. On the one hand, there was the official bourgeois culture; on the other hand, there was the culture of the trailblazing vanguard'. As a consequence, 'Middle-class intellectuals born during the last two decades of the nineteenth century reacted fiercely against the first and gave their allegiances to the second'.[21] This sense of generational revolt was important because, according to Wohl, when the 'war did break out over Europe, it was interpreted by intellectuals as an hour of redemption, a rite of purification, and a chance, perhaps the last, to escape from a sinking and declining civilization'.[22] This theme of war as redemption is highly significant, chiming with the previous identification of modernism's palingenetic drive towards transcendence to escape a modern world seemingly gone wrong. Much war fever among intellectuals can be seen as manifesting modernist tendencies, as it searched for a radically new world from the crisis of the war situation. Indeed, Wohl emphasizes that the generalized sense of a modernity as crisis among the intellectuals underpinned the myriad upbeat reactions to the war:

Upper- and middle class men born in the major European countries between 1880 and 1900 found themselves placed before a difficult set of tasks. They had to oversee the transition from an elitist to a mass and bureaucratic society, while at the same time resigning themselves to the relative shrinkage of the power both of their nation in particular and Europe in general. Upon reaching manhood, they were

required to fight a war for hegemony in Europe, a war whose multifaceted consequences would overshadow and render infinitely more difficult any action they
undertook. Witnesses of the breakup of the predominantly bourgeois world into
which they had been born, the most perceptive of them realized at an early age the
necessity of developing new forms of collective life.[23]

Extending further this important thesis – that war offered myriad myths of redemption
for cultural producers in the second decade of the twentieth century – Roland
Stromberg's study *Redemption by War* also develops a similar explanation for why
the war could be seen an ultimately positive development across Europe. Stromberg's
comprehensive, pan-European analysis highlights how the continent's intelligentsia
read the unfolding events as an escape from a modernizing, bureaucratized and
increasingly 'rational' world, and found in war a subjective sense of 're-enchantment',
for life to be somehow injected with a new sense of vitality and community. The 'old
rationale for war', claims Stromberg, 'whether as a necessity, as duty, or as justice, had
ceased to have much compelling power in the later nineteenth century'. In its place a
new vision of war developed that 'placed more stress on the motifs . . . [of] renewal,
adventure, apocalypse'.[24] Stromberg links these new imaginings of the nature of warfare
to the need to discover senses of authentic community among European intellectuals.
Therefore:

> A quest for identity and self-understanding marked the whole 1885–1914 Mod-
> ernist movement in the arts. We ought to be able to understand the magnitude of
> the psychic crisis that confronted human nature when it was first released from
> primeval group solidarity to face the anomic megalopolitan wilderness, the ter-
> rible freedom of total permissiveness. Then in 1914, as young intellectuals repeat-
> edly testified, the sense of community suddenly reappeared with the shock of war,
> and struck them with the force of a raw *reality* they could not resist. It is the most
> significant single motif. It was *felt* deeply, perhaps most strongly in Germany, but
> in fact everywhere.[25]

So once again we can see that across Europe the interpretation of the war through
the modernist lens of rupture, apocalypse and the promise of renewal was central to
its cultural dynamics. The '1914 spirit' was not only 'an antidote to anomie, which
had resulted from the sweep of powerful forces of the recent past – urban, capitalistic,
and technological forces tearing up primeval bonds and forcing people into a crisis of
social relationships', but also the 'primitive instinct to do battle against a common foe
was a remedy for this crisis'.[26]

Yet we should not see such positive readings that were developed at the outset
of war, and the desire for rupture to lead to renewal more generally, as necessarily
resolving itself in the new world that such a mythology promised. Rupture and change
were not only qualities that marked the outbreak of war, but as we have seen have
also been noted as standout qualities of more lasting its consequences. Regarding the
latter, one just has to recall the tenor of 'The Waste Land' or 'Hugh Selwyn Mauberly'
that Nichols highlights, not to mention the poetry of Sassoon, or the widespread fears

that Bolshevik revolution would engulf Europe as the war came to an end. In terms of cultural production, the end result of this yearning for escape in order to achieve nebulous forms of transcendence through war has been examined by the cultural historian Eric J. Leed, especially in his monograph *No Man's Land*. For Leed, the anthropological metaphor of the Great War as an event conceived by many as a *rites de passage* is central to understanding the relationship between the cultural climate in Western Europe in the eve of the war, and its embrace by so many intellectual figures. In terms of cultural backcloth, Leed presents the question of war as an event encoded in complex webs of renewal, and so he too highlights the importance of the general mood of optimism that greeted the conflict. Indeed, he asserts that this community of 1914 was 'a type that is peculiar to states of transition'.[27] Leed also emphasizes that a key trope among soldiers of all sides was the trend of talking of their prewar lives as 'dead' after reaching the trenches because the army initially offered escape from the 'structured society' of bourgeois life. Despite offering freedom from bourgeois conformity, the notion of modern war as the epitome of the chaos of modernity is also forcefully developed by Leed's analysis. As the war drew on, the myth that had initially suggested that 'civilian death' would lead to a new and more appealing life in the army had the effect of inducing a far more confused mentality in tens of thousands of soldiers. Once enlisted, many came to develop profound senses of estrangement from prewar society and civilian life, alongside deep ambivalence regarding their new soldierly identities. On the one hand, army life provided a realm where men were accepted and felt to be as one – a new brotherhood. Yet on the other hand, in the end it promised an ultimately thankless, anonymous and meaningless death and placed individuals in a realm that was indescribably atrocious and terrifying. Moreover, from our perspective, we can see how the trauma, and extended sense of living through a period of liminality, created by the war could lead to myriad diagnoses of decadence and yearnings for palingenesis among the cultural producers who, in various ways, experienced this horrific reality.

However, the most unsettling aspect of the conflagration for soldiers and others was the way war experiences tended to manifest 'incomplete' *rites de passage*. The purpose of such rituals of transition is ultimately to imbue individuals with new and positive senses of community, yet the experiences of First World War combat, and its wider cultural impact, tended to result in an extended sense of discontinuity, or liminality, of living between two worlds. For Many, the sense of disaggregation, of being ground down and awaiting a new identity was never credibly augmented by a sense of reaggregation and a new order during or after the war. Indeed, the lasting trauma of the war experience for many soldiers emanated from tensions surrounding an inescapable feeling of being 'outside' the norms of structured society when they returned to civilian existence. People had been prepared for an initiation into a new community as a result of their experiences in the trenches, not to mention the grand promises of the promoters of war, and others, yet were never credibly reborn into this reality, thereby rendering them profoundly 'homeless' and unable to achieve 'closure' regarding their experiences. 'No "rites of reaggregation"', Leed concludes, 'could efface the memory of utter defencelessness before authority and technology. No ceremonial conclusion to the war could restore the continuities it had ended, or recreate those "fictions" that had been left behind in the labyrinth of the trenches'.[28] So while wartime culture could promote the idea and need for cultural palingenesis, the reality was more often the generation of a lasting sense of liminality, and of the sense of being left between two worlds. This sense of war and postwar as continued liminal experience is also an important theme to identify in case-study analysis, and this anthropological lens will be developed further in the conclusion to this study, via the work of Victor Lewis and Anthony Wallace.

So to summarize, we have been able to identify in this opening discussion some of the central concerns for examining case studies in cultures of modernism during the First World War. Core questions include: How was modernity conceived as a form of decadence? How was the conflict seen as a liminal and potentially creative, 'palingenetic' event? And what responses were developed after the war, when hopes for renewal were not satisfied? This latter theme of the war promising rupture and renewal, being styled as the vehicle for realizing revolutionary change, yet ultimately offering few or no new solutions, can be seen in all the selected examples. Indeed, hope turning to exasperation can be clearly seen in the first of our case studies, A. R. Orage, who we turn to now. An early promoter of Nietzsche in England, editor of the modernist journal *The New Age*, and propagandist for the guild socialist revolution during the war itself, Orage exemplifies not the canonical modernist writer, but rather the modernist intellectual.

A. R. Orage and Modernist Publicism
in the Era of the First World War

The ideal type for interpreting modernisms outlined in the previous chapter developed a paradigm allowing for analysis of fundamental connections between cultural and political forms of modernist radicalism. To begin examining these concerns, one ideal location to ground a broad understanding of cultures of modernism in Britain in the era of the Great War is the radical journal *The New Age*, edited at this time by A. R. Orage. Indeed, by developing the themes set out in the expansive reconceptualization of cultures of modernism above – analysis that emphasizes that revolutionary visions for escaping a decadent-seeming modernity can be viewed as an essential component of modernist milieus – a new re-reading of Orage and *The New Age* becomes possible. With this interest in the blurring of political and cultural concerns among modernists, we must also begin by noting that Orage was also one of Britain's leading guild socialists. As we will see, within the core dynamics of this ideology, we can identify an idiosyncratic modernist call for a political and cultural revolution to transform a decadent modernity. Moreover, for guild socialists, Orage's *The New Age* was a central mouthpiece of their political movement, while Orage himself had become one of its central protagonist by the outbreak of the war. Despite this, often we find in secondary literature analysis the view that the guild socialists were not modernists, and so they are dismissed as reactionaries, merely obsessed with a mythic vision of the past. Though in part they looked to a mythologized past, our model of modernism stresses that such idealizations of previous eras were often developed in order to sketch out the vision of a radically alternate modernity, a new future that would offer a fundamental break from capitalism's decadent, modern existence.

As such, current analysis of Orage and *The New Age* misses the connection between the political modernism of the guild socialist project, and the wider cultures of modernism that were developed in the pages of *The New Age* magazine. This chapter, and the one that follows, will begin to piece together these highly politicized discursive fields of modernism, as developed by leading guild socialists, in the pages of *The New Age*. Chapter 4 will then widen an exploration of the cultures of modernism with *The New Age* and will examine some of the journal's wider modernist discourses found during the war period, to map the diversity of thought expressed in its pages at this time. So, to begin this survey of modernist cultures found in *The New Age*, it is only logical to start with the publication's central, animating figure, A. R. Orage, who combined an interest in Nietzsche with revolutionary, left leaning politics during the war.

Alfred Richard Orage

Originating from a lower-middle-class background, Orage began life as a provincial schoolmaster in Leeds. Interestingly, Samuel Hynes notes that Orage was essentially a classic example of a new type of cultural producer emerging at this time, the 'lower-middle-class provincial intellectual' who took his work seriously, was highly susceptible to intellectual conversions and regarded Victorian notions of science and liberalism as bankrupt.[1] In many ways a product of the late Victorian world, sensitivity to revolt against positivism soon came to the fore in his biography.

Already deeply interested in the philosophy of Plato, by the 1890s Orage had developed a fascination with new trends of mysticism and joined the Theosophical Society.[2] At this time, Orage described his entire outlook on life as spiritual rather than religious in nature. For him, spirituality promised growth and vitality, a connection with 'the new', whereas religion represented a more formalized, and therefore pedestrian, attitude towards the world. These sorts of distinction surrounding existential issues were typical of his self-presentation as a dynamic, expansive and creative thinker. Such spiritualism regularly combined with his left-leaning politics. He also signed up to the Fabian Society at this time, and helped found the Leeds Branch of the Independent Labour Party. His conversion to socialism was the result of hearing charismatic labour figures, such as Tom Mann and Tom Maguire in Leeds, and Orage himself was often described as a charismatic personality. He was an active intellectual from early on in life, for example writing a column in *Labour Leader* between 1895 and 1897. By this time he was also a regular speaker at theosophical meetings, and contributed articles to the *Theosophical Review*.

In 1903, he helped to create the Leeds Art Club, a society that sought to popularize Nietzsche in the Leeds area, developing a new coterie of forward-thinking intellectuals in the process.[3] Tom Steele has written the most expansive account of Orage's early intellectual development at this time, and provides much evidence to show how Orage and others connected to the Leeds Art Club not only developed highly radical critiques of modernity, but also were figures searching for new solutions to social and cultural life. Here, Orage gave many lectures outlining the need for radical changes in the thinking of modern cultural producers, including discussing the need for a new type of utopian politics to reformulate the modern age. In one striking talk, he developed a distinction between types of utopianism that were relevant to contemporary conditions: a defective variety called 'fanciful', and a desirable one called 'imaginative'. Only two thinkers fell into the latter category, Plato and H. G. Wells. Though he had critical comment on aspects of modern utopianism, he felt that Wells was among a few modern intellectuals who were, at the very least, introducing vibrant visions for the future into the modern consciousness.

But Wells was not Orage's primary guiding light. Epitomizing the modernist sensibility he developed before he moved to London to edit *The New Age*, we can see the influence of Nietzsche becoming central at this time. Indeed, Orage wrote three books on this key modernist philosopher. The first of these, *Friedrich Nietzsche: The Dionysian Spirit of the Age*, offered ground-breaking exposition of the *Birth of Tragedy* and *Beyond Good and Evil* for an Anglophone audience. The text not only discussed the idea of the superman, but more generally set out the modernist theme of Nietzsche's philosophy offering the key to mapping a 'moral regeneration of Europe'.[4] Stressing Nietzsche's concept of a dialectic between Dionysus symbolizing fundamental change and creativity, and Apollo symbolizing continuity and stability, Orage was convinced that the former had to triumph out over the latter if Europe was to undergo a much-needed transvaluation of all values. He also highlighted to a British audience how the moral revaluation that Nietzsche promoted sought the destruction of Christian morality, while also underscoring Nietzsche's assertion that entire cultures needed to be understood as being marked either by overarching ascent or decline. In sum, the trailblazing discussion offered a provocative discussion on how decadence was infecting early-twentieth-century Europe.[5] Moreover, the clearly palingenetic thrust of the message was developed too: from the decadent present came the need for a new redemptive figure. For Orage, this could emerge through probing new areas of human consciousness, and finding higher states of being.

Indeed, this search for a new type of human mentality, a response to the crisis of capitalist modernity, was extended much further in his subsequent book *Consciousness, Animal, Human and Superhuman*. This text was based on a series of lectures given to the Theosophical Lodges of Manchester and Leeds, and developed further the need for new supermen figures to emerge. The book's thesis proposed three stages of consciousness. The lowest grade, animal consciousness, was unreflective, and largely lacked self-awareness. Second was human consciousness, essentially a state of reflective self-awareness, and so was marked especially by the realization of one's own ability to think. However, the problem with human consciousness rested with its dual nature, torn between perceiving an 'exterior', material world and an 'inner', subjective one. The standard form of human consciousness was restrictive; it forced one to rely on the self-reflective intellect to interact with the world, a limiting burden according to the model. Indeed, for Orage human consciousness existed in a state of continual flux and, ultimately, confusion. Offering a potential solution, he proposed a higher, 'superhuman' form of consciousness that truly transcended the limited state of human consciousness. Here, the intellect was released of the burden and flux of conscious thinking and so, within this higher state of being, consciousness became 'winged' and intuitive. Superhuman consciousness was a state partially achieved by humans when in the presence of 'Religion, Art Love Nature, and Great Men', where one feels

> Lifted out of our duality into a sphere where for an instant we become one of Plato's spectators of time and existence. At such moment's time, space, and existence are indeed felt to be beneath us, outside of us. We are above ourselves, above our human mode of consciousness, freed and released, superconscious. Then the walls of egoity close around us, the ecstasy is past, and we are once more human.[6]

The book concluded with the claim that these glimpses of a 'higher', superhuman state of being needed to be developed into a coherent science, as they provided a way for humanity to transcend its current decadent predicament.[7] Elsewhere in the text, he talked of the pastoral role that the supermen would have. They would be 'Cultural Heroes', figures who 'stood above the contemporary humans' exerted 'the genius of their invention' and were essentially superior to mere men.

Such concerns continued in his final book on Nietzsche, *Nietzsche in Outline and Aphorism*, which again idealized the role of the superman. The book developed Nietzsche's theme of phases of human existence: the camel, the lion and the child. Currently, Europe represented the camel, set in its ways and stymying true creativity. The era of the lion was needed to tear down the era of the camel, and so Orage presented Nietzsche himself as one of the 'laughing lions' who were trying to achieve this creative destruction. Crystalizing the creative destructive tenor here, Tom Steele's analysis on these writings is worth stressing. 'Out of this holocaust', Steele argues 'would come the era of the child who now in Orage's text appears recognizably the superman of *Consciousness* . . . Orange comments that only students of mystical psychology could even conceive of this final metamorphosis and in this portrait of Zarathustra even Nietzsche had failed'.[8] So these writings drawing heavily on Nietzsche show a clearly modernist attitude to confronting modernity, diagnosing it as radically decadent. By engaging with Nietzsche, Orage developed his palingenetic, confrontational outlook. Interestingly, we even see attempts to identify limits in Nietzsche too, and, as we examine Orage, we will see that he was a highly syncretic thinker.

Indeed, it was shortly after developing these modernist critiques of modernity, and particularly the modern self, that Orage took over editing *The New Age*, relocating to London in the process. Here, his budding interests in using Nietzsche as a means to understand the need for new elites to emerge was combined with left-wing radicalism once again. Considering his editorial role for *The New Age* as one pioneering a new style of journalism for the modern age, he crystallized this point by claiming that there were two forms of publicism, the 'representative' and the 'presentative'. The former merely 'represented' common attitudes already in wide circulation, whereas the latter sought to 'present' fundamentally new points of view. Focusing on this more creative, presentative journalism, Orage's *The New Age* consciously marketed itself at the newly emerging British 'intelligentsia', indeed it even coined the term. The journal was broadly left-leaning in outlook, even before it embraced guild socialism, but it is important to stress that despite its political identity its remit also extended well beyond politics to discussions on psychoanalysis, radical philosophy and especially contemporary developments in the arts. This was all part of the project to explore the many new theories that were developing among European intellectuals at this time.

Orage came to embrace guild socialism after relocating to in London, and by the outbreak of the war was a firm propagandist for the movement. While the following chapter will delve much more fully into the dynamics of the guild socialist ideology, it is perhaps helpful to offer some further details. On the journal's central role for developing guild socialism, fellow proponent of the movement, G. D. H. Cole, described Orage's understanding of the revolutionary attitude, and his central role in its development, as follows:

. . . in the *New Age*, a small body of intellectuals, ably headed by A. R. Orage and S. G. Hobson, was developing new doctrines along another line. The *New Age* had long been an acute critic of orthodox Labour policies. It supported Victor Grayson in the troubles of 1908, and had preached, at all events from that date, a doctrine which made economic rather than political action the key to social change. Gradually this emerged as Guild Socialism. It began as a plea by medievalist craftsman, Arthur J. Penty, for a restoration of the guild system in industry. But after 1911, in the hands of S. G. Hobson and Orage it became a plea for the capture of control in industry by National Guilds essentially different from those of the middle ages . . . The proposed National Guilds were to be great corporations from the actual control and management of the various industries; and, according to the *New Age* plan, they were to be based on, and developed out of, the Trades Unions, which were to be widened to include all workers 'by hand and brain.' The workers, it was urged should organise not merely for defence but for the winning of control; the protective Trade Unions should turn into great workers' corporations which should demand and secure from a reorganised State the whole responsibility for the conduct of industrial affairs.[9]

The revolutionary thrust of the project is clearly discernable from such a characterization, and with this theme of fundamentally reorganizing the modern state we can summarize guild socialism as a palingenetic ideology, one that was largely led by the energies of Orage.

As well as this political project for revolutionary change, fully established in the journal's pages by 1914 and the outbreak of war, *The New Age* also developed radical critiques of existing standards in other ways too. Rejecting a Marxist, materialistic understanding of culture, and echoing earlier discussions on the need to access superhuman consciousness through the promotion of what Orage deemed 'great art', Orage's *The New Age* also promoted the need for a cultural revolution to sit alongside revolutionary political change. For Orage, socialism had always been something more than a method for developing workers' rights. Rather, it was seen as part of a fundamentally creative attitude, one that could lead to total cultural change. Orage felt that those who wanted revolution could not merely rely on the workers to develop the pathway to such palingenetic change, but rather there needed to be a vanguard of intellectual elites to lead the project. Figures such as himself, emerging from the newly educated professional classes, would be the source of this new vanguard, the new elite. In the future, the cultural sphere would be enriching to all in society, so long as it was not contaminated by the vulgarities of capitalist commercialism. Get rid of capitalism, and a new cultural era would follow. Yet echoes of Nietzsche were clearly still present: as Steele puts it, 'This was the politics of Orage's superman.'[10]

This thinking found some concrete articulation too. On literature, for example, Orage maintained that modern writing itself should be devoid of explorations of sociological questions, partisan political statements and scientific aspects of psychology. The intrusion of such approaches into modern novels epitomized the trend towards a sterile realism. Such an approach was flawed as modern literature treated fiction as something functional rather than beautiful. Only by rejecting such trends towards realism could such arts again truly focus minds on the deeper concerns of the soul, thereby revealing the true profundity and beauty of the human condition to its audience. This had occurred in earlier eras, in the texts of his literary cultural heroes, such as Dante, Shakespeare and Blake. What Orage claimed was truly great literature was text that he felt offered access to a nebulous, quazi-religious sensibility, a quality in short supply among modern writers, yet part of the future he believed was coming.[11]

Steeped in contrary values of promoting new elites from Nietzsche, and the rights of the masses from guild socialism, Orage was able to circumnavigate the disparity between egalitarianism and elitism by arguing that Nietzsche's thought was riddled with ambiguity. For Orage, Nietzsche lacked a clear doctrine because he did not live long enough to fully develop one. So his philosophy needed to be synthesized with other ideas in order for his incomplete prophecy of a transvaluation of values to be converted into a coherent and workable system.[12] Adding to the intellectual mix ahead of the war, Orage was even influenced by fresh reading of major spiritual texts such as the *Mahabharata*.[13] So by the outbreak of war, Orage's thought had thus become a highly idiosyncratic blend of radical critiques of modernity, and so offered a unique synthesis of a wide variety of modernist viewpoints, a vision held together by the underlying theme of diagnosing modernity as decadent and developing countervailing visions of renewal. With this intellectual backcloth established, we can now examine how these themes found expression during wartime itself.

The modern apocalypse

With the outbreak of war, Orage immediately began to seize on the conflict as the international crisis from which the guild socialist revolution would emerge. His central contribution to each edition of *The New Age* was the 'Notes of the Week' column, which fronted the publication, and comprised its first few inside pages too. Writing somewhere between three and six thousand words each week for the journal during the war period, Orage developed a clearly political modernist reading of the underlying significance of the conflict. In sum, it would be meaningful only if it could bring about revolutionary change, and pointless if not. Notably, his analysis was characterized by commentary that explored the political and economic changes that the world was experiencing, and stressed how they were radicalizing the 'spiritual' unity of the country ahead of the coming political transformation.

For example, epitomizing the initial war fever that developed widely across Europe, Orage claimed at the beginning of August 1914 that combat would result in 'a deeper sense of reality than has lately distinguished Europe and a return to spiritual sanities'. It was clearing Europe

> of much cant to her future advantage. We who are alive now may not, it is true, live to see the other side of Armageddon; but another side there surely will be, less black than this for our children and our children's children. Worse things than the war now at our doors the world has never seen; better things than the world has ever known may still come from it.[14]

Continuing such war fever, at the end of August 1914 Orage again argued that the conflict was a turning point in the history of the world, a tragic moment rich with the potential for the new to emerge. Indeed, the war was

> an event without parallel, a catastrophe almost sublime in its significance, a tragedy of almost unimaginable meaning and possibility. Upon its conclusions depends

the fate not only of our own Empire, but of all empires . . . The world is at the cross-roads of history. A turn to the left or the right will determine events for thousands of years to come.[15]

He also repeatedly offered clear assertions that the present now offered 'the most favourable [occasion] for revolutionary thought that ever was in the history of the world'. Indeed, not merely the map of Europe, but the 'the mind of Europe' was 'being recast'. Further, as a result of what he regarded as an overturning of hegemonic values, astonishing 'revelations are taking place everywhere and the more of them the better'.[16]

Though some of this initial exuberance soon wore off, throughout the war the underlying rhetorical strategy of these editorials was to present the conflict in terms of heightened nationalism and a sense of profound change. The idea that an apocalyptic sense of crisis and the prospect of fundamental social and economic renewal went hand-in-hand was self-evident for Orage throughout the war. In 1916, we see him reiterating this theme. 'National feeling runs high', he argued, at a time 'when everything is in the melting pot, and [when] all the old moulds are broken or breaking'.[17] The telling 'melting pot' metaphor was one frequently employed in Orage's war writings to evoke this sense of change, often used to articulate the belief that Europe was in a state characterized by fundamental transition and sociopolitical malleability. 'In the most precise sense of the metaphor', he continued in 1916, 'everything in the nation became fluid. Forms, habits, institutions, customs, prejudices, and all the rest of it were tossed into the cauldron, and there rapidly became molten, and so have remained even to this moment . . . it was as if God had taken us at our word and granted our prayer to make all things new'.[18] War was a liminal experience.

A war of ideas

The development of this revolutionary register allows us to see how Orage conceived the war as one underpinned by old and new ideas. He even believed that intellectuals were partly culpable for its outbreak, and had a clear stake in reformulating the governing ideas of the future of world society while they were in the melting pot of war. In sum, it was intellectual cultures that had contributed to the dynamics of prewar society, and in particular it was intellectuals had failed to persuade the Germans that the increasing threat of militarism would be a regressive step for both Europe and for Germany.

In order to see how Orage framed his reading of the conflict as a war of ideas, it is worth looking at some of the more reflective, philosophical discussions that he published early on in the conflict. Indeed, in some of these early wartime writings, Orage explicitly detailed his view of the war through the lens of Nietzsche's philosophy, echoing his earlier interests in Nietzsche already discussed in this chapter. Demonstrating the influence that Nietzsche still retained on his eclectic thinking, Orage proposed that he had been one of the few 'great men' to emerge from Germany since the Enlightenment. In one 'Unedited Opinion' column from this early war period,[19] Orage discussed this point in some detail. Emphasizing the vision of re-rooting European culture by developing a new morality, Orage again endorsed Nietzsche's philosophical confrontation with a decadent modernity. Here, he described the Nietzschean worldview as a form of secular Catholicism because it sought to remake Europe into a homogeneous, spiritual and rising cultural unit, rather than the enslaved and decadent society that it was otherwise becoming. Orage applauded this desire to return to Europe a sense of 'higher' purpose, and so Nietzsche was styled as a 'good European'. Like fellow countrymen Beethoven and Goethe – but unlike the German militarists and imperialists who were fighting the war – Nietzsche's thought offered access to a sense of the transcendent, and he knew how to connect with 'spiritual Europe'.

Moreover, Orage argued that Nietzsche would have hated the martial German ambition to impose a crude, materialist hegemony throughout the continent, precisely because such a programme was devoid of any sense of sacred purpose. Demonstrating Orage's own desires for Europe to be reordered into a new and 'creative' dynamic, he concluded that the war could become a radically modernizing event if the victorious powers could so will it. In 're-casting the map of Europe', he concluded, 'the concerted [goal of the] Powers should be, not solely to ensure peace in Europe, but to provide the conditions of high European culture in every group [i.e. nation-state] that is formed'.[20] This re-establishment of a higher culture at the centre of Europe would ensure that Europeans could regain a sense of spiritual vitality. Moreover, this would open the way for the continent to once again produce 'great Europeans'.

Alongside Nietzsche's philosophical modernism, Orage devoted space to discussing more general ethical issues raised by the war too. In outlining these views, he was clear that violence was philosophically justified in wartime. Like many, though not all, guild socialists, Orage was no pacifist. He argued that the duty of British citizens to fight resided not simply in an obligation to serve the good of the national community, but ultimately rested upon the responsibility to serve the good of the whole world. According to Orage, pacifists failed to realize that, although humans could aspire to perfectibility, it would never be the case that all human societies would do so. Consequently, there would always be people who hated the idea of peace and goodwill. Pacifists had demonstrated themselves to be intellectually naïve with respect to this innate flaw in the human condition. The pacifist method of pursuing peace by simplistically refusing to use force to repel an enemy was doomed to failure when confronted by ruthless opposition. For peace to exist at all, enemies of freedom and liberty needed to be fought periodically. In such times, reason and persuasion retreated, and violence came to the fore as the only effective response to aggression.[21] The war was one such occasion, and defeating Germany was just such a cause. This helps to clarify why Orage rejected what he regarded as erroneously 'progressive' notions of warfare as a phenomenon that could be eliminated through the steady introduction of reason into collective human existence. For Orage, this was not the war to end all wars. Rather, Orage saw the world in far more Nietzschean terms of continual struggle and conflict producing inescapable cycles of peace and war. Denying the essentially tragic quality of the human condition, pacifism and idealistic liberalism were principles destined to fail according to Orage's analysis. We will see this critique of pacifism recur in a number of figures writing for *The New Age*, including T. E. Hulme, but it was not shared by all guild socialists.

Rebellion abroad and revolution at home

We can also piece together how Orage conceived the origins of the war through a series of 'Unedited Opinions' from 1916. This again allows us to see how political developments and cultural themes were combined in Orage's analysis, and how he regarded the war as a fundamental turning point in the cultural life of the continent.

Beginning with the responsibility of Germany, as a state rising in political and economic power in the late nineteenth century, it was inevitable that the country would want to enlarge its sphere of influence and augment its power. One option was to expand territorially, which helped to explain the growth of its navy and army, alongside the general development of militarism in the country. However, this had resulted in European powers becoming increasingly wary of German aggrandizement, at the same time as many Germans felt the country had a right to pursue expansion. Conflating these tensions within Germany were concerns that other European powers had prevented it from trading fairly in international markets, thereby stymieing the country's potential economic, as well as territorial, growth. As a means to overcome these difficulties, Orage argued that Germany wanted to expand its sphere of influence in the Middle East, and so seized upon the idea of the Baghdad railway as the means for future economic development. In so doing, it became reliant upon Austro-Hungary to maintain peace in the Balkans. When Austro-Hungary confronted the Russian-backed Serbian threat, Germany foolishly took a gamble and began a general European war, hoping that the British would not intervene. Ultimately, this reading of events pointed to the hubris of German capitalism, especially its need to find foreign lands for investment, as leading to war, according to Orage.[22]

Turning to France, in the face of profane German aggression, its case was perhaps the starkest. Orage concluded that, for the French, 'the war spells spiritual annihilation or spiritual resurrection'.[23] He proposed that, although a popular motive among the masses, the war actually offered the country the opportunity to resolve a conflict that had deeper cultural roots than simply revenge for defeat in 1870 and the return of Alsace-Lorraine. The real war between Germany and France was one for cultural and intellectual hegemony over Europe. Orage claimed that, after the revolutions of 1848, Germany had set herself in opposition to French culture and its efforts to develop liberalism. So from 1870, Germany had become successful in creating an alternate cultural and political project that threatened the historic role of the French to lead cultural Europe. Defeat in the Franco-Prussian war and the Alsace-Lorraine question merely added insult to this deeper, cultural injury. Yet French victory in the current war would create a revolutionary shift in this trend, resulting in France being able to re-establishing its place as the leader of 'civilized' Europe. Defeat for the culturally, as well as militarily, aggrandizing Germany could well finish the country off. For Orage, the French were fighting a culturally defined war for their national *raison d'être*, an existential conflict at the core of the nation's identity.

In contrast to this cultural battle, Britain's Russian ally had the most to gain materially. Arguing that the country was effectively landlocked for most of the year – Archangel was frozen for six months, Sweden and Denmark restricted access to the Baltic, Vladivostok was too remote for trade and Turkey controlled access to the Black Sea – Orage foresaw a revolution in Russian trading prospects if the country could remove some of these blocks through war, thereby transforming ways in which Russia could exploit its enormous natural resources. Because of these economic forces, alongside the underlying weakness of the Tzar, Orage predicated from 1916 that the European war made possible 'a constitutional revolution in Russia even before the war is over'.[24] Yet in this analysis, the future of international trade both for Russia and for Germany rested upon the control of Constantinople, thereby also making Turkey a central country in the geopolitics of the conflict. Indeed, for Orage, one of the great losers in a German victory would ultimately be Turkey. Keen to secure trade interests in the Middle East by gaining unfettered access through Turkey, Orage believed that even a victorious Germany would not feel the need to respect the sovereignty of Turkey for very long, although the Turks had apparently failed to realize this fact. The only explanation for Turkey refusing to accept Allied assurances of neutrality, Orage concluded, was the delusion that, by joining the Central Powers, Turkey would become a vital regional player in Germany's capitalist economic expansion into the Middle East.

Regarding how the conflict should be resolved, in another of his 'Unedited Opinions' in 1916, we get a clearer idea of Orage's own views on the essential conditions for peace with Germany. Importantly, he outlined the necessity for the Allies to force a constitutional revolution that would destroy the 'militarist hegemony of Prussia', and heralding a new dawn of socialist-style economic and political democracy. Indicative of his attitude towards the future of Germany, Orage concluded by arguing against a simplistic, punitive approach towards the potential new Germany by the Allies, claiming that, by destroying the old regime, all necessary disciplinary measures would have already been taken. Discussing the creation of a democratic Germany allowed Orage to blur foreign and domestic concepts of revolution. Indeed, in order to 'bring about a constitutional revolution in Germany', he argued, 'the Allies must be prepared to accept an economic revolution in their own lands'.[25] Often, the end point of such discussions on the major changes in world affairs was also an opportunity to call for a revolution at home.

So with the entry of America into the war, Orage detected a welcome strand of utopianism in Wilson, needed simply because 'the times require it'. Indeed, once again evoking the theme of war as liminality, and therefore a time of revolutionary possibility, at this point Orage noted that three 'of the mightiest political events ever known in the history of the world have occurred within three years' – the other two being the outbreak of the war itself and February Revolution in Russia. So, as with other 'mighty' events, American intervention was presented as a turning point of such a magnitude that it carried 'with it such implications that our remotest descendents will date an epoch of history from it'.[26] Telling of this need to view wartime as a liminal period, Orage often argued that the diplomacy of Woodrow Wilson, and the rising significance of America on the international stage in general, marked the end of the old Vienna system of international relations. More generally, the intervention of America symbolized again a profound sense of change in world affairs, offering fresh hope for a new political reality to emerge from the war.

Regarding the final 'mighty' political event, revolutions in Russia, when responding to the February Revolution, Orage praised the fact that the country now enjoyed fresh liberties. With each war Russia fought in, he asserted the nation made great sociopolitical advances, citing the emancipation of the Serfs after the Crimean war alongside the creation of the Duma after the Russo-Japanese war as the precedents of this trend. In keeping with this tendency, the 'Russian Revolution', Orage stressed, 'even if it should now experience the dangers of reaction and counter-revolution . . . will stand to all time as an act of the greatest popular heroism'. However, he also warned that Russia had now entered into a capitalist era, which would 'only lay bare the economic facts, and, in all probability, enlarge them'.[27] Orage further claimed the event not only served as a lesson to Germany that the Allies were serious in overthrowing tyrannical and archaic forms of governance, but also was an event inspiring radicals in the Allied countries to overthrow the capitalist system.

Following the February Revolution, Orage consistently appealed for stability in Russia. Defining a revolution as 'a powerful movement Leftwards towards the extremist limits of idealist thought', he called for those fomenting further change to 'stop and rather coerce the diminishing minority of ultra-Revolutionists than apply coercion to the increasing minority of moderate Revolutionists'.[28] This identification of a worrying continued shift leftwards, and call for stability, also stressed that events had shunted Britain firmly to the political right among the Allies. To counter this, Orage again used such a diagnosis to state that it was necessary for Britain to move 'in harmony with the general tendency of the whole of the Alliance', that is to the left, if 'our new status will be one of increased strength and Russia will remain our ally with more heart than she has ever had before'.[29] Once again, the February Revolution at least, was to be seized upon as an event that inspired revolution internationally.

Yet support for change in Russian politics evaporated after the October Revolution, and Orage talked far less about the country's affairs than previously. When he raised the issue in November 1917, Orage claimed that the advances made by Lenin and Trotsky were regrettable, and came about as a result of Kerensky's failure to keep the Soviets on side.[30] By January 1918, he was clear that a Bolshevist dictatorship in Russia was a negative development, especially as it had left the remaining Allies 'in the lurch' by negotiating a separate peace with the central powers.[31] The surrender of Russia was clearly a great advantage to German continental hegemony, and it was the blinkered idealism of the political modernism being pursued by the Russian far-left that was to blame, according to Orage:

> Russia's 'blunder' lay in believing that a purely moral attitude would of itself induce a responsive moral revolution in Germany. With tragic idealism, Messrs. Lenin and Trotsky determined to stake everything upon their noble throw; and they have lost . . . If Russian idealism has failed to induce a response in Germany, can we expect that idealism alone in any other nation can succeed?[32]

The military threat from Germany appeared to be lost on both the leaders of the revolution and the people of Russia, Orage again suggested in April 1918: 'There seems to be no time-sense', among the radicals, 'in Russia that can foresee the situation in which she stands'. The likes of Trotsky and Lenin failed to look into the future, he felt, and erroneously 'advised their followers, today is considered to be sufficient without thought of tomorrow'. Orage also critiqued the Bolshevik revolutionaries for failing to realize that Germany still occupied around a quarter of the former Russian Empire. As we will see in the next chapter, other critiques of Bolshevism by guild socialists also highlighted a lack of direction and guiding purpose in its attempted revolution. In part this was because Bolshevism came to be viewed as a materialistic competitor ideology to guild socialism. Moreover, epoch-shifting world affairs had a direct impact on British affairs, so how was revolution promoted at home?

Revolution at home

Orage's guild socialism during the war argued that the impetus for the redemption of British society needed to emerge, primarily, from a revolutionary labour movement. He wanted organized labour to become far more involved in the management of the economy through seizing on the new opportunities created by war. For example, Orage regularly called not merely for the nationalization of key industries, especially shipping, but ultimately wanted organized labour to take over the economic organization of the country through the establishment of the proposed series of national guilds. We can see in the following chapter some of the technical details here, with regard to Hobson's analysis of wartime economics. Orage's commentaries, meanwhile, linked the major theme of revolution with the weekly flow of the war.

In terms of the underlying mood for this change created by the war, we see that Orage's core narrative for revolution was as follows: during the war, the labour movement would be able to raise a widespread sense of national betrayal and injustice in the working classes. This would be an attitude that would lead to workers becoming disillusioned with their alienation under capitalism, which would have an increasingly negative impact on their willingness to work. Ultimately, there would be a significant decline in productivity as a result. The downturn in the economy would be blamed on capitalist economics, forcing the government to consider the necessity of the transfer to the only serious alternative economic system, which according to Orage would be guild socialism. The cause would gain mass appeal as it alone truly championed a genuine patriotic fervour among workers.

Stressing his radicalism, the overarching tone of Orage's critiques of the labour movement during the war was to belittle it for shoring up capitalism rather than fomenting revolution. The labour movement only offered piecemeal reform, and so lacked political modernism's revolutionary stances. Epitomizing this tone, one of Orage's most programmatic statements on the way forward for organized labour came in September 1916. Here, he outlined seven key points that were necessary for the true war against capital to be successful:

> One: it is necessary that the Labour movement should create for itself a permanent General Staff, the nucleus of which is the Parliamentary Committee of the Trade Union Congress. Two: the single front of Labour is the union of all the societ- ies, leagues, parties and Trade Unions into which the thousand and one Allies are

now divided. Three: the objective of Labour is the control of Capital – the plan of Capital being the control of Labour. Four: every operation of reform that does not aim at acquiring or enlarging the control of Labour over Capital is regimental indiscipline; at best it is a waste of energy, at worst it is treachery or mutiny. Five: the most effective power of Labour is the power to strike. Six: the means to power are the abolition of the blackleg and the federation of the unions by industries. Seven: the war of Labour for the control of Capital is such a war that victory would herald a new era.[33]

Especially relevant here is how this confrontational statement sketched out a revolutionary programme, dressed up in a military rhetoric. Orage framed all industrial action in terms of a wider dialectic between oppression and liberation. Point four placed the sense of piecemeal change as an enemy of the revolutionary cause, while point five emphasized that economic action took precedence over political representation as the ultimate strategy for organized Labour to renegotiate its relationship within the capitalist system. Finally, point seven reinforced the political modernist message: the need for the emergence of a new era and a fundamental break with the past.

Like fellow guild socialists, Orage believed that the real power of labour lay in organized workshops and union power, not parliamentary politics. Therefore unions were 'the governing bodies of labour', and 'the cadres of the coming industrial system'.[34] However, lacking revolutionary verve their leaders seemed unable to grasp this point. By failing to extend economic leverage through industrial action, and instead deciding to play a political game of compromise during the war, Orage decried unions as acting as the 'watch-dogs of parliamentary Capitalism rather than the leaders of economic Labour'.[35] So although the labour movement was akin to 'a creature of vast body and many tails, but without a head', and although the TUC itself was something of a '*roi fainéant*' in his estimation, it was the duty of the labour movement to compel the TUC to work for the interests of economic revolution.[36]

To give an example of one area where organized labour was clearly wanting, we can look at Orage's assessment of its response to the Munitions of War Act, which, he stressed, was based on major incursions into workers' rights. Yet for Orage, the most mendacious aspect of this Act was the promise to restore the rights workers enjoyed in 1914 after the war. He regarded this as a conscious act of deceit by the capitalist system, seizing on the contingency of wartime conditions to destroy gains made by the labour movement over the preceding half century or so. As he put it: 'An earthquake does not pass like a cyclone and leave the foundations untouched. For good or for ill, the war has involved society in a social revolution the consequences of which will continue long after the war has become history.' Thus, the 'promise to restore the Trade Unions in their complete pre-war privileges' was 'as futile as to promise to set Humpty Dumpty on his wall again'.[37] There would never be a simple return to the pre-1914 world.

Moreover, when we look closely at Orage's commentaries on wartime industrial action, we find that he was keen for strikes to occur, but only if they developed truly revolutionary potential. He also argued that striking for piecemeal reforms, such as smaller improvement in working conditions or increased wages, harmed these grander revolutionary prospects and so such strikes were condemned. When discussing the strike on the Clyde in early 1915, for example, Orage's commentary was clear that a deeper significance than mere worker materialism ultimately motivated these actions. Moreover, as many strikers were not fully conscious of the revolutionary significance of their own actions, it was the role of intellectuals such as Orage to raise public consciousness of their wider, revolutionary significance. As he put it, 'in the case of industrial unrest we must learn to look at ourselves, and teach the workman to look, for a profounder origin than the desire for better wages'.[38] Although not all strikers had the necessary revolutionary consciousness, certain strikes at least were manifestations of the moral and spiritual battle that underpinned the guild socialist revolution. There was a clear *futural* drive to this view. As he put it:

> The world, and our nation in particular, will not emerge unchanged after the Great War. Power, organisation, responsibility – these watchwords will take the place of the old Liberty, Equality, Fraternity. We are in for a reconstructive epoch . . . the only certain thing is that power and responsibility will alone be the builders of it . . . Real power or illusory higher wages are the alternatives before them. Every wage-strike to-day is a waste of energy when it is not something worse.[39]

Workers who placed their material interests ahead of guild socialist revolution were thus merely motivated by illusions, and worked against the revolutionary epoch that he believed would emerge in the near future.

Orage was also highly critical of the lack of revolutionary leadership coming from within the labour movement. Labour organs such as *The Herald, The Call* and *The Labour Leader* were regularly criticized. However, the lack of a vision for a truly regenerated future was the foremost problem among leading lights in the labour movement. For Orage, the vision for the future was the proposed national guilds. For example:

> What is wanted to quicken the languishing atmosphere of Labour is the vision of a new world: a world not made in the image of Mr. Sidney Webb and his Fabian pigeon-holes, still less a world made in the likeness of a city-office. The prospect, on the other hand, of a world organised, responsible and national industries self-governed by their members would be a fitting and seductive sequel to the most agonising war that has ever been fought.[40]

The Parliamentary Labour Party was also weak, according to Orage. In his eyes, it was critically impeded because its MPs were intellectually wanting. Labour MPs not only failed to effectively criticize bills proposed by other members in the interest of the working classes, but, as with union leaders, lacked revolutionary drive. To take an example of this rhetoric, their 'views seem to go back to the age of the Christian Socialists, or the Benthamites; or, at the very best, to the early period of the Fabian society'.[41] Parliamentary Labour's stifling embrace of piecemeal change over revolution was again epitomized by the creation of a Minister for Labour at the end of 1916. Although glad that to see the Labour Party playing an instrumental role in the formation of the new government, the new Minister for Labour advertised both to the British proletariat and to the world in general 'that there not only exists in our midst a class of person different from the classes of active citizens, and needing, therefore, to be specially legislated for; but a class whose permanency is taken for granted, and whose status is fixed for all time'.[42] Such developments stymied revolutionary consciousness among the labouring classes, according to Orage, and again we see his radicalism emerging in such commentaries.

Aside from these limiting elements within organized labour, Orage equally frequently argued that capitalists had failed in their national duty too. To take an example from November 1914, we find him arguing that, unlike the proletariat, the business classes 'have not, except in pursuit of their own personal interests, performed any notable service to the nation'.[43] By identifying capitalists as essentially traitorous, he underpinned this analysis with a stark, binary opposition between the 'good' proletariat, symbolizing 'higher' spiritual qualities against the 'evil' capitalist who was always presented as the epitome of 'base' materialism and greed. This endorsement of a Marxist-style class war dichotomy also emphasized its dialectic relationship: capitalists were sowing the seeds of their own destruction during the war. We can get a clear sense of this position from a piece written at the end of 1916, immediately after the formation of the Lloyd George Ministry:

> . . . we may point out – not without a touch of malice – that in propagating the present war and in insisting so loudly upon the necessity of fighting it to a finish, the capitalist parties have really been calling upon a spirit, stronger than their own, and one which they will find hard to lay at their discretion – the spirit of the English working classes, the spirit of the English folk.[44]

From such pronouncements, we can also see in Orage's guild socialist vision a blend of English nationalism combined with a political modernist call for regeneration. These components of political modernism and mythic nationalism would be developed into more clearly extremist ideologies, in particular fascism, in the interwar period by a wide variety of protagonists.

Meanwhile, to develop this theme of capitalism as a force denigrating the national consciousness, from 1914 onwards Orage used issues where capitalists became prominent in the conduct of the war, especially war loans, to demonstrate the alleged antithesis between patriotic and capitalist goals. Ever-higher rates of interest on war loans were irrefutable evidence of capitalism's corrosive nature, placing private interest before that of the nation. Analysis of the first war loan of £350 million not only claimed that it would yield its investors £14 million a year in interest, but also that it would ultimately cost the state in excess of £500 million. For Orage, this financial cost would be borne by the nation as a whole. If the capitalist state remained after the war, workers would ultimately pay the bulk of this bill through their postwar tax bills. Indeed, he often pointed out that once war was over, the state would be 'compelled to act the part of official receiver on behalf of a practically bankrupt nation. Thirty-nine out of every forty of us will be in hopeless debt to the remaining fortieth, and the State must be the authority to see that we pay in full'.[45] So from this guild socialist perspective, war loans were nothing other than confidence tricks by the capitalist classes to make the rich richer and the poor poorer.[46]

Editorials also developed radical propositions to counter this trend. For example, Orage felt that the government should begin to seize credit itself from financiers, making his case thus: the 'Chancellor of the Exchequer can commandeer credit, with the authority of the Government and the nation behind him, as easily as any one of Lord Kitchener's representatives can commandeer a horse'.[47] He dubbed the commandeering of capital assets by the state 'the conscription of capital'. Indeed, reflecting his opposition to the policy of conscripting men to the army, the conscription of bourgeois capital was often presented as a *quid pro quo* for the conscription of proletarian men. Finally, according to Orage, strictly speaking, capitalists and financiers were not ultimately authentic components of the nation's 'spiritual' community – which we saw him discuss above. Rather, they were motivated by their own greed, not by an altruistic, national sentiment. In sum, they were spiritually bankrupt and divisive figures.

Reflecting his limited hopes for change being effected through parliamentary politics, following the 1918 Representation of the People Act, Orage called upon the Labour Party to defer ambitions of becoming the next government and prepare to become the official opposition preventing, rather than acting as anything approaching a postwar puppet of capitalism.[48] By the summer of 1918 Orage predicted that the now inevitable Lloyd George victory would result in the 'historic parties of Conservatism and Liberalism' finding themselves 'broken up irredeemably and their fragments, after the bulk has been absorbed by the Government party, left to dissolve into personal groups'.[49] Still hopeful of a new political system emerging in parliament, he predicted the fallout of Lloyd George's continuance of the National Government would be an end to the party structure. By October, he characterized the need to develop a new politics in the wake of the war thus:

> The sickness of the world is not a passing malady to be redeemed by a temporary change of diet; it is radical and profound; and its symptoms are indicative of a need of nothing less than a transformation of world-regimentation and policy . . . The blood of our slain is on the hands of our electorate, to be redeemed by a new world, shaped by good men, or left to corrupt and to cry to heaven for our destruction as a faithless generation.[50]

Yet regarding the guild socialist revolution itself, by this time Orage's overarching tone was one of despondency, not hope. The world, as he saw it at least, was still in fundamental decline, and despite epoch-shifting global events the revolutionaries had not created the desired breakthroughs. Perhaps the Labour Party could use its position as the dominant member of the disparate groupings forming the new parliament for 'gradually building up an alternative Government', he felt. So the labour movement's immediate future lay in creating the foundations for a new epoch by building the economic and political foundations for power in a new period of transition.[51] War had not lifted the world out of liminality.

Meanwhile, despite his praise for Wilson's presence on the international stage, Orage also believed that the new League of Nations would stymie attempts to overcome Europe's crisis. Indeed, the creation of the League following the war was the political development that he feared most. He had been critiquing the proposition from 1916 on the grounds that it failed to present an economic solution to the origins of war. Rather, Orage stressed that the only way to curtail the potential for massive international wars was for the inauguration of a new economic system internationally. The League itself had two fundamental flaws. First, it was composed of the diplomatic bodies of the existing nations, which Orage felt were 'the most reactionary and least democratic' branch of each government's bureaucracy. Second, and more dangerously, the League would play into the hands of capitalism because, as a result of the war, international 'diplomacy and finance are more closely associated than ever before'. Consequently, the League of Nations would become a powerful international body representing the growing influence of the will of international finance, the enemy that had profited from the war.[52] In other words, the demon force of modernity, capitalism, had extended its clutches.

By the signing of the Treaty of Versailles in June 1919, Orage was even more despondent about the future of Europe. Arguing that imagination, magnanimity and 'an exalted intellectual and moral courage' were all missing from the peace negotiations, he mourned the lack of a new era as a consequence of the treaty:

> No transformation of the world, such as the world hoped for, can be expected of the old wine thus spilled into the new bottles. Under new names the old evils are bound to re-appear and in a more dangerous form by reason of their change of name. Prussianism, for example, will be twice as dangerous when called precaution and defence as when it was exclusively associated with German militarism; and, similarly, the old Triple and Quadruple Alliances will only have increased their covering-power for evil on being named the League of Nations.[53]

From this dynamic, he divined three potential outcomes, each in pessimistic, modernist fashion evoking a sense of modernity descending further into decadence: first, world affairs would be dominated by the despotic rule of vast supra-national trusts, organizations with an international monopoly over a single product or cluster of products, the next advancement of the capitalist system. Second, the world would be reduced to fighting immense international wars dwarfing the previous conflict. In the worst version of this scenario, Britain would have to take on the new might of America. Finally, the entire international economic system could undergo a Bolshevik-style revolution. 'The present war and the present peace', he concluded, 'are only the prologue to the portentous drama now beginning to unfold itself'.[54]

By late 1919, influenced by his increasing appreciation of the role of finance in the dynamic of capitalism, Orage moved his economic critique of capitalism from guild socialism to the Social Credit ideas of C. H. Douglas. These too found a voice in the pages of *The New Age*, following Orage's endorsement, and are discussed here in Chapter 4. However, Orage moved on from this scheme for economic renovation after a few years too, because he felt the model to be far too complex to ever become a practicable solution,[55] and rather embraced the mystical philosophy of George Ivanovich Gurdjieff.[56] Reflecting on this postwar intellectual evolution in 1926, Orage described how the impact of the First World War had discredited guild socialism:

The Great War put an end to many things and many ideas; and among the latter was undoubtedly guild socialism. We woke from the evil dream shortly after
the armistice; and in the horrible light of morning we began to count our losses.
For me the realisation of the complete disappearance of the guild idea as a living
potency brought no sense of disappointment, but rather of relief . . . it was difficult to carry on a journal that lived by ideas in the absence of any living idea; and
between two worlds, one dead and the other powerless to be born.[57]

Conclusions

So we can see that, for Orage, guild socialism had offered a redemptive vision during
the war, ostensibly for all industrial workers, but in reality largely for himself and his
circle. Yet ultimately this was a failure. The world as he saw it remained in a liminal
state, despite the potential for change generated by the war. Moreover, we have seen
from this wide-ranging reconstruction of his wartime views and opinions some telling
detail on how Orage reacted to the war's various discrete events, casting them through
a guild socialist, and therefore revolutionary, lens. This was the journalism of a political
modernist. During the war years Orage genuinely believed the capitalist system was
on the verge of collapse. This tenor was also informed by his prewar promotion of
revolutionary solutions to the crisis he detected within a capitalist modernity. As we
saw, Orage's critiques had been largely drawn from Nietzsche before he took up the
guild socialism, and these earlier views also helped inform his negative appraisal of
capitalism during the war. Especially when we consider Orage's belief that cultures
were either characterized by ascent or decline, it is clear that he regarded the war as
a failure to bring about the revitalization of Western culture and society. Indeed, in
the end the war was yet another chapter in its decline. Orage's resolution to this crisis
of modernity afterwards was to drop his commitments to the revolutionary socialist
politics that had resulted in such a passionate outpouring of ideas and analysis during
the war, and in its place embrace the more mystical variants of modernist thought to
develop a personal solution to such concerns. In the following chapter, we will see how
fellow guild socialist ideologues developed their own articulations of guild socialist
political modernism in the pages of *The New Age* during the war.

3

War, *The New Age* and Guild Socialism's Political Modernism

While one can see from Orage that guild socialist ideology was steeped in a radical confrontation with capitalist modernity, we should also recognize that the movement could be viewed as posing a threat to society too. For example, the *Times* argued in September 1917 that there 'exists at the present moment a revolutionary movement in this country which has gathered considerable momentum; it has long passed the stage of mere talk, and has realized itself in formidable action'.[1] Such a striking attitude, taken from a lengthy feature on revolutionary movements across Europe, gives us one example of how the guild socialist movement was capable of raising genuine concern among sections for the British Establishment during the war. In an era of heightened propaganda, the piece linked the guild socialist movement to a wider trend emerging across Europe, one that included syndicalism, socialism and revolutionary action, developments epitomized by the situation unfolding in Russia at this juncture. Showing a reputation as one of Britain's leading revolutionary movements, here guild socialism was identified as 'the most popular of all reconstructive revolutionary schemes' by the report. Fears of the government being overthrown by guild socialists, and a descent into anarchy, were developed elsewhere too. The *Manchester Guardian* concurred, stressing that the guild socialists were exacerbating the crisis of war by calling 'for the class war, not satisfied with the national war that we have on our hands', and stressed that 'all this is the nature of a revolutionary movement'.[2] Much of this was media scaremongering, of course, while the real impact of the guild socialists was marginal. But such media reports give us a glimpse into the ways in which guild socialist calls for revolution were able to gain some purchase on the wider public imagination during the war. When they did so, the ideology could be presented as a dangerous threat from within, undermining the stability and order of the progressive liberal democratic project in a time of acute crisis.

We also saw in the previous chapter that Orage, editor of *The New Age* and himself leading guild socialist revolutionary, believed that the ideology offered a comprehensive critique of modernity. Yet often Orage was concerned with developing a running commentary on news events. Meanwhile, other protagonists also used guild socialist visions of revolution and cultural renewal to envisage a radically new modernity emerging in the wake of the war. Such revolutionary verve was used to develop a project proposing sweeping cultural change that was explored in some considerable depth. Such intellectual debate also needs to be discussed in the cultural histories of modernism, offering further examples of radical confrontations with decadence of modernity.

This wider analysis is also necessary because guild socialism's significance to cultures of modernism is often misunderstood. For example, Ann Ardis's examination of *The New Age* employs a more conventional, literary paradigm for conceptualizing modernism.[3] Consequently, she sees the magazine's commitment to guild socialism as a quite separate phenomenon to the aesthetic aspects of a modernist culture developed in the pages of *The New Age*. Contrastingly, the cultural historical model employed here claims that this type of approach unnecessarily limits analysis of the journal, in effect carving out major sections that do not deal directly with aesthetic issues, which are then often ignored or only superficially examined due to a narrow definition of what comprises cultures of modernism. The more embracing approach to analysing modernist cultures and sensibilities developed here suggests that politics and culture were interlinked, not siloed, and that there are clear connections between political perspectives that called for a new era to redeem a decadent modernity, and aesthetic arguments which also called for radical changes in cultural production. Meanwhile, Tom Villis characterizes guild socialism as a reactionary rather than revolutionary ideology, and so misses the palingenetic thrust of guild socialism.[4] As we will see, although the movement's protagonists looked to past models to inform their notion of revolutionary action, and possessed many socially conservative attitudes, their core belief in the need for an economic revolution that would redeem society from the antinomies of capitalist modernity gave the ideology a clearly *futural* dynamic: it sought to realize a new future, not a return to the past.

Avoiding these drawbacks, and based on detailed, textual analysis from the house journal of guild socialism, *The New Age*, what follows will be a new reading of this revolutionary intellectual movement during the war. This will highlight its modernist critique of Britain's decadent modernity, and detailed projections for revolutionary renewal, features largely missing from Orage's own publicism for the cause. What emerges is a complex picture. As with Orage, these radical socialist-leaning intellectuals found common ground critiquing the centralized, modern state, and rejecting piecemeal reform towards a new sociopolitical order. Culturally, their thinking often promoted a mythic nationalism and was also eager to reinvest a future, industrialized society with a spiritual dimension akin to a culture that its protagonists believed characterized the societies of the Middle Ages. So here we see a discourse that incorporated history, cultural commentary and revolutionary economics. Its debates found room for thinkers as diverse as Ruskin, Nietzsche and Marx. Finally, as with Orage, the outbreak of war allowed guild socialism's intellectual voices to view unfolding events as the catalyst for their revolution. Though *The New Age* will form the focus of this chapter, what follows will also introduce other books published at this time, relevant to the development of a revolutionary ideology by the guild socialists. However, before examining the wartime history of guild socialism, it is first necessary to plot its rise to cultural significance.

The roots of guild socialism

Situating itself within a tradition of British radicalism that included William Blake, Thomas Carlyle, John Ruskin and William Morris, a revolutionary yet national perspective was a central component of the ideological genealogy of the guild socialist movement. Indeed, the first consciously guild socialist text, *The Restoration of the Gild System*, was published in 1906 by A. J. Penty. Here we find an Anglo-Catholic architect who joined and left the Fabians before developing the first major statement on guild socialism as a revolution ideology rooted in a longer British tradition of radical left thinkers. Penty's primary concern was to critique the centralizing state model for the future of socialism being developed by the Fabians, and so, detecting a technocratic soullessness in the Fabian vision, proposed a radical alternative based on the guild system of the Middle Ages. In many ways, it can be seen as an embryonic variant of the corporate state ideas taken up by leading fascists in the interwar years. As highlighted in the previous chapter, the new guild system would be developed from existing trade union structures, and would then seek to take over the nation's affairs and replace the existing state. Penty also highlighted how this utopian idea would restore the dignity and status of modern workers. His initial variant of guild socialism thus provided left-leaning intellectuals with a more poetic alternative to the Fabian model of a technocratic central state to secure radical social change.

Penty's politics was also highly critical of capitalist modernity, and underpinning the vision was a radical interpretation of a need for creative destruction, required in order to escape the decadence of modern capitalism. To take an example of this crucial tenor, Penty stressed that in the coming years: 'Commercialism will reap as it has sown – a social catastrophe is clearly its fit and proper harvest', moreover, 'Though unable to save existing society, it may yet be possible to build something out of its ruins.'[5] In such rejections of the idea of steady progress, Penty stressed revolutionary political change needed to develop in response to the crisis being generated by an ever-advancing creep of social decay. The final chapter again emphasized a sense of an ending and the need for a new era, and drew on the past to create a new future as follows:

> . . . just as it was found necessary in the arts to seek a new source of inspiration in a study of Mediaevalism, so society by a reverence for the past may renew its lease of life. We live the life of the past to-day in our thoughts, to-morrow we may live it in reality. Thus hopes may be entertained that what has been may again be, and under new conditions with new possibilities, may be again in fuller measure and more complete perfection.[6]

With such statements, we find clear articulations of the myth of cultural rebirth underpinning Penty's call for revisiting the medieval epoch. On first inspection, such statements seem to represent a backward-looking ideology, a reactionary response to modernity, suggesting Penty merely wanted to recreate the past in pristine form. However, reading his text via the model of political modernism outlined in Chapter 1, we see the book operated on a clearly *futural* vision, evoking a reworked and highly mythic understanding of the past to underpin a radical response to Penty's damning critique of modernity. Essentially, Penty's statements were drawing on the past to envisage a future that could achieve, as he put it, 'more complete perfection'. As with other guild socialists, Penty's recourse to past was thus developed in the spirit of constructing a modern utopia, developing a modernist critique of capitalist modernity to provide a vision for transcending its alleged decadence. In this sense, though clearly honing in on a previous time to cull inspiration, Penty's politics should not be dismissed as mere nostalgia for a bygone age. Rather, even this early variant of guild socialism can be characterized as a radical critique of a decadent modernity, promoting creative destruction over piecemeal reform, and calling for revolution and a new future.

Penty's thesis remained largely unheeded within the labour movement until another disaffected Fabian intellectual, S. G. Hobson, intervened with a far more rigorous statement promoting guilds as an alternative to a central state model for socialism. His analysis was more clearly rooted in economic theory, and drew especially on Marxist calls for a revolution to transcend what Hobson perceived as a spiritual crisis brought about by capitalism. Hobson's initial work was also written during a period of increased industrial unrest, giving a timely impetus to the vision of modernized guilds that Penty lacked. Hobson began his guild socialism by writing essays on the topic for *The New Age* in 1912. In the wake of the interest they provoked, the magazine quickly identified itself as the house journal for the new ideology. Many of Hobson's prewar essays were subsequently published as *National Guilds: An Enquiry into the Wage System and the Way Out*, edited by Orage, and the ideology began to gain wider currency. As the *Times Literary Supplement* review of this central guild socialist text highlighted, by 1914 guild socialist ideas had 'already received a good deal of notice from the young "intellectuals" who almost for the first time in this country are beginning to constitute themselves into a thinking department of the Labour movement'. Acknowledging guild socialism's ability to capture young minds within the labour movement, the reviewer was ultimately critical, claiming the ideology 'though conceived with originality and elaborated with considerable cleverness, loses some illumination' once it was fully set out.[7] For the *Times Literary Supplement* at least, the mystique of revolution was more alluring than its practicability.

Hobson's essays themselves gave both an outline of how national guilds would emerge from trade unions, and described how a revolutionary moment could be created from the political crisis that could be generated by a general strike, with strikers backed economically by union funds. Importantly for understanding how its economic critique of society was especially relevant to those sensitive to cultures of modernism, Hobson's essays also stressed that guild socialism placed at its core the ability to escape from a world where the community was divided into fragmented parts, and would promote a new spiritual consciousness for a modern society. Telling of the cultural shift that would be achieved by the revolution, he argued the metaphysical dynamic of British society would be turned into a healthy 'organic' entity, once the devastating effects of capitalism had been overcome. This was because capitalism divided modern citizens into opposing types of people, a minority of 'active', capitalist citizens, and the vast majority of 'passive', proletariat ones. By not merely empowering workers economically, but also by ending labour's commodity status, the guild socialist revolution would turn the alienated, 'passive' proletariat of a decadent capitalism into fully 'active' citizens. For Hobson, passive citizens consisted of not merely the industrial wage earners but also the 'saletariat' of the emergent, lower middle classes too, all of whose labour was bought and sold, and therefore was commoditized, by capitalism. Meanwhile, the proposed alternate modernity of guild socialism would manifest a true form of 'economic democracy': workers would be given direct control of the deployment of the nation's economic resources through the new guild structures. In this vision, there was a deep concern with the spiritual qualities of the nation, a feature that helped to distinguish the guild socialists from the materialist critiques of capitalism forwarded by more conventional Marxism.

For Hobson, a clear way to emphasize the difference between capitalism and its guild socialist alternative was through a military metaphor. As in the army, all workers in the future society would receive 'pay', not 'wages', signifying the alienation brought about by the wage system. Such language was used extensively to emphasize the elimination of capitalism's reduction of labour to a mere commodity. To achieve this central goal, management of the nation's economic resources would be subdivided into approximately 22 democratic guilds, one for each sector of industry. Workers and not capitalists would ultimately own and control the means of production as a consequence of this revolutionary new state structure. This elemental shift in the status of workers would turn all citizens of the new order into the fully 'active' and spiritually content community of the guild socialist, alternative modernity. The nation would be reunited, not divided as under capitalism. Moreover, unlike previous visions of left-wing social revolution in Britain, such as William Morris's communism and even Penty's earlier incarnation of the ideology, central to Hobson's guild socialist vision for the future was a remodelled industrialized world, not a direct throwback to life before the Renaissance. Guild socialism's *futural* thrust was now clear: economic and social revolution was required to escape a decadent modernity and enter a new one.

By developing the vision of an alternate modernity that was opposed to capitalism, promoted discontinuity between the present and the future, and called for a new cultural epoch to flourish through the spiritual redemption of modern man, guild socialism offered a clear example of an embryonic political modernism ahead of the outbreak of war. Moreover, the war itself gave the movement further momentum, offering its proponents a liminal time in which, as we saw with Orage, the emergence of the radically new could be more easily imagined. We can begin this survey of the leading guild socialist figures by exploring the cultural critiques developed by one of the movement's most fertile writers during the early war period, Ivor Brown.

Ivor Brown

As we will see, economic issues were central to guild socialist debates on how the revolution would take hold and be successful. However, cultural considerations were also extensively discussed too. Epitomizing this concern was one of the most prolific writers of guild socialist publicism in *The New Age*, Ivor Brown. A lecturer at Oxford University and conscientious objector, Brown also joined the National Guilds League, an organization set up by fellow guild socialist G. D. H. Cole to promote the movement in 1915. After the war he became a journalist for the *Manchester Guardian* and developed an interwar profile as an influential theatre critic, before taking over the editorship of the *Observer* in later years.

He began his wartime critique of capitalist modernity in 1914 with a series of articles for *The New Age* entitled 'Geography and Human Grouping'. These essays explored the relationship between nationalism and the guild socialist revolution. Essentially, they argued that the cultural revolution that the guild socialists proposed should be based on a form of nationalism, as the pursuit of internationalist ideas for socialist revolution currently represented a 'barren pastime'. Rather revolutionaries needed to respect 'existing territorial distinctions as the necessary basis for an economic revolution', simply due to the 'extraordinary vitality which still lies in Nationalism'. Despite the irrational nature of national borders, as was being made patently clear during the war the public were fully prepared to fight and die for nation-states. Since the war broke out, the capitalist ruling classes simply had to play existing national sentiments against each other to retain their political dominance, using nationalism to divide the socialist movement. So revolutionaries had to find ways to 'take up this weapon which lies ready to hand and endeavour to make the best of it'.[8] Aside from the lasting resonance of nationalism, a related problem lay with the social role of religion. Christianity was no longer a guarantee of universal brotherhood, so that the decline in the power of faith required a new force to recreate an international sense of European unity. In a war that saw Catholics in Germany and France fighting against each other, traditional religion had 'faded into the mysticism of the individual, and as an organising power is no longer operative'.

The counterpoint to this crisis of modernity lay in the national trade unions. If their organization could become global, then an 'International Trades Union Conference would be one of the most important gatherings in the world'.[9] Typifying the guild socialist concern of resolving a spiritual crisis brought about by capitalism, the nation-states of the near future that would take on a socialist form would become 'organic' in nature. These political units would then be able to work in harmony, and they would realize that nations needed each other in order to survive and grow. Brown's international vision for the future of reformed nations in harmony was thus directly opposed to what he saw developing in capitalist modernity: nations placed in competition with each other. Indeed, central to his guild socialism was to develop what he called 'unselfish International Will' and 'spiritual bridges' that stretched 'across the moats of nationality', bonds that offered a sense of spiritual regeneration to his vision for escaping a decadent capitalism by building on existing nationalist sentiments.[10]

The year 1915 was the most prolific period in Brown's contribution to *The New Age*. He began with another two articles mapping the relationship between nationalism and revolutionary guild socialist economics. The first argued that his authentic version of nationalism was peaceable and respectful of other nations, and openly celebrated such diversity. Wars of national aggression, such as the conflict currently raging, were motivated by capitalist imperialism, and were counter to the future he envisaged under guild socialism. Economic revolution could only be successfully organized along the lines of 'historical geography', so revolutionaries had to develop a cultural understanding of a 'common fatherland', though expressly this was not a racial community predicated on the idea of a 'common blood'; racially defined communities were as aggressive as imperialist and capitalist ones.[11] Again epitomizing the radical critique of capitalist culture, a second article on nationalism again argued for fundamental reconfiguration of the European mind. Without a revolution in the perception of nationhood, competing nations would become like caged lions after the war. Europe would remain threatened by the unconsciously aggressive tendencies of a rapacious capitalism, combined with imperialistic and racial forms of nationalism. Counterpointing this gloomy projection with a guild socialist future, here Brown's peaceable nationalism would predominate. He stressed guild socialism's followers were 'ready to appreciate nationalism which keeps what it has of good and is prepared to build on the foundations of to-day by the introduction of a fresh architectural design'. Calls for such wholesale cultural renewal honed in on the Elizabethan era as a time when Britain possessed 'a great unity of will and purpose'. A later favourite of the British Union of Fascists, it was in such eras when 'the nation felt at one that the nation was most creative'. By creating a modern renaissance of this type, guild socialism would champion a new 'national spirit and a national art'.[12]

Having sketched out a vision of cultural revolution through organic nationalism, Brown also published a series of essays called 'Aspects of the Guild Idea', outlining programmatically his guild socialist vision. Typically, these critiqued both Fabianism and feminism, and railed against the idea of modern warfare. Evoking dissatisfaction with the intellectual milieu before the war, he stressed that socialism had failed in the last years of the nineteenth century and the first decade of the twentieth as a result of a decadent 'dreamy optimism' manifest in Fabians and related intellectual figures, such as H. G. Wells. Thus, 'in this world of dream and decay, of smouldering organisations and of political corpses that stank to heaven, Socialism was discredited, weakened and waned'. Yet guild socialism was the true British solution to reviving its revolutionary verve, rooted in extending the ideas of Robert Owen and William Morris.[13] Capitalism was again condemned as decadent, this time most clearly seen in the ubiquitous presence of a sentimental tenor in popular culture. The culturally alienated, modern worker, meanwhile, could find no aesthetic satisfaction in his work, so 'the revolting wash of modern sentimentalism is the outlet of humiliated man's desire for beauty'. However, though under constant attack by capitalism, the human drive towards achieving aesthetic satisfaction would never disappear completely, 'so long as there is some spark for self-expression and decoration . . . so long there is hope'. Revealing the concern with the cultural situation to be created by revolution, socialist revolutionaries needed to ensure that their ideas touched 'a real emotion in the English soul'. Failure to appreciate the social need for emotive concepts, such as beauty, had paralysed the Fabians and other reformist socialisms, and was a central characteristic of capitalism itself.[14]

Meanwhile, as with Penty's evocation of an idealized Middle Ages, we also see here clearly how Brown's guild socialism was predicated on a mythic, teleological sense of national history. It is important to highlight his revolutionary meta-narrative at the core of the ideology, detailing the death of guilds after the Renaissance and their projected rebirth in the future. The decline of guilds was a result of a series of historical accidents, starting with the Black Death in 1349, which had paved the way for the emergence of a new agricultural proletariat that was later absorbed by the industrializing cities. With the subsequent rise of industry on a national scale, the remaining structures of the old guilds had 'perished through negligence and the synthesis of [these] unfortunate facts . . . culminated in the Industrial Revolution'. The emergence of capitalism was thus presented as a sort of mistake of history, and needed to be rectified. The old guilds were not to be copied but merely used for inspiration, as they too possessed deep-seated flaws.[15]

As with other forms of political modernism, for Brown this new ideology was predicated on a totalizing vision of 'the new'. As he put it, the 'Guild idea was not so much a philosophy of anything as a philosophy of everything', and it was this total conception of life that distinguished the ideology from the 'vague "reformisms"' of the nineteenth century'. Portentously, for Brown 'If more control is needed anywhere it is in the world of ideas' as reformism failed to develop a 'theory that seemed to grip the whole problem' of the crisis of capitalism.[16] To what extent Brown considered guild socialism to be a totalitarian ideology is difficult to gauge. Nevertheless, the totalizing vision of a modern revolution was central to these articles. Historicizing the revolution, looking backwards to move forwards, was also central to this approach. Brown summarized his blend of backward and forward-looking perspectives thus:

> The Guild idea will return, not in its pristine form, but fused with the wider rela-
> tionships and vaster activities of the modern world. We cannot expect the future
> to carry us back to pedlars and fairs, to self-contained and self-sufficing boroughs
> ... But we can at least hope that the lurch of history will carry us one step towards
> medievalism, and let us pause there, not eternally and of fixed purpose, but merely
> to take up a load of old ideas, that we may sift them, and weave those worthy into
> the web of our existence.[17]

This synthesis of old and new into a radical vision for the future is important to underscore. As with Penty's use of the past, the Brown's *futural* thrust took its inspiration from idealized version of history, but ultimately this was done in order to flesh out a vision for elemental renewal of modern, British society.

Brown also discussed the war directly. It too was presented as the product of a crisis of modernity. He highlighted how the nineteenth century had seen a massive increase in the pace of modernization, which would, in all probability, increase still further. Consequently, all human activities had 'become business. All romantic activities of man are commercialised and made mechanical'. This was especially true of war, an activity that, in previous eras, may have possessed a romantic dimension but by 1915 he stressed that 'it is certainly not romantic when No. 171623 of the 2505 infantry regiment of the 250th division is destroyed by an equally remote number firing a gun twenty miles off'. The trope of modernity removing a poetic conception to life is clear from such commentary. Modern war was thus revealed as another dimension of the callous, impersonal world of a decadent modernity brought about by capitalist economics. These articles concluded by stressing that capitalism essentially created two types of mentality. First, unquestioning acceptance of the capitalist mindset, resulting in a repression of emotive engagements with its contradictions and baseness, and so ultimately a form of spiritual death; or second the rejection of capitalism's logic, which led to a dismissal of all reformist solutions to its antinomies, and ultimately pointed to the idea of National Guilds as the only way to retain an authentic sense of transcendent, spiritual life within modern society.[18] It was this need to escape from an all-encompassing crisis created by industrialized modernity, appreciated by a few outsider figures, which helps to reveal the modernist sensibility driving the ideology.

To develop his theory more fully, another series by Brown, 'Gilders of the Chains', explored aspects of the cultural and everyday decadence of capitalist modernity, thus mapping the dynamics of this spiritual death which Brown suggested defined modern living. 'The new capitalism of pleasure has made remarkable progress in the last decade', he claimed, and 'the whole effect of our ever-increasing music-halls, picture palaces, and corner houses has been to give colour to what was drab, and thus to persuade the worker – especially the office worker – that the world is not so bad after all'. To take some examples, his critique of Joseph Lyon's chain of tea houses argued they were a 'pan-Gentleman' movement attempting to induce an ostensible civility that legitimized the immoral division of labour intrinsic to capitalism. Typifying his sometimes obtuse polemic, Brown warned that, in the decadent, pleasure-seeking capitalism of the future, the 'Christians will be thrown to the Lyons, but there will be no fighting in the den for both will need each other'.[19] Another article in the series critiqued the rise of department stores, highlighting that owners of such institutions were interested in image over content. For example, they kept 'a lounge a restaurant, a reading-room, a rock garden, an observation tower – but a shop? Well, incidentally perhaps, but don't mention the vulgar fact'. In wartime, this capitalist culture of duplicity reached new heights, as the 'white-washing industrialism' wallowed in the myth that such outlets were engaged in national service rather than the pursuit of profits.

Tellingly, Brown also criticized Charlie Chaplin, seen as the epitome of capitalism's decadent cultural production. According to the critique, the human mind had innate, though currently repressed, tendencies towards enjoying joviality and idiocy as forms of entertainment. However, because capitalism focused minds merely on 'the struggle for wealth', the resultant population were unable to find humour in anything but the most inane entertainment. Chaplin exemplified this culture, acting as a release valve, the 'Great Release', for the insignificance of a capitalist existence. His was a 'farce, superbly unreal, eccentric, alien to any purpose or order . . . that is the Great Release'.[20] Chaplin was an ephemeral child of the era, and so to contrast this Brown stressed that cultural production had 'to recapture beauty and to reinstate emotion, to find virility somewhere, that is the task'.[21] Meanwhile, journalism, 'modern civilisation's substitute for literature', was another target. Picking out *T. P.'s Weekly, John Bull,* and the *Daily News,* among others, Brown argued that such journals were dominated by 'Sensation, Sentiment, Scurrility and Sex'. This practice of 'gilding the chains' of capitalism through populist print media had reached new heights during the war, again epitomizing capitalism's culture of decadence.

Brown's guild socialist articles thus reveal a writer railing against the cultural dynamics of what he regarded as a decadent modernity, a core aspect of the ideology's discourse. His writings also demonstrate the guild socialist trend of using history as a tool for developing a modern revolutionary consciousness, a tendency that we can see in other guild socialist authors writing for *The New Age.* Indeed, the use of the past to develop a radically *futural* vision, escaping a decant modernity and entering into a new one, is an important theme for appreciating modernist sensibilities, so it is worth exploring this issue in more depth.

William Norman Ewer

The diversity in such guild socialist thinking is important to emphasize. Countering Brown's stress on guild socialism promoting a new, revolutionary nationalism, W. N. Ewer's offered his own version of the *futural* vision, again deeply historicized, to promote internationalism. Ewer had been drawn into radical politics after joining the *Daily Herald* before the war. He was one of the 'Lansbury Lambs', a group of idealistic, young reporters working for the radical daily that also included G. D. H. Cole, recruited to the paper by George Lansbury MP. After the war, Ewer continued working for the *Daily Herald*, becoming its foreign editor, and reporting on the Paris Peace Settlement. He retained sympathy with radical politics too, and was a member of the Communist Party until 1929, before siding with reformist approaches within the labour movement.

Like Brown, Ewer was a conscientious objector during the war, as well as a poet. He was also one of the more minor guild socialist voices in *The New Age*. He developed his historical justification for the ideology in a series of four articles published between November 1915 and March 1916. He set out a potted history of the evolution of the modern nation-state. His narrative began in the Middle Ages, where the

> village and the manor found expression for its local life in moot and leet. As urban communities grew up they evolved spontaneously, without charter or grant, some kind of civic organisation. Religion, confined within the pale of one church, crystal-lised in innumerable associations, from the great monastic orders down to humble local guilds. The peace was kept, after some fashion, by a great network of associa-tions, from the local hue and cry to the great city-leagues of Southern Germany and the Hermandad of Spain. The social structure of Europe was an intricate network of groups, overlapping, inter-locking, shifting and changing: no rigid system, but a live organism of spontaneous, autonomous societies, acknowledging no master, but unconcernedly managing their own business in their own way.

Such a description is a typical example of how the Middle Ages could be idealized as a time when an 'organic' community flourished by guild socialists, a conception of life lost to the modern world he felt. Echoes of Ferdinand Tönnies's thesis championing premodern 'community' over modern 'society' are resonant in the development of such binaries, which were commonplace in guild socialist analyses of the past. Extending this theme, Ewer stressed that before the Renaissance Christendom was 'one articulate whole', yet by the close of the fifteenth century the modern State had come into being. Monarchs cemented their power by creating centralized national units, leading to the modern Leviathan state, characterized as an 'intolerant' and 'jealous beast'. Echoing Brown's arguments, again we see that the history of Europe since the Renaissance presented as an error that needed to be overcome in an elemental fashion through revolution. 'In the name of national unity and state sovereignty', Ewer lamented, 'the free associations of the Middle Ages, whether religious or political or industrial, were to be destroyed or reduced to a mere servile dependence upon omnipotent governments'.[22] Thus, in the fifteenth and sixteenth centuries, history witnessed the emasculation of

Britain's guilds, nearly to the point of non-existence. The 'spirit' had gone out of them, he stressed. In its rise to dominance, the Leviathan state 'slew, deliberately, and for its own purposes, the very idea of free and spontaneous associations'.[23]

In terms of its general structure, according to Ewer the modern state had remained essentially unchanged since the sixteenth century, though there had been some superficial alterations to its constitution, such as the decline of aristocracy and the rise of an ostensibly democratic parliament. Despite these 'minor' shifts, the centralized, secularized military prowess of the modern state was clearly again ravaging Europe, as it had done periodically since the sixteenth century. Modern guild socialism needed to 'establish an organic diversity in place of a mechanical unity'; and aimed 'at the revival of self-governing, self-existing corporations which shall not be servants but partners of the State in working to secure the full and free life of the individual'. Arguing that 'the national idea destroyed the guild idea', Ewer's historicism implored guild socialists to aim at destroying the national idea: 'We must effect a transvaluation of political values . . . We must uncrown the State . . . We must, as national guildsman, be internationalists: for international conflicts necessitate entire national unity and entire State-sovereignty'. By ending nationalist ideologies that underpinned international conflict, and decentralizing the Leviathan of the modern state, Ewer concluded that the current order would wither, and the Leviathan state would die alongside it.[24]

The association between solving a modern crisis and re-rooting Britain in the cultures of the Middle Ages was again presented as a reversal of a historical error, and was used to evoke the modernist theme of a new era emerging from a decaying cultural dynamic. War was the ultimate expression of the errors of the age, and so a cultural revolution was required to overcome the crisis of capitalism. We can see a similar theme in A. J. Penty's wartime interventions, which again laid the blame for war squarely at the door of capitalism.

Arthur Joseph Penty

To begin a survey of Penty's wartime arguments, it is worth initially turning to his 1917 publication *Old Worlds for New: A Study of the Post-Industrial State*. This essentially consisted of essays written for the *Daily Herald* before the war. However the text also offered a new introduction engaging with the wartime crisis directly. Here, Penty summarized how the revolutionary conditions created by the war gave guild socialism a new resonance:

For my changed attitude on this issue the war is responsible. Hitherto I had supposed that society was to be reconstructed by peaceable means – at any rate under the normal conditions which peace presupposes – for though I recognized the possibility of revolution, it did not appear to me to be in any way imminent . . . Capitalism, I thought, would have to be undermined; it would never yield to a frontal attack. But the war has altered the factors of the problem. Capitalism no longer appears impregnable. Indeed, I feel the war by its reactions will break it up, and in all probability precipitate a revolution. In this light the National Guild

propaganda acquires a new significance. The fact of the war has brought it within
the range of practical politics, for what was impossible in times of peace may be
possible in a time of revolution.[25]

The introduction went on to claim that the economic developments during the war
were leading to a revival of the guild system, not Fabian-style state socialism, as
many suspected. Critical of the idea of a postwar boom solving the looming crisis
of unemployment, he highlighted that this issue was likely to spark revolution in the
near future. Related to this, central to Penty's critique of capitalist modernity was the
idea that the modern, industrial economy simply produced too much, to the ultimate
detriment of mankind. The clearest example of this was his claim that the war was
the result of a German economic crisis, which itself had been brought about through
overproduction combined with a search for new markets within Germany. Thus
Penty was able to pin blame for the outbreak of war both on Germany, and on a wider
critique of the capitalist industrial system. Inevitably, the capitalist economic order
had to be overthrown, to achieve a stable future. Penty stressed that in his proposed
'post-industrial' new age, rather than reinvesting surplus capital in industry which only
encouraged increased production, excess wealth needed to be spent on adding to the
aesthetic richness of a modern world. As an architect by profession, unsurprisingly he
stressed that such artistic embellishment of an alternate modernity should be achieved
especially through architectural projects. Reinvesting in industry was only exacerbating
unregulated, and therefore dangerous, industrial production, the root cause of the war.
These complex arguments were developed by Penty in the pages of *The New Age*.

Stressing the sense of discontinuity and historical rupture brought about by the
conflict, an essay from 1917, 'After the War', asserted that the conflict marked 'the close
of an era in our civilisation' and was 'the inevitable catastrophic ending of a society
which has chosen to deny the laws of its own being'. Here, Penty again stressed the
conflict was the result of German economic instability, an aggressive war undertaken
by the nation as the only way for the country to prevent its capitalist economy from
crashing down through overproduction. This central truth was stressed thus: 'I do not
exaggerate when I say that so far as our welfare and happiness is concerned it is a matter
of life and death with us that this fact should be publicly recognised'. Overcoming the
crisis of modernity, especially industrial overproduction, required the reconstruction
of society on a new set of principles. He again sketched out the need for guild socialism
to cure industrialized society. After the war he predicted an industrial conflict in the
wake of rising unemployment, opening 'the floodgates of anarchy and revolution'.
The realization of Penty's political modernist vision was crucial as this alternative
modernity alone would be able to redress the balance between man and machine,
pulling back the present trend for workers to be replaced by mechanized production.[26]
Though sceptical of many aspects of the industrialized world, Penty's variant of the
ideology was also inherently revolutionary, using a mythic reading of the Middle Ages
to imagine a more hospitable, modern world.

He also discussed the function of the state. Primarily its role was to 'give protection
to the community: military protection in the first place; civil protection in the next;
and economic protection in the last'. The creation of guilds would provide people

with an enhanced level of economic protection, a feature that the decadent capitalist state was essentially failing to provide. For Penty, this issue needed to be justified philosophically. Thus, Enlightenment thought also became a key target, and the most important problem facing the state was an 'acceptance by reformers of Rousseau's doctrine of "the natural perfectibility of mankind"'. Unlike the majority of socialists, who were subliminally recapitulating what he regarded as this central tenet of liberalism, like Orage Penty did not believe in an ultimate human perfectibility. Alternately, the conception of human nature accepted during the Middle Ages, based on Original Sin, offered a polar opposite to Rossueau's Enlightenment philosophy of human perfectibility. For Penty, Original Sin ultimately created order in medieval society, as this concept justified the state's role of providing potentially intrusive forms of protection and structure for imperfect humans, thus legitimizing the guild system. However, such revolutionary critiques of the Enlightenment project were still the preserve of a minority of intellectuals. Although the war was helping to break down the idea that Western civilization would automatically progress to a perfect human society, it was not destroying the pernicious idea of the perfectibility of man. Until this ideal was also demolished, it would be impossible to reinvest a new world and the new state with the strict sense of morality that Penty believed brought order to the Middle Ages.[27]

Continuing this religious theme, Penty stressed guild socialism held a spiritual as well as material dynamic elsewhere too. For example, with the emergence of Soviet Bolsheviks, he compared the guild socialist movement favourably to materialistic revolutionary ideas of nascent British Bolsheviks – for him, to be found within the auspices of the Plebs League and the Socialist Labour Party. In the essay 'National Guilds v. The Class War', for example, the central struggle for ideas preceding a revolution was between guild socialists and what he dubbed 'Neo-Marxians'. In the coming revolution brought about by the war, he was clear that socialists 'must cleave either to a purely materialistic or to a spiritual conception of the nature of the problem which confronts us'. By recognizing the centrality of reconstructing the spiritual reality of the Middle Ages, along with aspects of its economic relations, guild socialism was the only alternate modernity with a solution to both the profound spiritual and material problems of the day. The aim of guild socialism was 'nothing less than to restore the unity to life which the Renaissance destroyed', and 'unlike other movements which have aimed at spiritual regeneration it deems it advisable to begin at the economic end of the problem in the belief that it is only by and through attacking material and concrete evils that a spiritual awakening is possible'. By thus recognizing that the crisis created by modernity was 'both spiritual and material', guild socialism distinguished itself from the materialistic 'Neo-Marxian philosophy' that was developing in the wake of the Russian Revolution. So here we see a striking example of how a spiritual solution to the crisis of modernity was styled as the movement's unique selling point.[28]

By the close of the war, Penty went even further in developing the myth of revolution leading to an alternate, guild socialist modernity. His essay from September 1918, 'On the Class War Again', renewed his critique of 'Neo-Marxians' like Walton Newbold, and framed the postwar milieu as one of a 'great struggle between Capital and Labour'. The labour movement had to embrace the returning, victorious army. Though this development was now likely, such a victory would not be the end of the matter. 'In our anticipated revolution', Penty projected that, 'the moderate party will come first'. This took the form of the progressive Labour Party, which, lacking in radical drive, would drift towards collectivist principles, and would essentially 'dilly-dally' and so 'all its actions will be feeble'. Following this period, Penty predicted that 'the great crisis will arrive and our future history will depend entirely on the way it is met'. At this point, the war between the two competing sets of revolutionary ideas, two forms of political modernism, came into view. As he foresaw, the 'Neo-Marxians (our Bolsheviks) will get their chance', potentially resulting in Soviet-style anarchy for the country. To avoid this, guild socialists had to dismantle the impoverished ideals of 'British Bolsheviks' immediately, preventing those sympathetic to political modernism from believing that the Russian model formed the only solution to his crisis of modernity. Specifically, guild socialists had to demonstrate how their competitor's ideology lacked a clear social theory from which to create a new society, and reveal how it was obsessed with the process of gaining power for its own sake. 'They do not propose to change the system', he concluded, 'but only its ownership'. Guildsmen, on the other hand, 'not only have questioned industrialism, they have some idea of what to put in its place', thereby saving society from successive wars and steering it towards the security achieved by looking 'back to the Middle Ages for inspiration guidance'.[29]

To conclude the discussion on Penty, it is worth noting that, in 1920, he published *A Guildsman's Interpretation of History*, based on articles published in *The New Age* from November 1918. Again we see Penty's idealization of the Middle Ages, and his critique of Marxism's historical materialism that derided the period. We also see in his study guild socialism's highly selective, and ultimately mythic, version of history, used to justify the teleological vision of revolution. Picking up on these problems, the *Times Literary Supplement* was withering in its critique of Penty's use of the past, likening it to fiction, an important quality to note. In its strident examination, the review rightly argued that the utopian imagination at the core of Penty's thinking did not allow for the development of a realistic vision of medieval life: 'The main thing about paradise is of course the general idea, and precision is a mistake. To attempt to locate historically this communal heaven of the Middle Ages would be as futile as to send a column from Mosul to survey the Garden of Eden.' As with other guild socialists, recognizing this essentially modernist, utopian use of history is important, and is an issue that contrasts with those who would characterize Penty as simply seeking a return to the past. Rather, his politics were ultimately *futural*, using the past to promote an alternate future – even if he characterized the vision in part as a return to the supposed sanities of an earlier age. Meanwhile, as with Penty, others in the guild socialist movement were vocal on the need for revolution to solve the postwar crisis, a theme exemplified by Maurice B. Reckitt.

Maurice B. Reckitt

Turning to Maurice B. Reckitt, co-founder of the National Guilds League, we find another Anglo-Catholic supporter of guild socialism. Following the war, from 1923

Reckitt was the chairman of the League of the Kingdom of God, an organization emerging from the Church Socialist League. Showing its relevance to Anglo-Catholics, T. S. Eliot among others was drawn to the league, and from 1932 the organization published the journal *Christendom, A Journal of Christian Sociology,* edited by Reckitt.[30] Regarding his wartime guild socialist activism, from 1915 we get a sense of the centrality of his revolutionary vision for the future from a series of essays collectively titled 'The Prospects of the Guild Idea'. Echoing others, for him guild socialism offered a revolutionary solution to capitalism, as well as a break from other forms of left-wing revolution.[31] The future transformation of the state was central, and here too the escape from capitalism would allow for a reconfiguration of the relationship between citizens and the state. Moreover, for Reckitt the future society would be an organic one, thus: 'Society is more than a mere horde of consumers; its past memories and its future destinies, all that concerns its public life, centres in the State – and the State is born, not made.'[32] However, this new, guild socialist state would be 'born' only if trade unions developed the required new partnerships with the state.[33]

Aside from such wartime publicism, typical of the movement, Reckitt's most significant pronouncements on the revolutionary nature of the ideology came at the end of the war in his book *The Meaning of National Guilds.* Written with the journalist Carl Eric Bechhofer, it summarized the key guild socialist themes for a general audience, highlighting areas of debate among the ideology's activists. Demonstrating the impact of the war on Reckitt's own approach, the book was dedicated 'to those who, having no "stake in their own country," yet fought for its honour abroad, in hope that they may one day fight for their own at home'. Typifying the ideology's identification of a crisis in capitalist modernity, he devoted one chapter to critiquing the idea of progress, claiming it to be a capitalist myth:

> The gospel of 'Progress' is a gospel of quietism and greatly have the forces of tyranny and avarice profited therefrom. It has stolen from the workers, and from that movement which they have raised as a challenge to the machine of Power and Gain that we know as Capitalism, the very quality which alone could supply the inspiration for their crusade – the quality of faith. It is faith alone which can move the mountain of the wage-system. To-day the apathy of the worker is largely due to the fact that he does not believe this can be done . . .[34]

The links between revolution and a new form of politics based on faith clearly resonate in such extracts. Meanwhile, his conclusions regarding the likelihood for a guild socialist revolution stressed the theme of more gradual transition to a guild socialist state, rather than a violent revolution. He hoped that guilds would emerge in one or two sectors to begin with, before overtaking the whole sociopolitical order. However, Reckitt feared that an aggressive capitalism might suppress postwar strikes by setting the army against protesting workers. Such state violence could lead to a revolutionary climate in the country. Out of this climate guild socialism would also emerge victorious, however, this was not the desired route to victory. Reckitt's publicism thus clearly promoted a postwar revolution. Others chimed with this call for a peaceful path to revolution, most clearly G. D. H. Cole, one of the movement's most high-profile theorists.

George Douglass Howard Cole

A Fabian intellectual and later Oxford University academic, Cole became a central figure in the guild socialist movement during the war. He had broadly aligned himself with *The New Age*'s guild socialist project in his influential 1913 work *The World of Labour*, an analysis again critiquing state-directed socialism and calling for left-wing radicals to develop a more decentralized alternative. In his alternate vision for modernity, the working classes would again be economically re-empowered, as had been argued in Penty's and especially Hobson's discussions on the rise of guilds from unions. Cole soon became a regular author for the journal, but, in an attempt to move the ideology away from the intellectual debates of *The New Age* and promote it more widely within the labour movement, in 1915 he also helped to found the National Guilds League. Soon, this institution became another hub of guild socialist activity, competing with Orage's *The New Age*. It even produced its own journal, *The Guildsman*, designed to generate a widespread propaganda for the guild socialist project.

In tenor, Cole was much less combative in his publicism when compared to figures such as Orage. Representing the more moderate end of the guild socialist spectrum, he emphasized in his first book to engage with the war, *Labour in Wartime*, how the conflict would lead to a new spirit within the working classes. Though not predicting immediate revolution, Cole nevertheless stressed the regenerative aspect of the war, claiming it 'seems at least as probable that those who return from a life spent in the open air will be far more intolerant of the routine and the petty oppressions of workshop life, and far readier for some sort of revolt against it'.[35] Meanwhile, his new preface to the 1917 reprint of *The World of Labour* outlined his basic attitude towards labour in wartime. The war was a conflict of ideas, a battle between industrial autocracy and industrial democracy. The former came in two forms, state socialism of the Fabian type, and state assisted capitalism, epitomized by the more severe working relations introduced by the Munitions Act. As with Orage, Cole was fearful that this precedent for greater state control over workers would continue after the war, leading to an ever more enslaved relationship between worker and employer. The potential saviour was the trade union movement, which needed to reject compromise with capitalism, develop its own revolutionary agenda and adopt the long-term goal of creating autonomous guilds. This need not happen overnight, and Cole stressed that perfecting the revolutionary structure of the new trade unionism for victory sometime after the war was far more important than rushing the project during the conflict.[36]

To examine Cole's version of the guild socialist revolution in more detail, we can turn to a set of articles for *The New Age* from 1917 titled 'Reflections on the Wage System'. Unlike Orage, here Cole did not present the war itself as a cataclysmic moment allowing for the swift transfer to guild socialism. The war merely opened space for credible discussion on changing the relationship between capital and labour, potentially ushering in a phase of 'transition' between capitalism and National Guilds. At some future point, an apocalyptic yet revolutionary moment would still be necessary for the switch to become complete. 'For the present', his second article concluded, 'the task of the workers is to concentrate on increasing and perfecting their control of their labour, which is the basis of their industrial power'.[37] He also argued for the democratic control of factories, as a first step towards the abolition of capitalism. The ultimate solution though was to remove the underlying functions of capital: 'we shall succeed in overthrowing industrial capitalism only if we first make it socially functionless ... This means that, before capitalism can be overthrown, there must be wrested from it both its control of production and its control of exchange'. Only through a strong, nationally organized trade union movement could this process commence. By extending trade union responsibilities to the management of labour, one could generate a transition period of 'joint management'. Cole stressed that such temporary 'join management' was not permanent partnership with employers in the management of industry, and was confident that a taste of authority would encourage a greater thirst for power and revolutionary verve within the trade union movement.[38]

Vital to a successful transitional period was not mere control of the means of production, but to 'secure control of the product'. He described how labour needed power over both the organization of the workshop, and 'the product', namely the means of investing capital, purchasing raw materials and selling of finished products. During the war, state control over industry was increasing, while workers were also gaining greater power in their workshops. The continuation of these two processes alone could not bring about the fall of capitalism, though it may result in the Fabian's state model for the economy. However, wartime conditions were creating what he called 'a breach in the system', which allowed the goal of a guild socialist revolution to be pursued. Nevertheless, it would still need to deploy a final weapon to destroy capitalism: a revolutionary, general strike. 'The more we are inclined to foresee catastrophic action as the last stage of the coming social revolution', he stressed, 'the more prepared we must be for the evolutionary steps which alone can pave the way for the great catastrophe'. Blackleg proof unions and the united will of workers were both essential conditions for the success of this political modernist deployment of the myth of a revolutionary transformation of modern society.[39] For Cole, 'Only the manpower of an awakened people can defeat the economic power of a clever capitalism'.[40]

In sum, for Cole guild socialism's alternate modernity could only emerge if it was properly prepared for. This meant long-term planning for revolution some time after the war, otherwise capitalism would be victorious. Meanwhile, the ideology's original economic architect offered the fullest elaboration of the guild socialism's ability to seize on the revolutionary potential of wartime itself, developing a complex, economic critique of wartime Britain. To see how this modernist sensibility, which promoted the revolutionary 'new' in order to fatally subvert a liberal-bourgeois hegemony, found further articulation through economic concepts it is worth examining S. G. Hobson's perspective in some detail.

Samuel George Hobson

Before Cole's interventions, S. G. Hobson was guild socialism's most influential economic writer. He too joined the National Guilds' League in 1915, but was intimidated by Cole's weightier intellectual credentials, and so he focused his wartime guild socialist activism on *The New Age*. From the outset of the war, Hobson too saw an opportunity for a new politics and society to emerge. He again stressed that a profound crisis had united the nation as a single, communal unit, thus 'giving a sense of universal fellowship with all our nationals, as of men bound together in some great enterprise or overwhelming danger'. From 1914, he argued that the proletariat from each warring country, 'having experienced this most thrilling of all human fellowships', would try to recreate their revitalizing experiences in domestic industry. Meanwhile, like Penty and others, Hobson characterized the postwar scenario as one where acute unemployment, resulting from a lack of credit in the financial system, would lead to a downturn in national industry. A workforce unified by common combat experiences would negotiate with capitalists 'not as individual employees but as an organisation' and demand a partnership in the management of industry. Thus, from 1914 he was clear that 'war has prepared the path for Guilds'.[41]

Building on these themes, a series of articles from 1916 called 'The Permanent Hypothesis' critiqued various voices calling for moderate reforms of working conditions. The eponymous 'permanent hypothesis' was simply Hobson's preferred way of signifying the proletariat being treated as a commodity. Left-wing reformers and capitalists believed such commoditization was unavoidable, while revolutionary guild socialists believed this 'permanent hypothesis' was a myth and should be eliminated, the only way to truly democratize society. On the subject of leadership within the labour movement, Hobson was, like Orage, highly critical. For example, when discussing how various models for reconstruction acknowledged the necessity for a shift in the status of labour, he insisted that when 'these concessions are spontaneously offered by employers, it is not for us to accept them with whispering humbleness . . . labour must demand the maximum. If only the Labour leaders . . . Alas! There is none; no, not one'.[42]

He also again stressed the 'spiritual hiatus in English life', characterized as a lack of dignity, sense of unity and self-respect within the country's population, as a phenomenon brought about by capitalism. This had a moral dimension, as 'the permanent hypothesis destroys the self-respect of Labour, compelling it not only to value itself on a commodity basis, but to acquiesce in the morality of its masters'. To combat this, he called for a new social contract, one governed by four key points: '(a) a more or less blind revolt against degrading conditions; (b) the imperative necessity of a more scientific and efficient system of production; (c) the call for a higher spiritual and moral life; and (d) a revivified passion for freedom'. The 'old social contract', he claimed, 'has been dissolved by the war' as both the employers' and the workers' conceptions of each other were being radically altered. A new social contract would offer 'a revolution in all our ways – our way of thinking, our way of acting, our way of faith. Invariably so, because the mass of mankind shall have mounted to a higher plane'.[43] Such ideals of spiritual regeneration forming an escape from capitalist modernity were central to guild socialism's political modernism.

Later essays emphasized the necessity of an active, revolutionary tone to achieving lasting change, important to stress because passive ideas suggesting an inevitable transition to a socialist economy were the unsophisticated myths of an earlier age.[44] Capitalism needed to be radically confronted and challenged; it would not simply wither away on its own accord. The final essay, 'In War', examined the relationship between the permanent hypothesis and the wartime conditions. Several further points emerged here. First, Hobson noted that the wage system had been pushed to one side in some sectors of industry by the war – especially in the army – allowing many ordinary workers temporary freedom from the status of wage-slave. Second, both industrial leaders and the state acknowledged that co-operation with organised labour would be essential to winning the war. Hobson emphasized that these gains should be built upon, and detailed how joint councils of trade unions and employers, along with government representation for directing each industry for the national war effort, were positive steps towards guild socialism. Moreover, wartime had created a sense of urgency, allowing for comprehensive reform of the nation's political economy. Thus,

> Truly may we say that in the midst of death we are in life; that in the stress and tumult of war our vision of peace is clear and vivid. Never in times of peace have we realised how false is the permanent hypothesis; nor did we see the true bearing and incidence of unemployment; nor did the urgent need of industrial autonomy assert itself so instantaneously; nor did we understand how vital is functional definition and freedom.

Rejecting the permanent hypothesis was 'the one emancipating movement that can demand of us that emotional and spiritual energy without which no new era can be approached, much less begun'.[45] Calling for people to reject the 'permanent hypothesis' was a statement demanding a wholesale rejection of the capitalist version of modernity.

With the war turning against Germany in the summer of 1918, Hobson offered further detail on the transition to the guild socialist alternative. The first, a standalone piece, 'The Criteria of Peace', stressed the discontinuity brought about by war, claiming that any peace conference must not simply 'reconstruct civilisation', but needed to 'register and formulate a new-born civilisation of which the horrors of the war are but the birth pangs'. Labour needed to be strongly represented at any peace conference, as such 'economic democracy' was necessary for the future of the world. British and German labour representatives had to ensure international leaders grasped the underlying point that 'the economic solution is as much Labour's affair as the capitalists'' and of major importance in the discussions'. Labour movements thus had to demand and insist on 'a new economic *regime*'.[46]

Following this polemic, Hobson offered a series titled 'Chapters on Transition', detailing the revolutionary transfer to guild socialism. He stressed that society was not merely a lump of clay, able to be remodelled into various new forms, but was a 'vast living organism, all its parts evolved in the slow process of time and by patient, human effort'. Hobson's political modernist vision of creative destruction saw this organism in dire need of dramatic surgery: 'since society is a living organism, it often contracts ailments that call for treatment, diseases that need the surgeon's knife'. He argued that the successful revolutions of the past had been such surgical operations, cutting away at diseased aspects of society. The current social malady was the commoditization of labour, therefore, if any revolutionary 'surgical operation becomes imperative, it will be the extirpation of wagery'.[47]

Offering more detail on constitutional changes, Hobson claimed that the new society 'must compel unquestioned obedience to the new order'. This was especially true for those empowered by the revolution as 'Government is a function; but unless strictly subject to the will and policy of the citizen-State, it becomes a tyranny. An economic revolution unguided by sound citizenship may also become a tyranny.' Hobson's vision thus decried an autocracy, and was motivated at least by a desire for a more democratic society. How democratic such a model actually could be is more debatable. Symbolizing his empowering vision, the monarchy would have no place in the new order: 'In an economic democracy, a monarchy is not only incongruous but impossible; citizenship itself assumes the sovereign quality.'[48] Furthermore, the war was creating a unique social dynamic, it had 'entered into our being', and was shattering the principles of labour as a commodity:

> It is not the labour commodity the Army asks for; it is men. Neither is it the labour commodity that munitions factories demand; it is men . . . The economic distinction between man's body and the labour power in it . . . has been torn to shreds in the violent reactions of war.

Again, although war was creating conditions for change, it was still necessary to actively work towards achieving guild socialism. 'War is certainly a potent solvent', he concluded, 'it is our business to understand and apply the solutions it throws up from the depths of its cauldron'.[49]

These essays were followed by a longer series titled 'The Workshop', a further contribution to Hobson's 'Chapters on Transition'. He reaffirmed his distinction between the compromise position of labour gaining 'part control' in the management of industry, and the need to usher in a temporary period of 'joint control', with the ultimate aim of transferring all management duties to labour alone. This vision stressed the amalgamation of unions, in addition to democratic principles entering the workshop. He also raised the idea of unions securing collective contracts with employers. Unions would then distribute members' salaries, a 'halfway stage between existing workshop conditions and Guild organisation'. Whereas the creation of workshop committees possessing a voice in the management of industry was 'static in conception, based on the permanent hypothesis, the principle of collective contract possesses within itself the magic of its own metamorphosis'. This new type of union, an Industrial Union, could even develop sufficient capital to inaugurate its own banking system and begin to control the supply of raw materials, as well as that of labour. Collective contracts negotiated by Industrial Unions would thus break 'into the sacred arc of the capitalist covenant', setting in 'motion the forces hitherto deemed to be strictly within the control of the employer'.[50]

Central to new trends in the industrial workshop was the emergence of the radicalized shop stewards, 'the stormy petrel of approaching industrial unrest'.[51] The labour movement needed to be decentralized too, and so 'The real line to pursue was to develop the local spirit', alongside encouraging 'local autonomy, to decentralise power, to recognise the efficiency of that democracy for which we had presumably gone to war'.[52] The new shop stewards, the 'new men' as he called them at one point, were the epitome of the realization that the workshop, not the local branch of a Trade Union, was now the nerve centre of the consciousness of the proletariat. Shop stewards would force the amalgamation of unions, 'bringing the worker of every grade into organic cohesion'.[53] These figures constituted a visionary avant-garde who possessed:

> a new and fresh point of view . . . He no longer regards the bench as the perquisite of his particular craft; the shop presents itself to his eye as a ganglion of labour nerves, all related to each other, touching each other, within reasonable bounds of equal significance and industrial value. Viewing the workshop in this light, he immediately awaits industrial amalgamation, with unified command, that he may more quickly achieve strategic victory, where formerly only minor tactics prevailed.[54]

Hobson's concluding essay defined this idea as 'the stuff of a new life, the seeds of a new epoch'.[55] The quest for social rebirth was clearly evident in this vision.

Finally, it is worth underscoring that from November 1918 he began another series titled 'The Influence of the War upon Labour', reviewing labour conditions resulting from the war. These reprised ideas developed in the summer of 1918, and stressed a changed mood in workers. War had encouraged individual initiative. Moreover, world events, especially the Russian Revolution and the Stockholm Conference, alongside food shortages and other domestic crises, had 'stimulated interest in world-problems'. During a war, 'where they have faced, unflinching, grave reverses, and won through by a national tenacity', workers underwent elemental change. Thus, 'they will not be slow to turn to industrial purposes. A victorious citizen army will not submit to industrial oppression, if its leaders are as wise as the men are brave'. The war had demonstrated that 'it is not state control but rather industrial control that will provide our salvation'. Labour could regard the war period 'with pride and satisfaction', for it had emerged from war:

> with an invigorated faith, a widened horizon. Our men return trained to vast operations, their minds coloured by great conceptions. The fusing of new principles with these unexampled experiences opens vast vistas of an industrial destiny more consonant with sanity and the humane. Labour has glimpsed the meaning of economic freedom. In the terror and devastation of war, in the sombre memories behind us and the sordid necessities before us, this stands sure: there is a new vision, and the people shall not perish.[56]

So the spirit of the trenches, for Hobson, had radicalized the grass roots of the labour movement, given it new vigour, an overarching sense of purpose, and a renewed belief in its destiny.

However, after the war this vision for revolution did not last long. Losing faith in Orage's journal after its embrace of Social Credit in 1919, Hobson tried to initiate a guild system of his own in the building trade in the early 1920s. However, economic realities revealed the many difficulties behind his scheme and his brief postwar experiment with guilds came to an end. He detailed this disillusionment in his autobiography. Here, he also highlighted that his ideas took on what was for him a surprising new role, as they had been translated into Italian by another member of *The New Age* circle, Odon Por. Hobson was convinced that he had been read with interest by a young Benito Mussolini.[57] Such speculation highlights the link between guild socialism and nascent fascism, which is important to document.

Odon Por, guild socialism and fascism

To conclude that guild socialism, and indeed *The New Age* more generally, was a purely British cultural phenomenon would be erroneous. As the following chapter will make clear, the journal's many contributors, some of whom closely identified with guild socialism, were part of a Europe-wide nexus of radical thought. Ideas developed in the journal, such as syndicalism, were borrowed from Europeans, while guild socialism's own impact could spread back to the continent. For example, the Hungarian intellectual Odon Por provides a clear instance of a figure linking guild socialism with European political modernism, especially Italian Fascism at this time. Working as the London correspondent of the Italian socialist paper *Avanti!* before the war, Por became part of *The New Age* network. He later became a pronounced supporter of early fascism in Italy, writing on the affinities between guild socialism and Italian Fascism. By the 1930s he was a contributor to many fascist journals, and also became closely associated with Ezra Pound as he developed his own sympathies for Italian Fascism.[58]

To give a flavour of his active engagement in *The New Age*'s wartime promotion of guild socialism, in a 1914 article, 'War and After', Por argued that political socialism had failed because of the fragmented nature of modern society. Central to Por's critique was the claim that there existed no socialist unity 'holding, so to say, man's body and soul'. All the socialist parties of Europe had so far failed to provide a unifying vision for revolution. In order for revolution to occur, the proletariat needed to attain a far greater level of self-organization; therefore, 'National Unions are wanted which, beyond being ready to stop the nation's work, are also capable of assuming the functions of production'. Typically, Por proposed that new National Unions should be able to stop and start national production at will. They would comprise 'every vital function of society', and would possess a vital, organic quality that would compete with the sense of community offered by military organizations. Such unions required a 'revolutionary tendency, aiming at the reorganisation of economic relations'. Crucially, this

> organising vision, emanating from a living organism, comes into play only when the insurrectional tendency is accompanied by an active tendency towards expropriation of function. The union only becomes alive when it passes from passive resistance to attack, for only then does it release the powers of all-comprehensive activity.

With the outbreak of war, he stressed that the 'historic moment of the proletariat is drawing near'. National Unions would provide unique institutions to harness 'the common work and the communal spirit . . . which alone can change the armies of destruction into armies of creation'. In other words, as with other guild socialists, Por's publicism linked war and revolution as an escape from a decadent, capitalist modernity.[59]

Then in February 1919, he developed a series of three articles discussing the emergence of a guild system in Italy after the war, 'Towards National Guilds in Italy'. Such contributions demonstrate how the guild idea was not limited to Britain. Meanwhile, turning to his subsequent 1923 book, *Guilds and Co-operatives in Italy*, here we see that Por more clearly established the transferability of guild socialist ideology. Indeed, showing an affinity between guild socialism and the emergence of fascism, he also presented Mussolini's Fascism as a movement that flirted with reactionary politics, before entering into a truly constructive project of national regeneration, key for Italy's future.[60] Por was not the only link between the guild socialists and nascent fascism. Several guild socialists, most prominently A. J. Penty, became fascist fellow travellers by the 1930s. Moreover, at least aspects of the ideology also influenced some British fascists. One clear case here was Oswald Mosley. An avid reader of *The New Age*, according to his most recent biographer Stephen Dorrill, Mosley even considered purchasing the journal. He also found the ideas highly relevant to his own developing radicalism in the 1920s especially. For example, preceding his turn to the Labour Party in 1924, he avidly read the guild socialist economic theories. So in turn these ideas, especially as they developed corporate state themes, combined with the movement's spiritual nationalism, became a significant aspect of Mosley's intellectual transition to fascism.[61]

Yet although such links are significant to plot, care should be exercised here too. In itself, guild socialism was not simply a nascent form of fascism. Rather, it was a fully developed, socialist ideology in its own right, and clearly lacked the potent ultra-nationalist qualities needed to fit the leading definitions of generic fascism. Rather, it is useful to characterize it as a unique form of political modernism, part of a new genus of revolutionary political ideologies that decried capitalist modernity and called for an alternate modern world through revolutionary action, a broad trend which also included fascism and communism. Such categorization stresses guild socialism's potential compatibility with these other ideologies, all of which were operating within a wider matrix of radical thought that decried the capitalist order and worked towards establishing plausible alternatives through revolutionary politics during and after the war. Thus, in Britain alone, interwar movements that also responded to the underlying concerns that animated guild socialism include Kibbo Kift, the Social Credit Movement, the British Union of Fascists, the British Communist Party and Distributism.

Conclusions

From this survey, we can come to a number of tentative conclusions regarding the development of guild socialism, and its relevance to cultures of modernism. Most importantly, we can see the modernist themes of the ending of an era, and the need for an alternate culture to replace the milieu developed by capitalist modernity, were central aspects of the guild socialist project. The revolutionary thrust of the ideology also gave *The New Age* a key selling point during the war, and so its identity in the marketplace of modernist journals at this time was indelibly marked by this potentially exhilarating revolutionary thrust. For its readers, engrossing visions of wholesale cultural and political change could be engaged with as a result of its promotion of this wide-ranging, revolutionary discourse. Moreover, voices were diverse. From the perspective of Hobson, the revolutionary cause needed to be developed through detailed economic arguments, while other figures, such as Ivor Brown, were far more interested in understanding the cultural impact of capitalism and the need to develop an alternate vision for British modernity. Despite these differences in emphasis, what was inescapable in the wartime print run of the weekly journal was a sustained, forward-looking vision, radicalized by the war. Indeed, guild socialists were figures that placed at the centre of their thought a critique of capitalism that argued the commoditization of society fragmented the social landscape and prevented a truly spiritually sustaining form of existence from developing in modern times. Only by seizing on a revolutionary moment could this esoteric critique of capitalism achieve its desired reconfiguration of society, and accomplish the modernist redemption that such intellectuals craved.

However, like much of art produced by cultures of modernism, this vision remained largely esoteric in its own time – even if it was able to create the occasional scare for bourgeois sensibilities, as we saw at the beginning of this chapter. Although the guild socialist discourse was not concerned primarily with discussing aesthetic innovation – for many marking it as a movement lacking direct relevance to British cultures of modernism – uncoupling our understanding of modernism from aesthetics alone allows us to see guild socialism's affinities with wider modernist sensibilities. Meanwhile, intellectuals working on many other, largely esoteric visions of renewal at this time could find common cause in the politics and cultural debates housed in the pages of *The New Age*. To develop this theme in some more depth, we need to examine the wider discursive field gravitating around capitalist modernity as decadence, cultural palingenesis and war that developed within the journal during the 1914–18 period. This will allow our analysis to reveal further how critiques of the conflict, competing visions of cultural and political revolution, and modernist concerns were developed in the pages of *The New Age*.

The New Age's Radical Intelligentsia and Modernism

With a focus on its guild socialist agenda, we have already seen how *The New Age* developed a diverse discursive field promoting the war as a watershed event, a cataclysm bringing about the potential for cultural renewal. This re-reading of its wartime years takes us beyond some earlier assertions found in the secondary literature, such as Samuel Hynes who suggested that the journal 'became little more than a weekly review of the war'.[1] As has now been established, *The New Age* offered readers sustained access to revolutionary political thought. Yet we should also be sensitive to the highly variegated nature of its discourses during the conflict. Orage's editorship allowed the magazine to promote many ideas, and numerous contributors developed sets of radical essays engaging with themes of Britain and Europe experiencing revolutionary endings and beginnings.

Given its weekly nature, in total this wartime output consisted of many thousands of pages of writing over the course of the 1914–18 period, and so developing a comprehensive analysis of this material is simply impossible to achieve in a single chapter on the journal. In order to offer an overview of this discursive field, this final chapter on *The New Age* will précis the positions of a selection of at least some of the notable contributors to the journal's pages during the war, as well as some more minor voices that help convey a sense of the diversity here. Study of such lesser-known voices in the journal is still embryonic, and so what is presented here is analysis that merely scratches the surface of the variegated nature of thought and opinion set out in *The New Age* at this time. Nevertheless, what emerges from this albeit limited survey is a picture of a diverse range of culturally modernist discourses in *The New Age*, each finding idiosyncratic registers to diagnose cultural crisis as a consequence of modernity, and propose radical alternatives that were not being considered by the cultural mainstream at this time.

War fever and early responses to the conflict

Aside from the excitable early rhetoric of Orage's 'Notes of the Week' which we have already encountered, immediately following the outbreak of the conflict war fever could be detected in a variety of other articles too. For example, the 'Military Notes' column by Romney conveyed the tone of the initial phase of war fever among European intellectuals. One article from August 1914 exemplified the tenor when stating 'I think we may say with Goethe on a former occasion that we are assisting at the birth of a new epoch.'[2] Similarly, Alice Morning's 'Impressions of Paris' series manifested similar, palingenetic themes in her reports on the war fever in France. For instance, she claimed that some of her socialist friends were 'already building free utopia in the futuristic German and Austrian republics', promising 'an entirely new reconstructed idea of the art of life'.[3] In the war's early days, many contributors developed such themes, caught up in the initial hopes of a short and meaningful war.

By the end of the month, regular contributors began offering more detailed analyses of events, again laced with modernist tropes of decadence and rebirth. An excellent example of this style of publicism came from Oscar Levy's article 'Nietzsche and this War', an early piece bravely defending Nietzsche.[4] A Jewish émigré from Germany, before the war broke out Levy was, along with Orage, one of the early champions of Nietzsche in England. His development of Nietzsche's philosophy in prewar articles for *The New Age* and elsewhere had led him to compose his own, modernist interpretation of history by this point. This has been summarized by Dan Stone as follows:

> Modern European society is degenerating because it is bound to an effete moral value system; these effete values derive from Judaism . . . this Jewish ethic was taken a step further by Christianity, which is 'Super-Semitism'; Luther, the Reformation and Puritanism took Europe even further away from its manly origins; modern revolutionary movements such as led the French and Russian revolutions, though they believed themselves to be atheist, are in fact continuing to further the causes of Judeo-Christianity by their insistence on a utopian vision of equality and their contempt for the 'strong'; the archetypal example of this barbarism masquerading as civilised values is Germany; only an aristocratic revival – based on the attitude of the ancient Jews – which scorns Christianity, the week and feeble can save Europe from terminal decline.[5]

This modernist perspective was one that Levy developed through the course of the war in *The New Age* and elsewhere. So when we look to his first piece after the war broke, here we see Levy not only dismissed the notion that Nietzsche represented the epitome of German militarism, as was so often argued in the contemporary press, but he also developed aspects of this wider reinterpretation of European history to critique modernity. In particular, here Levy took issue with the pro-German ideology presented in Houston Stuart Chamberlain's *The Foundations of the Nineteenth Century*, and he suggested this type of thinking, and not Nietzsche, offered the intellectual underpinnings for the current German militarism. Specifically, it was Chamberlain's delusion that the Teutonic race formed a new ideal capable of redeeming the world that was to blame for German aggression. Nietzsche was contemptuous of such crass German nationalism, Levy stressed. He also noted how Nietzsche developed a pan-European vision, embracing the cultural influence of France especially. Like Orage's wartime defence of Nietzsche, Levy thought that, if he were alive, he would have welcomed the war. But this was not because Nietzsche was a rabid militarist, as so many in Britain wrongly thought. Indeed, Nietzsche would have been highly critical of the vulgar and, in his eyes decadent, nationalisms that war epitomized. Yet looking to the bigger picture, he felt that Nietzsche would have embraced the war because it could clear away such decadence, and in this light Levy presented the war as a potentially constructive event. 'There is no doubt', concluded Levy,

> about the growing consumption and decadence of Europe during the last and our own century; there is no doubt that everywhere wrong values have been creeping into men's consciences, the values of the weak, the tame, the lame, the social, the humble, the crooked, the cunning, the dishonest, the botched and the bungled.

So for Levy, this view of modernity as decadence allowed him to see how it 'poisoned' both the people and the leaders of Europe to the extent that 'no-one could any longer have preserved an upright and honourable peace, and all have drifted into a general conflagration. So the brutal cure has come at last'.[6] With Levy, we see both the specific trope of war as purification and the wider theme of violence as the ultimate solution to a decadent European modernity clearly underpinning his reading of the profound cultural significance of the war. It is also worth stressing that Orage was bold to be publishing not merely a defence of Nietzsche, but one by a German author, at this time. Moreover, Levy's views offer us another instance of the modernist culture developed in the journal: modernity is decadence, the mainstream is delusional and caught up in misguided utopian projects, while a new elite needs to emerge to redeem Europe. As we will see, these core themes recurred throughout the war in the contributions from Levy and others deeply influenced by Nietzsche's philosophy.

Meanwhile, discussions on prominent German intellectuals continued the following week, in A. E. Randall's weekly 'Views and Reviews' column.[7] Arguing that Friedrich von Bernhardi's notorious glorification of war and militarism, *Germany and the Next War,* had been entirely misunderstood in Britain as only a polemic of German aggression, the essay claimed that Bernhardi had, in fact, 'done us a service by insisting on the necessity of war'. Randall too was concerned with demolishing false perspectives among those who considered war as a thing of the past, and continued that 'civilisation tends to negate war, it tends to unreality'. Consequently, civilized people often failed to see that war and peace had a dialectical relationship: one was depended upon the other. Periodically the violence of war was a necessary; it kept civilized peoples from descending into a state of decadence. Despite this home truth, Randall stressed the supposedly civilized people of Western Europe often forgot the periodic need to embrace its antithesis, in order to revitalize the conditions for existence. As with Levy, then, Randall too argued that Western civilization had in recent times chosen to embrace decadence and comfort. Such softness, he claimed, was really the new barbarism, not the blunt militarism of Bernhardi's school of thought. In short, his deconstruction of the received opinion on figures such as Bernhardi argued that 'Civilisation is a conspiracy to avoid calamity', yet sometimes 'calamity cannot be avoided'. In his embrace of this tragic and cyclical worldview, Randall also argued that one had to recognize that 'the destructive power of calamity is inherent in the process of growth', and that war is without purpose if 'it does not set free the creative activity of man'. He concluded by eliding the destruction of war with the creativity of genius:

> Genius, seeing the need for destruction, will destroy . . . destruction is only an incentive to and an opportunity for creation; militarism and culture do not really stand in antithesis but in sequence to each other; and war remains intrinsic to reality and necessary to civilisation.[8]

In October 1914, we can find another instance of war being presented in such a modernist form as an act of creative destruction, bolstered by an accompanying rhetoric for mythic renewal, in Randall's 'Views and Reviews' column, usually devoted to lengthy book reviews. Here, he claimed that the war was putting an end to an English complacency that regarded the nation's empire as a God given fact – 'what God spoke in Hebrew, he meant in English', the article mocked. Through combat, the nation was discovering its true spirit of honour, destroying the idea that, for the English, 'the religion of valour has been superseded by the religion of velleity, that Thor was beaten once and for all at the beginning of the eleventh century'. By engaging in war with a country possessing the 'grandeur of soul' of Germany, Europeans suddenly found themselves 'back in the sagas, battling with heroes for the dominion of the world'. 'We shall win', he stressed, 'only because we can still revert to the religion of valour, because we also regard Christ as the eternally crucified'. Although he was sure that Germany would lose the war as a result of military errors, eventually 'our empire will be challenged . . . by some other heroic nation; for it is intolerable to the soul of man that the bourgeois should sit in the seats of the mighty'.[9] Such arguments, then, were predicated upon the notion that only through continual military challenges could the nation remain vital, preserve a mythic sense of authenticity and prevent itself from descending into decadence. In this embrace of the aesthetics of a warrior mentality, the article even quoted the final lines of Henry Wadsworth Longfellow's poem 'The Challenge of Thor', framing Germany's actions as the challenge made by the Norse god of thunder and war. It was this belligerent, mythopoeic register that the confrontation with German drew out.[10] The following week, he confirmed the view that the war was an event effecting fundamental change to the moral makeup of the continent: 'Nietzsche did not make this war, this war will make Nietzsche; for it is effecting a transvaluation of all values; or, at least, is forcing people to define their ideals of the purposes of civilisation and the nature of man.'[11] Once again, the presentation of the war as a cataclysm from which elemental change would emerge is clear from such dramatic interpretations of its significance.

Writers for *The New Age* were diverse. In these early months we see other issues shot through this lens of war as a watershed event. For example, several discussions regarding the role of India in the war, especially ways in which the conflagration would serve the purposes of altering the country's political status, appeared in the journal from October 1914. To take one instance of this theme, 'An Oxford Indian' argued that India was more than a bottomless well of mercenaries for the British to draw upon. Rather, the country was 'fighting for a just and honourable and *equal* place in the Empire', and that 'young India sees in Indian loyalty this purpose'.[12] Following on from this shorter discussion, in December 1914 we see the topic of political rewards for Indian loyalty being revisited by Ananda Coomaraswamy.[13] Coomaraswamy himself was a very curious, occasional contributor. An Anglo-Tamil, broadly speaking his philosophy sought to blend Eastern and Western thought. Drawing on influences as diverse as William Morris, William Blake, Peter Kropotkin and Nietzsche, alongside Hindu and Buddhist writings, what we can again style as a modernist style of thinking identified a profound spiritual crisis in the West, and again projected into the future a unique vision for fundamental renewal. In his article for *The New Age*, he argued that Indians had no natural enemy in a European war, and that Indian sympathies primarily rested with the heroism of all the troops and all the various innocent victims of the war. Nevertheless, he felt that an Allied victory was the 'most desirable' outcome, and argued that, after the war, 'Austria should be disintegrated and Poland and Youga Slaviya [sic] new built; and we may hope that out of such a conflict may emerge a saner and more loving Europe . . . we may expect that social revolutions will follow international bloodshed'.

This was not his ultimate focus though, and Coomaraswamy's argument then shifted into a more philosophical and redemptive register regarding the future of the world. He believed the war had highlighted 'a crisis in the history of Western culture', demonstrating the hypocrisy of Christianity, the errors of imperialism and, perhaps, even signalled the end of industrialization too. From this decadence, 'European culture is at the point of renewal', he declared. Moreover,

> since the Reformation, Europe has suffered from an undue exaltation of knowledge and a disvaluation of doing and feeling, but she has begun anew the education of her hands and heart. At the present moment her life and art are witness to the results of centuries of aimlessness; and the individualism and internecine warfare of the various activities of the mind are the diagnosis of the imperfection and discord of the modern European character. But a new age is in a process of development; after the war, Europe will enter upon a period of creative activity, the endeavour to realise in outward life the truths discovered in her age of criticism. This will be parallel to the Indian social evolution after the Upanishads and Buddha.

In response to the current European crisis, India also had to undergo a national awakening. It needed to actively engage with the problems of the world in order to both gain its own freedom and play an active part in the profound renewal of the world's moral makeup. The war was nothing less than 'a universal *kultur-kamph*' from which a new era of humanity would emerge. India's primary asset was its development of 'the most profound philosophy of the world', and the way this had been developed into 'a social organism, the Brahmanical theocracy'. Here was 'the science of peace' for Coomaraswamy. European history had been misguided for 300 years because its leaders had regarded the advice of 'artists, saviours and philosophers' as lacking practicality. Yet when philosophers once again ruled over states and societies, a sense of overarching purpose could guide society, and the whole world could achieve 'well-being and enlightenment'. India had to help Europeans find this sense of higher purpose, a reconnection with the transcendent; and in so doing, the country would 'rediscover her own inheritance'. He concluded that the 'evolution of a new humanity' was necessary, one that was 'at once national and international, a culture with widely varying local standards, but essentially the civilisation of all men, and the conscious creation of all'.[14] So in terms of developing a nascent post-colonial outlook, Coomaraswamy's vision of Western and Eastern rebirth offered in a short compass a profound articulation of the sense of fundamental change that could come about during the war, arguing that India needed to become an active player in a new world order, one concerned with spiritual as well as political realities.

Major wartime contributors

The pool of essayists offering articles for the journal was substantial, yet some sets of essays do stand out as forming central planks of *The New Age*'s core publicism. One of the central contributors during the war, exploring the relationship between the war and the future of European society, was the Basque intellectual Ramiro de Maeztu. A regular writer for *The New Age*, Maeztu's output was prolific. Drawing on many ideas closely connected to guild socialists, he developed his own, distinct critique of Western European society that represents a further, idiosyncratic example of political modernism in the journal's pages. Maeztu essentially claimed that modern society no longer offered a culture that was structured according to a hierarchy of authentic values, and as a consequence many people, especially the wealthy, operated without a clear 'function' that served a wider community. During the war, he developed his political writings on the potential for a new type of society to emerge from the cauldron of war into a book taken from these articles, *Authority, Liberty and Function in the Light of the War*.[15] Showing the trajectory from sympathy for the guild socialist discourse to supporter of revolutionary ultra-nationalist politics, in the interwar period Maeztu returned to Spain where he became a prominent figure within the proto-fascist *Acción Española* group. This movement was not only sympathetic to Italian Fascism and *Action Française*, but after the civil war broke out became a fervent supporter of Franco. Indeed, a striking tenor of embryonic totalitarianism can be detected when examining Maeztu's modernist political philosophy. For example, in one section of *Authority, Liberty and Function in the Light of the War*, we find him arguing that not only was forced conscription desirable due to the current wartime crisis, but that forced motherhood could also become a consideration if the war became a prolonged affair.[16]

To give an overview of the perspective that could lead to such assertions, Maeztu's radical reworking of guild socialist theory identified a need to overcome two unwelcome forces that were set against each other by the war: liberalism and authoritarianism. While Germany epitomized the latter, the Allies were founded on the former. Essentially, for Maeztu neither was desirable and so something new was needed to take their place. The war was thus timely, and so, drawing on a range of thinkers and developing his themes in an assiduously philosophical register, Maeztu presented the conflict as an event creating the opportunity for fundamental political change, helping to foster the new mentality that would push society into a radically new order. Tellingly, his political modernism styled the conflict as a watershed event akin to the Renaissance in terms of significance.

The guild socialist trend to idealize the Middle Ages was again strongly developed in Maeztu's wartime writings, and for him the entire modern era, which had begun with the Renaissance, was now coming to its final climax. Moreover, in terms of historicizing his analysis, Maeztu stressed that from the eighth to the twelfth centuries, Europe had operated as a harmonious, dreamlike society, before being torn out of this ideal period by the forces of modernization. As he put the onset of this transition, and its contemporary significance: 'In my judgement the awakening of Europe in the twelfth century was due to a cause analogous to that which is bringing about the awakening of England in the twentieth. That cause is war.'[17] His history of Europe subsequent to this point stressed that the Crusades brought the continent into conflict with the Muslim world, leading to strategic political truces, expediency and new knowledge. All of this change through war effectively destroyed the harmony of the earlier, idealized era, and ultimately led to the emergence of the modern, centralized state in either its authoritarian (i.e. German) or liberal (i.e. British) formats. It is important to stress that, as with others inspired by the guild socialist vision of creating a new social system based on an idealized reading of the Middle Ages, Maeztu was clear on the point that such idealizing of the past was part of a *futural* vision, not a mere return to a previous age. As he put the theme of drawing on the past to shape a new era: 'thus, as the men of the Renaissance by turning their eyes towards antiquity prepared the modern era, so may the men of the *New Age*, with their mediaeval conception of the Guild, lay well and truly the foundations of the future.'[18] Maeztu's variant of political modernism went on to propose that high ideals, such as 'moral satisfaction', serious art, scientific achievement and so forth should be regarded as the most important social values of any civilization, and so a fully functioning society needed to aim towards these ideals above all others. Yet to achieve these higher goals, the freedom of the individual would have to now play a subordinate role. The ideals of individualism promoted by liberalism and humanism had to come to an end in the future society. Rather, Maeztu's political philosophy asserted people had to fulfil their wider function within society, and stressed the idea that the masses of a modern state needed to be subordinate to a powerful governing ideal defining the social order. But unlike traditional authoritarianism, conforming to the new social ideals would not be policed through a centralized state structure.

Moreover, throughout his writings Maeztu was a staunch critic of both 'liberal' pacifism and 'authoritarian' militarism. Yet telling of the inherent problems in his search to define a new, 'organic' community, one finds a striking level of praise for the military here too: indeed, Maeztu saw in the army a perfect model for outlining the mechanisms of the new society. Meanwhile, revealing his attempt to rework left-wing radicalism into his own revolutionary proposals, we also find him developing syndicalist tropes. With the idea of the individual subordinated, Maeztu stressed that a person's function in a modern society should provide one's life with meaning. Knowing one's place in the wider order of things, and ensuring that all social functions worked towards the greater good was the preferable way of structuring the new society. The decentralized series of guilds provided a specialized structure empowering specific aspects of production, and so, as with the Middle Ages, again there would be no need for a centralized state. Society could once again reach a sort of harmony naturally. Though people would hold different roles and standings, the wealthy would not be above society, as had become the case in the centralized modern states. The rich needed to be disempowered, and their wealth be used for the common good.

Thus Maeztu's answer to the challenge of liberty and authority was to create a new political philosophy justifying this view, based around 'function', where people would be compelled to work for the organic community at the expense of their individual liberty. One telling discussion on the theme of compulsion in the new order ran as follows:

> It is not necessary to set a policeman behind every citizen to make him do his duty. It is sufficient to withhold social assistance from him (food, clothing, shelter, etc.) if he refuses to do it. This is being done already where the poor are concerned. But we Socialists want this compulsion to be extended to the wealthy; and the best means for applying it to them, we think, is to make the community the inheritor of their wealth. Our principle is compulsion all round.[19]

Space does not permit full elaboration of Maeztu's ideas here, but clearly one can see how the guild system, itself an embryonic version of later corporate state ideas, could lend itself to a radical new style of rule, fascism. Thus it is not surprising that Maeztu later became attracted to this perspective, as it emerged into a clear ideology in the interwar period. In sum, the radical fusion of the idealized past with a powerful new type of decentralised state, and a new elite, could all be found in Maeztu's wartime philosophy, which far more than guild socialism was an embryonic proto-fascism.

Major contributors developed examinations of European society undergoing a fundamental renovation in culture in a number of ways in *The New Age* during the war. Writing in a very different idiom to the political modernism set out by Maeztu, the numerous contributions to *The New Age* during the war made by Ezra Pound also expressed this concern. Many of these writings have been discussed in the wider literature on Pound, but it is useful to briefly examine this trend in his wartime output. To take one example, from the beginning of January 1915, Pound contributed a series called 'Affirmations'. In particular, an article entitled 'Analysis of this Decade' captured the sense of European crisis and desire for a sense of modernist cultural regeneration. His argument claimed that 'only recently have men begun to combat the Renaissance', not in terms of extending the ideas of the counter-reformation, but because a fundamentally new approach to perceiving the world was coming into view. Artists such as Pound, he continued, had 'begun deliberately to try to free ourselves from the Renaissance shackles, as the Renaissance freed itself from the Middle Ages'. The characteristics of this new art were epitomized most fully by the new age of machines, of modernity, and this 'enjoyment of machinery is just as natural and just as significant a phase of this age as was the Renaissance "Enjoyment of nature for its own sake"'. In the following chapter on Wyndham Lewis, we will see an exploration of this theme of the spaces of modernity as inspiration for a new era of art examined in more depth.

Moreover, reflecting the impact of new, global influences on cultural production, Pound believed that the recent influence of Chinese and Japanese cultures on the European sensibility 'cannot help but bring about changes as great as the Renaissance changes'. Unlike the Renaissance, which sought to rediscover 'a lost reality, a lost freedom', for Pound, the current cultural and political renovation sought 'a lost reality and a lost intensity'. The new aesthetic avant-garde, then, was attempting to develop a guiding programme that would combine the qualities of individualism and community, one that was 'in contradistinction to, but not in contradiction of, the individual impulse'. Concluding with a mechanical image, Pound went so far as to suggest that this synthesis created a new form of consciousness; or, to use his metaphor, this formed the steam to drive the engine of a new age.[20] Such contributions thus chimed with the overarching tone of other articles in the journal, especially with respect to setting out the need for a fundamental cultural renovation. Pound's statements calling for innovation, and an epoch generating revolution in aesthetic styles, explored into the same underlying concerns with modernity as decadence that also characterized guild socialist publicism and the ideas of Maeztu. The real enemies of both political and aesthetic modernism were those who respected the past to the point of rendering it inert. Like the guild socialists, Pound saw it as his task to encourage an active engagement with the past, especially its cultural production, which was capable of bringing a sense of radicalism to the present. This creative energy could then be harnessed to forge a fundamentally new future.

As well as contributions from regulars such as Pound, Oscar Levy also continued to publish in the journal during the war. In particular, he stressed the need for a return to earlier religious sensibilities as the means to regenerate the regenerated future. Such ideals were developed in his 1914 essay 'Nietzsche and the Jews'. Here, Levy argued that the Jewish understanding of community was superior to that which had been created by the historically far more recent concept of the nation-state: that 'which is presently called a "nation" in Europe', he stressed, 'is really rather *res facta* rather than *nata* – a thing made rather than born'. He also claimed that 'such "nations" should most carefully avoid all hot-headed rivalry and war!' Levy was clear on the point that Nietzsche believed that, though his ideal of the superman had not yet materialized, he regarded the Jews as 'the nearest, though imperfect, approach to it'. Levy continued this call for the redemption of Europe through this higher, racial spirit that, in his opinion, was possessed by the Jews, and claimed that the 'world still needs Israel, for the world is in a period of quick change and requires a centre around which the best of all nations may rally and recover'. The world 'has fallen a prey to democracy', he continued, and the 'terrible wars, of which the present one is only the beginning, are in store for it . . . the world needs a race of good Europeans who stand above national bigotry and national hypocrisy'. Such a Jewish aristocracy, steeped in Nietzschean morality, could provide for the world the 'strongest spiritual guidance which is to be had on earth', a message that 'can only be given by a strong and pure race, a race which has previous experience in guiding humanity and in deciding its good and evil, its right and wrong, its aim and direction'. Levy concluded by noting how Nietzsche's attacks on Judeo-Christian ethics stemmed from his concern with developing a new, higher morality, and that his critique of modern religions was the result of his intuition of truly authentic religious impulses.[21] Again, a redemptive narrative is here couched in tropes of modernist thought: the war was the epitome of the age of flux and crisis for Levy, and nations were not imbibed with the racial purity of the Jewish people (who themselves were also largely decadent). The resolution would be for Jews to return to their earliest, and allegedly most authentic, form of existence – 'the manly Jew, the warrior Jew under his kings, the Jew yet unbroken by the misery of later years', as he put it – in order to construct a new moral order for an age he believed to be profoundly adrift and, as a consequence, in global conflict.[22]

Continuing this theme, from June 1915 Oscar Levy offered a longer series of five dialogues between two figures, dubbed 'The German' and 'The European', arguing that the causes of the war lay in the domination of Christian morality, and that it marked the beginning of a series of wars for the future of Europe. The drama in these articles centred upon the ways in which 'The German' failed to grasp the wider historical and philosophical contextualization offered by 'The European', as 'The German' essentially acted as the degenerate straight-man to the radical, Nietzschean assertions of 'The European' in this dialectic. The first article established that Germany was a particularly Christian nation, arguing this point through a Nietzschean lens so that the widespread take-up of socialism in Germany was also seen as Christianity 'without a God'. Moreover, this growing faith in the state resulted in a 'State-Church', allowing for the German belief in national superiority. However, as a result of war, the world had reached a turning point where the decadence of Christian morality could be transcended.[23]

The second of the dialogues again picked up the theme of critiquing religion. 'The European' argued that a virile religiosity was a masculine ideal, stating that 'there is no more manly occupation for thought than religion', while also critiquing the idealism of thinkers such as Kant – 'it is a short way from Kant to cant' – by arguing that one could either be idealistic and enslaved, or intelligent and free; Christian morality was the former, 'The European's' virile, masculine religiosity was the latter.[24] The third of these dialogues again developed the argument that democracy was a secularized variant of Christianity. In a very condensed narrative of historical cause and effect, 'The European' elaborated this point thus:

> Without Christianity, there would have been no Protestantism, without Protestantism no liberty of conscience, without liberty of conscience no Republic of Geneva, without Geneva no Rousseau, without Rousseau no French Revolution, and without the Revolution no universal vote and no Democracy.

Finally, it was the failures of modern, democratic institutions that had, in turn, led to the war, 'The European' continued. Indeed, the decadence of the modern world was revealed in the ways in which the war quickly turned into a stalemate. The conflict had become a vast symbol of the failure in modern Europe to cultivate 'great men' who alone were capable of generating the much-needed sense of renewal. 'How else', 'The European' asked rhetorically, could one explain why the continent was characterized by 'a dullness of the age, the absence of all stirring action, the universal paralysis of brains and hearts, the outrageous decay of character and will-power?'[25]

The subsequent article continued this identification of decadence in the present, arguing that patriotic people were essentially slaves to their nation. 'The European', as a man committed to the truth, could not countenance patriotism, as it placed the good of the nation above the pursuit of 'truth'. Patriots were either actual or potential liars. Instead, 'The European' regarded truly great men, such as Napoleon, as heroic figures who the masses should hold in awe. Their superior attempts to fuse Europe into a coordinated whole, not divide it into nations, were much desired unifying myths and the continent was in dire need of new great men, figures who aimed at nothing less than the reunification of Europe. The decadence of the age was explained in part because: 'For generations Europe has taken no notice of its higher men, that is to say, of those who are the guardians and the prophets and creators of divine truth'. Ignorance or misunderstanding of the likes of William Blake, Lord Byron, Heinrich Heine and Nietzsche, alongside the growth of materialist atheism during the nineteenth century, played their part in the emergence of this culture, where unthinking patriotism and a 'moral muddle' dominated the divine truths of poets and great men.[26] Levy's final article in this set tied these strands together by commenting most explicitly on the 'intellectual bankruptcy' and neglect of great men of the age, and its relationship with the war. 'This war', 'The European' emphasized, '*is* the consequence of our contempt of the spirit, of our neglect of ideas . . . If the world despises the spirit of great and good men . . . it is no wonder that it stands in need of moral purification and spiritual regeneration'. In the final analysis, the war was a sign of the weakness of the age, not a war for national power. Levy aligned the mentality of Christianity with feminine qualities; the spiritual cure for the age was refracted through the lens of a muscular – and what was presented as a spiritually purifying – masculinity. Likewise, 'The European' detailed how he had sensed the emergence of the war over the preceding years. As with Hobsbawm's metaphor of 1914 as a gathering storm, 'The European' claimed that he had felt the war as akin to a thunderstorm: he saw it as a violent tempest, one offering the hope of a fresh dawn after it passed:

Suddenly the most terrific thunderstorm is upon us . . . And now the sniff of fresh air . . . The first signs of a change for the better . . . The first ray of hope despite the gloomy skies . . . you understand the tears of joy now? You understand that I am not a pessimist but an optimist, only an optimist with better reasons than you?

Indeed, war 'was the only way' for Europe to achieve this glimpse of a new sense of the transcendent, a 'sniff of fresh air':

how could anyone go on living in such a stinking world! A world full of fat, bourgeois, screaming women, starving poor, revolutionary slaves led by decadent dynasts, mad reformers, and impotent talkers! A world without health and beauty, without spirit and courage, without true joy and without true grief. A world aiming at wretched comfort, at love and cotton-wool, at peace and happiness at any price. A world which had room for anyone, nursed everyone, pampered everyone, respected everyone, obeyed and honoured everyone – but hated and suppressed only one sort of being – a man. For such an age there is only one remedy and that is war, for it is only in times of danger that a man can show his value, and thus war brings men to honour again.

Continuing this tirade, Levy drew upon medical metaphors, claiming that 'war *is* a medicine, a cruel medicine, maybe, but the only one that promises a cure'. His final lines congratulated Germany for taking Europe into the war, a necessary, purifying act according to this view. The German aggressors were the 'physicians of Europe', who, in the long run, would cure Europe of its decadence. 'Europe is looking for new Masters', he concluded, 'and it will find them in the end'. The palingenetic core of Levy's ideas is clear from such rhetoric.[27]

Elsewhere, demonstrating the eclectic range of authors within the journal, between late 1915 and early 1916, one of the key instigators of modernism in English literature, T. E. Hulme, published his last two sets of essays in *The New Age*. By this time, Hulme had already been at the centre of Imagism, a prominent promoter of Bergsonian philosophy, and was an early protagonist within the embryonic Vorticist movement, yet by the war had fallen into an irresolvable conflict with Wyndham Lewis. The first of these wartime essay series for *The New Age*, 'A Notebook', offered what was probably the most comprehensive survey of his developing modernist approach to philosophy, one that dismissed figures such as Nietzsche as part of the problem, rather than the solution, to the crisis of modernity. Written in his typically dense yet at the same time conversational tone, these essays rearticulated Hulme's core thesis that a new 'classical' cultural order was now emerging, while the liberal humanism that had come to dominate Europe from the Renaissance period onwards was beginning to wane. So once again, we see analysis arguing that Europe's culture was on the cusp of entering a new age. This modernist theme, styling the present as a liminal period, was also characteristically set within a pessimistic tenor, and in particular Hulme wanted to dramatically distance himself from the idea of the perfectibility of the human condition found in Enlightenment philosophies, or even the more hyperbolic style of Nietzschean-influenced writers, which he again believed to be defective as it was marred by the erroneous romantic outlook. To help develop his deeply 'anti-romantic' tenor, Hulme proposed two broad types of society, one dominated by the view of liberals and humanists, and another dominated by what he described as a religious outlook. As with Orage and others, religion for Hulme was not to be understood in terms of regular attendance at church. Indeed, he talked little of organized religion in these essays, and was dismissive of the modern church for its failure to offer a truly dogmatic expression of man's flawed and sinful nature. Despite this implicit critique of organized Christianity, Hulme's worldview rested very fundamentally on the notion of Original Sin, of man's imperfect nature, which Hulme stressed was the most essential and inescapable truths for understanding the human condition.

Historicizing his ideas, for Hulme this distinction between the naïve optimism of liberalism and humanism, and the pessimism of the religious attitude, allowed him to propose a philosophy of history. He claimed that the former outlook had developed in Europe from the time of the Renaissance, after which almost all religious expressions simply became representations of human emotions rather than representing anything truly sacred. Even the major religious works of art produced after this time could not be regarded as expressing an authentically spiritual perspective, and simply regurgitated human concerns. In contrast, for Hulme a truly religious art had an essentially ahuman quality to it, and so abstraction was the marker of the religious mentality. Indeed, the abstract art developed by non-European civilizations, such as in Africa, offered more primitive examples of a truly religious culture. Yet the most problematic aspect of post-Renaissance humanism and liberalism for Hulme was its promotion of the idea of human perfectibility: the notion that Western civilization was progressing humankind to a higher plane of existence had erroneously placed man at the centre of the world, according to Hulme. Such misguided views tried to mask people from man's true, flawed nature, as expressed by the authentically religious attitude. As Hulme put this issue of perfectibility, 'while he can occasionally accomplish acts which partake of perfection, he can never himself *be* perfect ... As man is essentially bad, he can only accomplish anything of value by discipline – ethical and political. Order is not merely negative, but creative and liberating. Institutions are liberating'.[28]

Moreover, as with the guild socialists and others such as Maeztu, Hulme identified the Middle Ages as a period in European history when the more desirable, religious and tragic nature of mankind was enforced through the dogma of Original Sin. Also in harmony with the guild socialists and others, for Hulme this did not mean he wanted to simply see a reversion to an earlier time. Rather, his notion of the coming change was specifically *futural*: 'I do not in the least imagine that humanism is breaking up merely to make place for a new medievalism. The only thing the new period will have in common with medievalism will be the subordination of man to certain absolute values'.[29] So the Middle Ages merely offered a major reference point, primarily because it was an exemplar of a kindred culture that regarded men as limited beings, and expressed a religious dogma that enforced the unquestionable limits on human perfectibility. Unsurprisingly perhaps, Maeztu drew upon Hulme's ideas in his own identification of desirable aspects of the Middle Ages when mapping his vision of the emergent new order. As with other modernist intellectuals we have encountered so far, Hulme was a highly eclectic thinker, and in order to develop his perspective drew on many recent trends in continental philosophy, including Henri Bergson, Wilhelm Worringer and Edmund Husserl. Blaise Pascal, one of the few post-Renaissance philosophers who developed the 'correct', religious outlook according to Hulme's modernist philosophy, was a further, major influence.

Hulme's second set of essays, 'War Notes', meanwhile, were published under the pseudonym 'North Staffs', itself reflective of a culture of writing under false names in the journal. Rather than developing his overarching philosophy further, in this collection Hulme engaged directly with the war itself. We can see some notable characteristics of the modernist attitude being developed here too. Criticism of the Allied prosecution of the war was the striking aspect of early articles. Hulme was clear that the army was poorly led by the General Staff, figures he suggested lacked an ability to innovate and respond to the new conditions of modern warfare, only helping to confirm the popular prejudice that the army was stupid. As with Orage, Hulme was no pacifist, and he wanted to see Germany defeated as he felt the nation was a dangerous promoter of romantic ideals that denied mankind's imperfect nature. Reflecting his playful yet provocative tenor in these articles, in the place of the current system for leading the army, he proposed the following model to achieve military victory:

> Staff work, and in certain cases, higher command should be entrusted to a new civil service, modelled somewhat on the lines of the Indian Civil Service. There should be no uniforms for these superior officers; they should all wear top-hats. They should have no titles and none of those special privileges attached to the soldier as a man doomed to sacrifice. Such a civil service would, I think, spontaneously generate in itself a kind of atmosphere and the kind of organisation which makes for efficiency along its own narrow lines.[30]

Meanwhile, the first of these articles also developed Hulme's reading of the significance of the war. Here he set out his stall criticizing liberal, and especially pacifist, attitudes to the war as follows:

> The common phrase about things being in the melting-pot is neither hyperbole nor cliché when applied to the present war. It is, on the other hand, an exact metaphor. Literally every boundary in Europe, of political, social, intellectual and cultural importance, is at this time in dispute, not of argument alone, but of force; and as the war subsides, so will these boundaries be left where it places them, to determine the *form* of Europe during the coming period of peace.[31]

Typifying Hulme's pessimistic attitude, he suggested there was nothing inevitable about an Allied victory; it would be a hard won yet vital outcome for the development of the new era he had alluded to in his philosophical writings. Though Hulme was no militarist, he was determined that Germany should be defeated on the battlefield, and that liberal and humanist ideas that informed pacifism were blind to the very real, existential threat that Germany posed to the type of culture he promoted. In later columns, to help develop the antithetical nature of this German threat Hulme even cited key figures such as Werner Sombart and Max Scheler, quoting their own praise for war at length, to highlight the nature of the enemy and his ideals.

Regarding the problematic nature of the culture in wartime Britain, Hulme also strongly critiqued pacifists, especially what he believed was their naïve reliance on the myth of progress. According to Hulme, pacifists liked to delude themselves with the idea that Germany was on the verge of a social democratic revolution. Yet Hulme stressed the only way of achieving any sort of democratic revolution in Germany would be for the country to be totally defeated in war. As he put his critique of pacifism in one article: 'The pacifist often finds it almost *irrational* and unnatural to believe that a fundamental thing like liberty can depend upon a *trivial* material thing.'[32] As with Orage, Hulme was acutely aware that the outcome of violence would shape the coming peace. The attack on pacifists came to a head in the essay series when he challenged Bertrand Russell's attitude to pacifist radicalism. This intriguing development, in Hulme's 'War Notes' have been well discussed elsewhere.[33]

Interestingly, in these notes we also find Hulme becoming more positive towards the idea of democracy itself, but again he wanted to make distinctions between a good form of democracy that was compatible with his pessimistic, religious perspective, and a bad form that was the political expression of liberalism and humanism. Hulme's preferred type of democracy had a precursor in the seventeenth century. Indeed, he likened himself to a latter day Leveller: a figure who not only believed in democracy but who was prepared to fight for it. As for the pacifists, 'It seems demonstrable to me', he asserted, 'that the kind of ethic it fosters will never develop the force which is likely to radically transform society'. Meanwhile, the ideals of 'seventeenth-century' democracy 'had a certain virility and had not fallen into the sentimental decadence of *humanitarianism*'.[34] The war had also helped clarify other political ideas that Hulme had entertained before the war. The notion of the organic state had previously been attractive to him, but he now believed war was revealing the notion as a horrific concept, as it was exemplified by the German state. Also, some of the French theorists who he had previously been attracted to, such as Charles Maurras, now seemed to be developing organic conceptions of the state which ran counter to his emerging democratic intuition during wartime. So Hulme was surprised to admit that the war seemed to bring him closer to a democratic perspective than he would have endorsed before the war. Yet clearly, his thinking was again heavily peppered with tropes of decadence in the present, and rebirth for the future, markers of the wartime intellectual discourse of seeing the war as a major modernist event.

Regarding his view on revolutionary politics, we see that Hulme also published an authorized translation of the Georges Sorel's *Reflections on Violence* in 1916, offering his own introduction that linked the revolutionary Sorel with his 'classical' religious attitude. Indeed, we can note that Hulme was no mere Tory either, and his thinking blurred left- and right-wing themes. Tellingly, the final paragraph here reveals Hulme's fulsome endorsement of Sorel's revolutionary attitude:

> Sorel is one of the most remarkable writers of the time, certainly the most remarkable socialist since Marx; and his influence is likely to increase, for, in spite of the apparently undisturbed supremacy of rationalist hedonism in popular thought, the absolute view of ethics which underlies his polemic is gradually being re-established. A similar combination of the classical ideal with socialism is to be found, it is true, in Proudhon, but Sorel comes at a happier moment. The ideology attacked by Proudhon has now reached a fuller development, and its real consequences can be more easily perceived. There are many who begin to be disillusioned with liberal and pacifist democracy, while shrinking from the opposed ideology on account of its reactionary associations. To these people Sorel, a revolutionary in economics, but classical in ethics, may prove an emancipator.[35]

Again, the search for a philosophy offering a sense of radical emancipation from capitalist modernity helped to frame Hulme's interest in Sorel.

The release of the book also revealed an influence of such syndicalist views on the British intellectuals who were attracted to *The New Age*. Orage had been engaging with, and critiquing, these themes even before the war. Telling of this interest in Sorel during the war, Herbert Read contributed a pithy commentary on Hulme's translation of *Reflections on Violence* in June 1916. Describing Sorel essentially as a social critic rather than a true political philosopher, Read argued that he had exposed the ways in which capitalism had moved on since Marx's era, stymieing the potential for revolution. To counter this, Read stressed the importance of two radical, Sorelian ideas for ending 'our social decadence', which would be especially useful when combating those reformers who simply attempted to ameliorate the worst aspects of capitalism, such as co-operative movements. First, Sorel stressed the need for a myth of the general strike, one that could evoke an authentic sense of 'heroic virtue'; and second, he discussed proletarian violence. Regarding the latter, Read stated that it 'is for us to consider to what degree the present war will do the work expected by Sorel to be done by a general extension of proletarian violence'. His wider commentary argued that, on the one hand, the war was strengthening capitalist classes, yet, on the other, it was also imbuing the proletariat with a greater sense of mission and *esprit de corps*. The 'mob of the past', he claimed, 'will be the army of the future'. He also noted the shift in general mood, sensing that, as a result of the war, '[t]here has passed over us like a wave a grand revival of the sentiment of glory – a new realisation of heroic values'. Read concluded that, regarding the transcendence of capitalist decadence and the inauguration of an alternate modernity, 'the outlook is not one of despair . . . the fatalistic revolution is in sight'.[36]

We can see a clear distinction between the theme of Original Sin set out by Hulme and other, major contributors. While Hulme regarded Nietzsche as a throwback to romanticism, it is important to stress that it was not just Oscar Levy who developed Nietzschean critiques of Western modernity in the pages of *The New Age* during the war. Another significant contributor here, Edwin Muir, also presented a major series of essays drawing on Nietzsche. According to his autobiography, Muir was even briefly being groomed for taking over the editorship of the journal later in the war.[37] Writing under the pseudonym Edward Moore, Muir developed a particularly striking set of essays titled 'We Moderns' between November 1916 and September 1917. These were not directly concerned with the war, but were rather affirmations of the Nietzschean perspective that the present could be interpreted a period of fundamental renewal, marked by a highly decadent order coming to an end, and a new world emerging from the wreckage. Interestingly, Muir took issue with the trope, regularly found elsewhere in the magazine, of praising the Middle Ages. He was also critical of the promotion of dogma and the core notion that Hulme predicated his views upon, Original Sin. These traits were far from positive features of modern thought, according to Muir; indeed he believed these themes were restricting true moderns from developing the superman consciousness that was so desperately needed. As he expressed this point:

> Original Sin and the Future are essentially incompatible conceptions. The believer in the future looks upon humanity as plastic: the good and the bad in man are not fixed qualities, always, in every age, past and future, to be found in the same proportions: an 'elevation of the type of man' is, therefore, possible.[38]

Linked to this damning critique of Original Sin was a similar criticism of dogma. Muir styled the originators of religion, and truly religious people, as figures quite distinct from later followers of highly organized and codified faiths. This latter category had lost connection with an authentic religious outlook, and instead had become reliant on dogma. Contrastingly, those who possessed true 'religious feeling', according to the analysis, brought with them authentic vitality and passion. For Muir, religions were also presented as having lifecycles, and so with the passing of time such 'religious feeling' wanes, leaving only those who become dependent on the crutch of dogma to interpret the faith. These un-inspirational dogmatists represented the antithesis of a true 'religious feeling', and the dogmatic faith was merely 'religion for the irreligious'. With these ideas in mind, he argued the present was marked by the notable tenor of the death of Christianity:

> The fount is dried up; there is no longer an inward force seeking expression; there is only the fear of the dogmatist lest his foot, his guide, his horizon be taken away from him. Religion is then supported most frenziedly by the irreligious; weakness then springs with a more poignant eloquence than strength itself. And that is what is happening with Christianity. Its 'religious feeling' is dead . . .[39]

At best, in such an era there could be some sort of stop-gap restoration of the Christian attitude, but what was really needed for Muir was a fundamental break with tradition, not an attempt to shore it up. When highlighting such concerns, Muir heaped praise on Nietzsche, who he presented a few weeks later as the 'only modern who has dared to be a poet through and through, that is a liar in the noble and tragic sense', moreover, 'In Nietzsche, again, after centuries of trying, the poet has appeared in his great role of a creator of gods, a figure besides whom the "poet" seems like nothing more than the page boy of the Muse.'[40]

Nietzsche's philosophy helped Muir develop a vision for the future, a prophecy projecting humanity beyond a crumbling religious system. Muir proposed the crisis of the present age could be replaced with a new, 'elevated' type of humanity. For example, at one point he argued that Schopenhauer presented life as defined by the 'Will to Live', while Nietzsche took this further by highlighting the 'Will to Power', yet Muir proposed an even more elemental level to this line of enquiry: the 'search for expression', which itself had produced the 'Will to Power'.[41] From such assertions, as with Orage we can see that Muir was looking for ways to move beyond Nietzsche, but there were also limits to the expansion of these points. Later, Muir heavily critiqued his earlier self for the naivety in such writings. A further theme running through this interpretation of Nietzsche was a distinction between what he described as 'creative love', and a profane or barren type of love. The former type of love was found in the search for genuine creativity, and genuine expression, and was to be celebrated. The latter type of love was marked by a weaker, sympathetic outlook, was expressed by humanitarians and liberals, and found its pinnacle in dogma.[42] A few weeks after this entry, Muir continued the theme by opening his commentary with a description of Heraclitus as the central proponent of a doctrine of Becoming, and continued as follows:

> Nietzsche, the modern counterpart of Heraclitus, re-affirmed this doctrine; but he coupled it with the idea of creative love: that is his chief distinction. Certainly, those who do not comprehend Nietzsche's Love do not comprehend Nietzsche. It is key to his religion of Becoming. Becoming without Love is meaningless; Love

without Becoming is meaningless. But, united, each gives its meaning to the other, each redeems the other.[43]

So such linkages between Nietzsche, creative love and a philosophy of becoming were all central themes that Muir used to evoke a coming era, offering this approach as a means to critique the static perspective of dogma and Original Sin. Yet did not cite Hulme in such critiques, and rather chose to land his blows on figures such as G. K. Chesterton.

Muir also commented extensively on his concerns with modern developments in the arts. He criticized the Decadence movement of the 1890s at various points in these discussions, which he styled as ultimately superficial. Yet he also believed it was a development that pointed to Europe's entry into an era of elemental transition: 'it [Decadence] appears at the time when old values lie deliquescent and the new values have not yet arisen'. Moreover, Muir stressed that a new art had a profoundly important role to play in this period of transition, offering a coherent reference point during a tumultuous period of change: 'an art arises greater even than that of the eras of tradition. The pathos of the dying and the inexpressible hope of the newly born find expression side by side; all chains are broken, and the new world appears suddenly to be immeasurable'. This period of transition, epitomized by overcoming a decadent culture, sought new solutions, and so he concluded this column by asserting that, rather than 'going back to the old dogmas, we should have strained on towards the new'.[44] The *futural* and palingenetic dynamics of this vision are again very clear.

Aside from criticizing writers associated with the Decadence movement, as with Orage, Muir also took issue with realism in modern writing, finding it a debasement of what a great literature should be aiming to achieve. He praised the genius to be found in a figure such as Shakespeare, someone who he felt could truly articulate a sense of genuine tragedy. Yet the modern realists, for Muir, represented a contemporary attempt to trivialize literature, and so sought merely to popularize the art of novel writing; realist fiction was no better than newspapers. In the modern age, art was not treated as an object of admiration, and was not approached with a sense of awe. 'Art', he argued, 'must be approached with a sense of reverence, or not at all. A democratic familiarity with it – such as exists among the middle classes, *not* among the working classes, in whom reverence is not yet dead – is an abomination'.[45] Indeed he also promoted the idea of the future society developing a special role for artists as a leisurely elite. The coming age needed to develop 'a privileged class of artists and philosophers, with *absolute* leisure, who would work only when the inner compulsion made them'. Wider society also needed to have access to leisure time, in order to enjoy the profound fruits of this elite.[46] Yet in the present, capitalist realm this type of society was not possible. The industrial world, according to Muir, was the most advanced form of enslavement that mankind had yet devised for itself. One of the most striking aspects of modernity was the way it promotes the average, and discouraged the true artist:

In this age, therefore, in which a man appears as the helpless appendage of a machine too mighty for him, it is natural that theories of Determinism should flourish. It is natural, also, that the will should become weak and discouraged, and, consequently, that the power of creation should languish. And so the world of art has withered and turned barren. The artist needs above all a sense of power; it is out of the abundance of this sense that he creates. But confronted with modern society, that vast machine, and surrounded by hopeless mechanics and slaves, he feels the sense of dying within him; nor does the evil cease there, for along with the sense of power, power itself dies.[47]

So this critique of modernity marked Muir's columns, which also offered a clear counterpoint to the very limited vision of the perfectibility of mankind in the future found in, say, Hulme and Maeztu's contributions. Muir's essays presented the Nietzschean perspective in a dynamic and vibrant manner, revolving around the modernist nexus of identifying the present as essentially a liminal period, set alongside a potent vision of mankind developing the superman figure. He lamented modernity's failure to allow humanity to soar to new heights, rather enslaving people in a world marked by industrial and capitalism. This was a decadent realm with a degenerate interest in superficial literature, and an inability to transcend a dying form of religion, that had resolved itself in an unthinking dogmatism, and lacked a truly 'religious feeling'. An authentic form of 'religious feeling' could be discovered in the genius figures of the nineteenth century, including Ibsen and most importantly Nietzsche.

Interestingly, Muir soon moved away from this position, describing the outlook in his autobiography as emerging from an inward excitement but not forming a lasting philosophy that he wanted to endorse. Nevertheless, he also points out that these essays attracted commentary from readers of *The New Age*, who were drawn to his vibrant depiction of a world marked by decadence and the potential for an elemental shift, the key theme that animated the 'We Moderns' series. Their messages, then, clearly struck a cord, a fact underscored by their subsequent publication as a book in 1918, *We Moderns: Enigmas and Guesses*. The volume itself was dedicated to Orage.

Alternate visions for a new era

As these debates among more high-profile contributors were developed, elsewhere in *The New Age* a diverse range of modernist views and critiques were expressed by less well-known figures. On example of this was a series of eight essays signed by 'Kosmopolites', running from July to September of 1916, which inquired into the underlying societal mainsprings of the war. Early articles explored the ways in which European culture was one riddled with prejudices, used by the powerful to control the masses, and it was these divisive preconceptions that ultimately had led to the war. 'Kosmopolites' identified the role of education, both at the level of school teachers and university professors, as the key figures in disseminating populist presumptions, constructing them in terms of skin colour, nation or religious creed. Further, the media was highlighted as another major disseminator of prejudice, especially in the years immediately before the war. Referring to these discriminatory ideals, the author claimed that the 'destruction of these monsters', which for 'Kosmopolites' were essentially ideologies of power, 'would inevitably bring with it an amelioration of international relations'.[48]

'Kosmopolites' then identified methods whereby the various rulers of the European nations – figures who did not themselves believe in the populist prejudices they manipulated to retain power – used them to their own advantage of selfish wealth-creation. For example, the article stressed how rulers had created an ideology of empire that served well the purposed of divide and rule, allowing the powerful to dominate both European populations and global ones. However, as these ideologies of power were socially created, not innate properties of collective human psychology, they could theoretically be destroyed, their hegemony could be overturned. The final articles of the set augmented earlier claims that a peaceful future depended on a fundamental re-education of European society, albeit not primarily through the creation of new international institutions, such as the League of Nations. Though 'Kosmopolites' arguments were sceptical of a palingenetic shift in society as a direct result of the war, they nevertheless again tried to identify a profound failure in the liberal Enlightenment project. Moreover, they were also informed by a highly idealistic vision of the continent's future, one that would see its inhabitants detached from the ideologies of race, religion and nationality – perceived as dividing Europeans. If such a revaluation were achieved, this would have marked a radical change, a revolution, in the value systems of the continent's population.

Also in terms of the negative consequences of Empire, the situation in Ireland was often discussed in *The New Age*, especially following the 1916 Easter Rising and its aftermath. One article penned by the poet, journalist and Irish ideologue, Æ,[49] in January 1918 demonstrates how the journal's publicism fused a palingenetic tenor with political issues such as the future of Ireland. The article argued that the idea of the country being divided into two competing races was misguided. 'We should recognise our moral identity', Æ stated, and stressed that the style of politics pursued by both 'Ulstermen and Nationalists' was fundamentally distinct from elsewhere in Britain. Moreover, this nationalism was based upon the twin principles of blood and common mythology. Æ also argued that interbreeding had meant that, in the veins of all Irishmen, there now flowed 'the blood of the people who existed before Patrick', therefore, together, both Ulsterman and Nationalist could 'look backward through time to the legends of Red Branch, the Fianna and the gods as the legends of his people'. The invasions of Ireland by the British, he continued, 'however morally unjustifiable, however cruel in method, are justified by biology. The invasion of one race by another was Nature's ancient way of re-invigorating a people'. Æ's argument also highlighted the idea that all civilizations operate 'in waves, that races rise to a pinnacle of power and culture, and decline from that, and fall into decadence', and cited Flinders Petrie's *Revolutions of Civilisation* in support of this endorsement of cyclical history. Invasion had stimulated renewed vitality, and this now required a united and spiritually reborn Irish nation: 'We are a new people, and not the past, but the future, is to justify this new nationality'. Both the sense of common sacrifice in the war and the Easter rising were aspects of a national awakening, according to Æ: as the article phrased this point, they were instances of 'the modern Irish character just becoming self-conscious of itself'. He concluded by highlighting how, as a consequence of his Anglo-Irish identity, the Easter Rising had helped stir a sense of national unity in his outlook, and the article finished with a seven-verse poem idealizing the sacrifices being made in European battlefields, alongside those made by Pearse and other members of the Easter Rising. This concluded on a clear note of harmony:

> And to see the confluence of dreams
> That crashed together in our night,
> One river, born from many streams,
> Roll in one blaze of blinding light.[50]

Highlighting the diversity of topics for debate within the journal, the issue of Ireland's future identity was yet another subject for the *futural* discourse to developed in *The New Age* during the war.

This diversity of interests can also be seen in the contributions from émigré writers from Eastern Europe who contributed articles to the journal during the war. For example, writing in a prophetic, poetic and philosophical register, a Russian monk, R. A. Vran-Gavran, offered a series of articles on the need to fuse a pacific spiritualism that was derived from Christian teachings, alongside the wisdom of other religions, with the transcendent idea of mankind becoming regenerated through the creation of a divinely inspired form of communism.[51] The first two essays on this highly esoteric topic, entitled 'Ideals and Methods', elaborated the idea that fundamental changes could only occur if both one's ideals and one's methods for achieving these principles were pure. His forecast was clearly marked by a profound visionary pessimism, for example stating early on that: 'The existence of ideals has a double meaning: a poverty in the present and an abundance in the future. Our ideals are painful because they represent a burial feast of the present and birth agony of the future.'[52] The articles found that the model for the future was a man 'whose ideal and method are neither opposed nor separated from each other'. This vision for Vran-Gavran meant nothing less than 'the shaping of a new species of man, i.e., a new creation by good will instead of a forcible geological creation'.[53] Given these articles' poetic and prophetic register, they offered few details of what this new man would be like; rather, they lyrically discussed the idea that such a creative force would usher in a new era, and that it would be pure in both ideals and action. In the article 'Modernism and Antiquism', Vran-Gavran lamented the use of religion as a justification for war, as was often currently the case, alongside the separation between what he distinguished as religion and knowledge. This contribution concluded with an appeal for a new generation not to recapitulate the decadence of the present, but to find a profound, new impulse. Turning to metaphor, he contrasted the flow of rivers with the inspiration of a spring, arguing that 'it is much easier to flow than to spring. Yet you can spring if you make an effort to plunge into the source of the life-river – which is everywhere deeply hidden – and bring back with you a new, clear wartercourse.' God, he stated, had retired from earthly matters, offering His creative powers to mankind alone. 'He', Vran-Gavran continued, 'is now looking at and waiting for a creative mankind to assume his own duty on Earth'.[54]

In a following article in the series, 'Jesus the Carpenter', Vran-Gavran celebrated the figure of Christ, whose story and faith created a powerful sense of religious clarity.[55] The final article, 'Communism of the Saints', further outlined a communistic future based on sacred principles, claiming: 'Lo, the spirit of holiness is the best stone for the loftiest building of human organisation'. He critiqued Nietzsche's idea of the superman as a figure lacking the spiritual purity needed to redeem mankind from its present 'disharmony'. This was because interest in Nietzsche's superman figure cast an unwelcome shadow over the very aspects of the past that needed to be better understood. Vran-Gavran continued by stating that 'a new tale mankind needs, the yet untold, unapplied. It is the tale of the holy ones, the only superhuman ones that do not kill and drink blood'. To find this new tale, it was necessary to look backwards to truly move forwards: 'The only sparkles of light in the past were the saints, killed by your shadow-casting superman . . . From his tomb he warms the earth, stretching his hands through the shadows to meet the sun'. Such saintliness was precisely the quality lacking in the leaders of communism and revolutionary socialism, and ultimately the true communist question was 'a question of souls and not of codes'. Vran-Gavran concluded by rhetorically asking if the next generation could be educated to become such saints: 'If you say yes – yes, you are saved, and the world is saved, and a superhuman super-historical, superindividual construction is coming to be'.[56] Clearly the discursive field developing themes of regeneration and renewal in *The New Age* offered an eclectic set of messages.

Indeed, from this endorsement of Christianity in the face of Nietzsche, an alternate émigré perspective came from Janko Lavrin,[57] whose contributions included a discussion on the need for a deeper appreciation of tragedy, set out in the article titled 'The Tragic Individual'. Here, Lavrin outlined a plan for an authentic attainment and growth in life, which first needed to set about destroying the 'mechanical values, ideologies and "golden rules", which have been imposed a priori'. This was presented as a 'titanic task' requiring 'great spiritual honesty'. It was only figures aspiring to achieve this state who would be able to 'attain that creative idealism, the aim of which is not to mask reality but to transvalue and transmute it consciously by the individual will'. To develop his theme, he maintained there existed two types of idealism, the sentimental, romantic variant, as epitomized by *Candide*'s Dr. Pangloss, a personality incapable of creating the necessary transvaluation of values; and the tragic idealist who could see the world in all its nakedness, and therefore was uniquely capable of transforming reality. The greatest tragedy of the current era was that there existed no truly tragic figures, instead the present was a hedonistic epoch, one characterized by a distinct sense of 'spiritual poverty and decay'. At least with the war, Lavrin continued, many of the 'comfortable illusions have been destroyed . . . many philistine ideologies have been drowned in blood. The naked reality showed its Medusa's head and changed one part of mankind into stone, another into beasts, another into heroes'. As a result, Lavrin concluded, 'it is possible that this total catastrophe of all our former values will give birth to the true transvaluer, i.e. to the tragic individual'. The war, according to Lavrin's deeply palingenetic longing, could be justified were it to generate a figure capable of redeeming a decadent era.[58]

Postwar themes

Immediately after the war, we see renewed attempts to examine this new scenario, and its implications for Britain and Europe, through the modernist lens of rupture and renewal. As space is limited, we can develop two key examples here, first Oscar Levy's Nietzschean reading of the postwar situation, and second Major C. H. Douglas and his new theory of Social Credit. To begin with Levy, reflecting on what the war meant for Europe in his idiosyncratic, Nietzschean register, we can note that he contributed a series of articles called 'The Idolatry of Words'. These had been originally published in *La Revue Politique Internationale*, early in 1919. 'The Idolatry of Words' examined the war as a product of Europe's long-term descent into an enfeebled state by the twentieth century. By 'weakening men', the discussion stressed the decadent, prewar world had developed into a tinderbox for violent conflict. Levy felt that, ultimately, such decadent cultures 'do not turn their thoughts towards peace', but rather they made people 'quarrelsome and vindictive', stressing in counterpoint to this: 'Only the strong and healthy can remain at peace, provided they desire to do so.' Indeed, Levy's provocative tenor here argued that, in principle, 'pæans of praise' should be sung to 'the dauntless Hercules who attacked this dungheap', a typically condemnatory description of prewar Europe. Yet sadly, in practice, Levy stressed there were no such 'heroes'. The sacrifices made by countless soldiers were a sign of their weakness and decadence and not of their heroic virtues. No-one had satisfactorily attacked the true causes of the war. Indeed, the war effectively marked a failure by Europeans to cultivate their egos, their inability to direct them towards a 'higher' cause. 'It is this very point that the modern man had failed to grasp', Levy continued, mankind 'had entirely neglected to cultivate his ego; his desire for gain and mastery were no longer centred on any but base objects. When the war came, he was at once ready to sacrifice his ego, a fallow field, to the "sacred cause"'.

Of course, this 'sacrifice through stupidity' had its ultimate roots in the morality of religion;[59] for Levy, the war could easily be read a symbolic failure in Christianity's code of ethics. For example, in the third of these articles, Levy grounded this point in a sustained critique of Judeo-Christian morality that discussed at length what he dubbed the 'fiasco of the categorical imperative'. For Levy, this was an idea that could be traced back to 'decadent Judaism ("love thy neighbour") or, if you will, Christianity'. Specifically, he argued that Kant's notorious ideal had engendered a long period whereby Germans in particular had denied themselves 'every effort towards happiness', creating a mass psychological 'suppression', resulting in 'a disease that can only be cured by violent reaction'. With the outbreak of the war, 'the strain became too great, the nervous system exploded, the categorical imperative was blown sky-high'. For Levy, this explained the much discussed and mythologized barbarism intrinsic to Germans, leading them to be conceived as criminals across Europe.

Further, given the fact that the war was, in Levy's opinion, a conflict between Christian moral principles and the secular religion of Teutonism, he suspected that:

> this war is a war of religion, in an up to date form. The world no longer believes in God, but does believe in Christian morality. Germany is endeavouring to establish and spread this morality through the agency of an organised state system: she is, in fact, the modern Church. Her enemies hate a church which they look upon as a dungeon for the imprisonment of men's consciences, and aim at the triumph of true Christianity, that is the individual freedom of sovereign peoples, no matter

what the cost. The Church and the heretics are once more at daggers drawn, but with weapons of war more formidable than have ever been known before.

Any peace settlement could create an end to this condition in the short term. However, because the emerging peace failed to grapple with the fundamental causes of the war, the conclusion to the hostilities would necessarily be a temporary one. The true, spiritual undercurrents of the war were understood only by an enlightened few, those who aspired towards the development of a radically new form of morality adjusted to the conditions of modernity. Only such an intellectual vanguard realized the full extent of the decadence into which Western society had descended. Without overcoming the spiritual antinomies of a centuries old and now decadent Judeo-Christian ethics, there could be no new era. The future, Levy concluded, would surely be beset by further wars of this type, conflicts that, according to his thesis, were both symbolic and all-too-real expressions of moral weaknesses in modern humanity.[60] In his final article, he emphasized this last point:

> Such a peace could only come about through a katharsis, a universal purification of souls. The world must endeavour to free itself from its moral mysticism, which in Germany assumes a 'State' form and elsewhere an 'individualist' form . . . But nothing is more difficult, nothing causes us more danger and loss of blood than this operation, which has to tear from our hearts a doctrine rooted there for thousands of years past.[61]

Writing in a notably dissimilar register of economic revolution, a second key writer for the journal, Major C. H. Douglas, proposed a new analysis of the contemporary crisis and the immediate postwar milieu. In a number of essays, he began to establish the Social Credit theories that came to inform a variety of radical and even fascist grouping in the interwar period and beyond. This set of ideas was essentially a further evolution of guild socialism, yet rather than critiquing the holders of capital in society, it gravitated its economic critique around those who issued credit: financiers. Moreover, Douglas regarded both state socialism and market capitalism as erroneous economic models for a modern society, yet his most potent comments were directed at the ways in which credit was managed within the current structures of capitalism. In its place, he developed a notoriously complex set of economic arguments that stressed that financiers were akin to parasites, sucking out of the economic system a significant proportion of the overall value available to wider society through their management of credit facilities. Such financiers also made the economy highly inefficient. In his first essay in 1919, 'A Mechanical View of Economics' Douglas began to develop the theme of modern industry becoming extremely wasteful, as workers were required to create unnecessary products:

> The effect on the worker [of financiers] is that he has to do many times the amount of work which should be necessary to keep him in the highest standard of living, as a result of an artificial inducement to produce things he does not want, which he cannot buy, and which are of no use to the attainment of his internal standard of well-being.[62]

A follow-on essay then talked of the revolutionary nature of the ideas he was developing. His new vision proposed the creation of a sort of leisure economy, one where people would put in minimal working hours in order to sustain an advanced lifestyle. It was this idealized image of the alternate modernity that Douglas believed was being stymied by the presence of private finance as the mechanism for issuing credit. The breakthrough that was necessary was for credit to somehow be issued by society, not financiers, as it was the creative, collective whole of society that ultimately created the possibility of issuing credit in the first place. Again embryonically setting out these ideas, the essay 'The Control of Production' concluded with a clear statement of his revolutionary vision:

> The community creates all the credit capital there is; there is nothing whatever to prevent the community entering into its own and dwelling therein except it shall be by sheer inability to seize the opportunity which at this very moment lies open to it; an opportunity which if seized and used aright would within ten years reduce class-war to an absurdity and politics to a disease.[63]

Such polemical extracts not only point to Douglas's palingenetic vision calling for society to be fundamentally reordered within a short period, but also reveal his sensitivity to the immediate postwar period as a time of special historical opportunity: all that was required was to develop the consensus for his new, visionary reordering of economics and it could become a reality.

Soon Douglas was setting out these ideas in much more detail in *The New Age*. The journal serialized his first systematic exposition of Social Credit, *Economic Democracy*, between June and August 1919. Again, the opening chapter presented the possibility for change in culture that had emerged in the wake of the war: 'As a result of the conditions produced by the European War, the play of forces, usually only visible to expert observers, has become apparent to many who previously regarded none of these things', moreover, the war had 'riveted the attention of an awakened proletariat as no amount of positive propaganda would have done'. Meanwhile, capitalism was again presented as failing modern society, and styled as an economic system in decay. Consequently, the present was essentially a period of transition: 'from every quarter come the unmistakable signs of crumbling institutions and discredited formulae . . . a clear indication that a general re-arrangement is imminent'.[64] With this framing of the issue in place, subsequent chapters helped to set out Douglas's alternate vision in some more detail.

Strikingly, he developed a sense of jeopardy if his ideas were not heeded, focusing on the potential for capitalism's ills to become far worse if left unchecked. He argued that, unless transcended, capitalism had a will-to-power that drove it towards ever greater consolidation and centralization of the institutions that it created: 'the coalescing of small businesses into larger, of shops into huge stores, of villages into towns, of nations into leagues', was the pattern to observe, each time justified 'by the plea of economic necessity'. This centralizing tendency unleashed by capitalism, if left unchecked, would ultimately destroy the possibility for individuality and freedom, and so needed to be countered by a decentralized model for the future society.[65] The description of the stark choice people now faced was articulated again in chapter seven, styled as a fundamental decision between freedom or authoritarian rule:

> Ultimate authority is now exercised through finance . . . it seem certain that either a pyramidal organisation, having at its apex supreme power, and at its base complete subjection, will crystallise out of the centralising process which is evident in the realms of finance and industry equally with that of politics, or else a more complete decentralisation of initiative than this civilisation has ever known will be substituted for external authority.[66]

Fleshing out the vision, he cited some examples of the decentralizing forces that he believed would become a part of the new order, including a trend also developed by Hobson: the shop steward movement. Yet there were limits to the detail here, as the full dynamics of the coming system were still obscured by 'the fog of war', he felt. Nevertheless, Douglas styled his ideas as an economics compatible with a modified version of the national guilds model, and again developed the positive reference point that guild socialists had earlier found when discussing the Middle Ages. He also proposed radically adapting this to the new conditions that would follow on from capitalism:

> It does not seem possible to agree with the conclusion of the Medievalist that we are in a cul-de-sac from which the only exit is backwards . . . We may in time regain the best of the advantages on which the Medievalist rightly sets such store, retaining in addition a command over environment which he would be the first to recognise is a real advance; a solution which may be described as Ultra-Modernist.[67]

So the *futural* dynamic within Douglas's vision is redolent in such passages. Yet ultimately the serialized book failed to systematically outline a clear model for the new society.

We can find some further clues that give at least some parameters to the type of lifestyle Douglas believed people could enjoy in this 'ultra-modernist' utopia. For example, it is interesting to see some of the specifics he set out for the lives of future workers, once the inefficiencies of finance had been removed, and a decentralized society had been established. Details were limited, but Douglas's description of the hours a worker would contribute to the future society is revealing: 'It has been estimated that two hours per week of the time of every fit adult between the ages of 18 and 45 would provide for a uniformly high standard of physical wellbeing under existing conditions.'[68] From such radical speculation, we can note Douglas envisioned an efficient society offering substantial leisure time developing in the wake of an authoritarian, inefficient capitalism. Retooling the economy to operate in the interests of the worker was key here, and though there would clearly be a reduction in working hours, this was not to be a new era revolving around excessive luxury either. One aspect of capitalism that he felt epitomized its wasteful character was the trend of promoting a desire for luxury items through advertising, creating unnecessary demand. Indeed, he stressed that currently 'a large proportion of the world's energy, both intellectual and physical, is directed to the artificial stimulation of the desire for luxuries'.[69] A new society based on Social Credit principles would not be concerned with allowing such waste to develop, allowing people to work fewer hours.

The final chapter of the book also discussed the theme of propaganda. Mainstream press misinformation was another key issue to be tackled if the new society was to emerge. Douglas again asserted the need to develop an economy based on:

> the administration of credit by a decentralised local authority; the placing of the control of process entirely in the hands of the organized producer (and this in the broadest sense of the evolution of goods and services) and the fixing of prices on the broad principles of use value, by the community as a whole operating by the most flexible representation possible.

And concluded with the deeply palingenetic vision: 'Thus out of threatened chaos might the Dawn break; a Dawn which at the best must show the ravages of storm, but which holds clear for all to see the promise of a better Day'.[70] Social Credit was promoted by *The New Age* until 1938, when the journal finally ceased publication. In the interwar period we see a number of originations develop links with Social Credit ideas, from Douglas's own Social Credit Secretariat, to the Social Credit Party of Great Britain and Northern Ireland, both established in 1933. Finally, Orage's later interwar journal, the *New English Weekly* also promoted Social Credit theories. Moreover, as with guild socialism, these ideas were also influential on British fascists such as Oswald Mosley.[71]

Conclusions

The main conclusion that we can take from this final survey of *The New Age*'s modernist publicism is its highly diverse nature during the war. The considerable range of competing views that can be found in its pages at this time, revolving around the themes of war as creating the possibility of a new era emerging, and of liberal democracy as being essentially decadent and corrupt, demonstrates the vitality of this concern among such intellectuals. As we have seen, the magazine's diverse intellectual roots reveal a dynamic and variegated culture operating within *The New Age*, one creating a unique venue for the elaboration of many radical responses to modernity. From the outset of the conflict, we saw how war fever allowed some contributors to regard the war as an act of creative destruction. We have also found figures such as Oscar Levy offering readings of the modernity and the war through the lens of Nietzsche's philosophical modernism. Such positions not only presented the conflagration as the epitome of a decadent morality, but typically included glimpses of hope for redemption in the form of a moral transvaluation of Judaeo-Christian ethics as well. Meanwhile, artists were developing modernist thought during the war in the journal. Ezra Pound's numerous essays offer just such an example of aesthetic modernism as a form of regeneration. Muir and Hulme also epitomize the concern with developing the philosophy for a new culture and a new art in the coming period. Yet aside from aesthetic concerns, the journal also acted as a focus for the importing of ideas by the likes of Ramiro de Maeztu alongside émigrés from Eastern Europe such as Janko Lavrin and R. A. Vran-Gavran, the latter highly critical of the Nietzscheanism that Levy so enthusiastically developed within the journal's pages. Finally, Major C. H. Douglas reveals the postwar concern with developing radical new solutions to the crisis of capitalist modernity.

So in sum, between 1914 and 1918, highly diverse forms of cultural and political modernist thought – that is, not just guild socialism – were disseminated in wartime Britain via the pages of *The New Age*. Indeed, the pages of *The New Age* present an ideal case study in the diversity of ideas that can be identified as conforming to wider cultures of modernism, and merit further examination. For some, war offered the opportunity to realize transcendence to a new order, a new modernity; for others it merely signalled the decadence of the age. Moving to our next case study, Wyndham Lewis, we can find these modernist concerns being developed once again, through his own, highly idiosyncratic body of fiction, essays, radical journals and paintings in the era of the Great War.

5

Wyndham Lewis and Modernist
Aesthetics in Wartime

From the fiction that he began publishing in 1909 to his editing of *Blast* in 1914, Wyndham Lewis was a figure whose star rose quickly ahead of the war. By the outbreak of the conflict, he occupied a prominent position in British modernist circles and his work offered original perspectives. His new aesthetic, Vorticism, was itself a visually distinct response to modernity when compared to its nearest equivalents, Futurism and Cubism. Moreover, we can see in the prewar Lewis a clear concern to examine the unsettling conditions of modernity, and render these into discrete, new aesthetic forms. So already within this matrix one can detect the core aesthetic modernist trait of confronting a decadent modernity through radical artistic innovation. Before 1914, and ever more so during the war, we also see in Lewis's work the emergence of coded, political modernist messages underpinning calls for a new and revitalized form of civilization, ideas that in the 1930s would eventually drew Lewis to fascism. Indeed, regarding Lewis's politics, Alan Munton's description of his political trajectory as 'left-right-left' offers an overview of the political stances taken by Lewis, with these particularly right-wing interests, discussed at the end of this chapter, developing in the interwar period.[1] Though he never rendered his critique of Western modernity into a concrete, revolutionary ideology, such as guild socialism, during the wartime era we will see that Lewis increasingly sought not only to critically engage with the political impact of modernity on intellectual and social life in his work, but also to promote an engaged role for the radical artist to change society. As such, Lewis can be seen as more than an aesthetic innovator, and, as with the intellectuals already encountered, by the end of the war he too called for a new epoch to emerge from the senseless trauma of European conflict. Only by giving a voice to a new epoch through continued aesthetic innovation could the experiences of warfare be transcended.

As such, Lewis offers a clear example of an aesthetic modernist, yet one possessing some clearly political modernist tendencies too. Indeed, we can understand this characterization more fully by looking at the development of Lewis's thinking ahead of the war. In order to explore Lewis's volatile modernism, this chapter will begin with an examination of his prewar ideas, assessing some of his earliest published writings before focusing on the critique of modernity that he developed during his Vorticist period, epitomized by his writings for his journal, *Blast*. Here we find many of the modernist tendencies that made Lewis stand out as a key figure among radical intellectuals by 1914. The analysis will then survey the impact of the war on his continued ability to promote Vorticism, as well as on his first published novel, *Tarr*, initially serialized in the *Egoist*. Lewis's period as an official war artist will also be considered, revealing again his complex responses to modernity and warfare, especially as it rendered the absurdity of individual human experience in the face of an industrialized war machine. Finally, the analysis will end with the immediate postwar years, focusing attention on his book calling for new movements coming from the arts to redeem wider society, *The Caliph's Design*, as well as the subsequent creation of another journal to promote an art calling for a new era, the *Tyro*. In the wake of war, we find that Lewis was a figure looking for the radically new in art as well as politics, rendering him susceptible to the allure of fascism, seen as a political expression of the need for a radical confrontation with a decadent modernity.

Lewis before *Blast*

Lewis's transformation from an undistinguished student at Rugby School into a truly original thinker and artist began in earnest in 1898, when he took up study at the Slade. Here, he began to show promise until expelled in 1901. Following these formative years, Lewis then set out on an essentially nomadic existence, travelling in France and across Europe. Encountering the ideas of Bergson in Paris, and reading Nietzsche among other key intellectual influences at this time, Lewis's broadening intellectual horizon during these travels was the focus of his earliest written works.[2]

When we turn to this early writing, we find explorations of what Lewis regarded as primitive human forms, an analysis that he based in particular on his travels to the Breton region. In 1909, the *English Review* published the first of these sketches of life in Brittany, 'The "Pole"'. This was a critical exploration of primitive form of humanity he believed Breton life epitomized. In his first published piece, Lewis's description of such figures began to reveal some of his emerging aesthetic strategies for critically assessing human societies. The everyday existence of characters in these early texts was carefully elaborated via a detached, anthropological perspective, with a narrator's voice unpicking the inner dynamics of the closed worlds he surveyed. The Poles in this early critical narrative were presented as usually Slavic artisans, though sometimes German too, who took advantage of the naivety of Breton women who ran the local *pensions*. The analysis highlighted that, after paying an initial fee for several months' board and lodgings, such Poles would remain in place, living frugally like monks, yet paying no more money to their landladies. To these superstitious women, enamoured by the presence of potential artistic geniuses, such Poles became akin to 'household gods'. Through such primitive superstitions, the Poles would remain an accepted presence for years, no more likely to be ejected 'than most old women would get rid of a blind and callous old cat'. One beat his landlady, while later encouraging her to fall in love with him, only to reject a marriage. Another Pole was depicted as possessing a purely childlike nature. Aside from being based on the superstitions of Breton landladies, local peasants also hoped to make money from Parisian art dealers, eager that metropolitan figures would purchase pictures given to them by Poles to cover debts.[3] Importantly, throughout this dissection, Lewis's narration sought to evoke a curious and alien world, one briefly inhabited by the narrator, who was even mistaken for a Pole himself. This fragmentary analysis of what was presented as a more primitive realm, examining an alien culture where people carved out a meaningful existence through self-delusion, exemplified the detached gaze that became a hallmark of Lewis's art. Such scrutiny of the failings of others deemed subordinate to his artistic genius was an idea that Lewis would later dub 'inferior religions' in a key wartime essay reflecting on these early writings. Indeed, the diagnosis of ritualized delusions, such as those found in Breton women, was a common thread in Lewis's commentaries on more primitive as well as more modern cultures.

Peasant life as a manifestation of such 'inferior religions' was again developed in 'Some Innkeepers and Bestre', again published in the *English Review*. Similarly, the descriptions here were rich in detail, and, as with the figure of the Pole, oscillated around the theme of examining manifestations of national characteristics, another central trope that Lewis would develop during the war too. To cite some examples, the English personality was critiqued as inherently divided between the 'business' and the 'private': two entirely separate mental worlds that the English created for themselves. Meanwhile the French personality blurred its business and private life, and so had a less hypocritical psychology. The French national character was also here styled as calculating, except in terms of money, which supposedly had a mystical quality for the French. Once again, this analysis was developed via Lewis's detached, objective narrator who revelled in his superior ability to dissect the foibles and failings of his individual subjects, while also couching his analysis in comic exaggerations of their character flaws. Moreover, there was some interesting, critical reflection on what it meant to be modern here too: the idealized Frenchman criticized 'modern man's' inability to be truly friends with another person: 'my savage and inner being has been used so long to solitude . . . at this sudden and direct contact with another human being it retreats hastily still deeper into its seclusions. Civilisation has resulted in the modern man becoming, in his inaccessibility, more savage than his ancestors of the Stone Age.'[4] So here, while the primitive was evoked, the contemporary, modern man was also styled as inferior too. As such, Lewis's commentaries do not point to easy resolutions to the tensions they highlight, but rather revel in ambiguity.

Developing these themes, in May 1910 Lewis published an essay in *The New Age*, 'The Wild Body', which sought to bring greater coherence to the ideas that were being explored in these early, short dissections of Breton life. 'The Wild Body' set out Lewis's concern that modern social conventions stifled a more elemental form of human existence. It is also interesting to note that the essay was published shortly after Marinetti suggested in his '*Discours Frutuiste aux Anglais*' that the English, if little else, should at least be credited for their love of sport and physical endeavour. Contrastingly, in 'The Wild Body' Lewis stressed that such love of sport was something to be rejected as quaint and colloquial. Moreover, we again see the examination of national identities theme employed to develop a larger critique of a decadent modernity. Lewis stressed that the English in particular had created for themselves an unhealthy attitude towards the human form, with the nation's bourgeois culture attempting to tame the body's wild qualities. This was ridiculous, the essay made clear; indeed, Lewis was a figure who often liked to ground his critical assessments of cultures in the comic, and through caricature. Here, Lewis likened the idea of using sport to connect with manly, heroic qualities as akin to a mother who, despite having a real baby to nurse, would cast aside an infant and play with wax dolls. So underpinning Lewis's rejection of the English bourgeoisie's attitude to the body was a stress on diagnosing a culture that was disconnecting modern man from something truly elemental and vital, replacing it with something false and absurd. The French bourgeoisie, he asserted, was at least more comfortable with the animal qualities of the body, and this could be considered an improvement on the English. Yet even this more animalistic, French culture too was far from the ideal, 'healthy' man that such texts by Lewis tried to evoke.[5]

Yet the essay, though critical of existing cultures surrounding the body, only vaguely pointed towards a more preferable attitude, one where the 'wild body' could enter into a favourable relationship with wider society. The idea of a fundamental shift in accepted valued, drawing from the primitive, yet rejecting bourgeois conventions too, comes to the fore here, far more so than in the earlier Breton writings which the essay helped to give some intellectual coherence to. Moreover, we can detect within such early proclamations from Lewis an embryonic attempt to establish components of his idiosyncratic, critical scrutiny of the culture of contemporary European society. The self-styled anthropological observer pithily critiquing Breton peasant life and the English bourgeoisie both placed Lewis somehow 'outside' the identifiable quirks and foibles found in others, and implied the need for a fundamental renovation of attitudes in modern consciousness. In part, this position drew on Lewis's extensive, early reading of Bergson and his search to break through conventional boundaries of perception and into a realm of intuition. Lewis too was fascinated by developing appreciation of a non-rational realm of perception, giving aesthetic representation to a reality that transcended the common-sense boundaries of the rational world. Meanwhile, as we will see Nietzsche was a further influence on Lewis's thought. Yet we should also note that he was attempting to move beyond these seminal figures too, and wanted to develop his own, distinct reading of modernity, even in his early writings.

After returning from his European travels, between 1910 and 1914 the young, aspiring writer transformed himself into a central figure in England's nascent embrace of continental forms of aesthetic modernism. The narrative of this achievement has been developed in detail elsewhere,[6] so we need not dwell on this here apart to stress a few core points. Temporarily moving away from writing and towards visual arts, Lewis pioneered a novel, clearly modernist aesthetic style, one drawing primarily on Cubism and Futurism. Indeed, 1912 saw Lewis's lost major work in this embryonic style, *Kermesse*, exhibited at the Allied Artist Exhibition, a painting that caught the attention of Roger Fry.[7] Then Lewis exhibited his work at the 'Second Post-Impressionist Exhibition: British, French and Russian Artists', organized by Roger Fry at the Grafton Galleries between 1912 and 1913, helping to establish his position as a leading aesthetic modernist in Britain. Other key pieces from this period, especially his *The Life of Timon of Athens* series, also contributed to Lewis developing the distinct visual style that would later be dubbed Vorticism by Ezra Pound.

To create this new visual language for scrutinizing modernity, Lewis at this time was adapting aspects of Cubism, and at least the rhetorical bluster found in Futurism. Yet his concern to develop an idiosyncratic style allowed him to become a genuine innovator not a mere imitator. Futurism was an aesthetic he ultimately rejected because he found it too excitable and superficially interested with the world in motion, and so he dismissed it as a romantic throwback. Cubism, meanwhile, was also problematic because it had a tendency to become too analytical, and often lacked a vitalistic energy and engagement with the wider world. Added to this, after the war especially, we will see how Lewis came to believe that art needed to connect to a sense of political and social change, though one can find such themes in earlier works too. Revealing a growing confidence with his stature, Lewis broke with Fry in 1914 and set up his own Rebel Arts Centre to pursue his innovations. He also broke formally with Marinetti and Futurism at this time, signalling a wider fragmentation within the English avant-garde by 1914.

Despite these radical breaks, there were continuities here too. Intellectually, reinterpretations of Bergsonian themes of the artist's gaze being guided by spiritual intuition were still central to the development of his new visual style, though Lewis openly rejected this key figure too, preferring the antagonistic ideas of Nietzsche. (Indeed, we find Bergson and his proposal of a higher realm achieved through a turn to institution 'blasted' in the 1914 edition of *Blast*.) Yet Bergson's identification of the *élan vital* as an arena where human perception was freed from the boundaries of Newtonian physics, and allowed to enter into a more authentic awareness of pure creative energy, does appear to have influenced Lewis's understanding of a 'higher' reality that he proposed a truly civilized art needed to engage with. Nevertheless, within Lewis's emergent Vorticist aesthetic, the pure sense of a transcendent realm that Bergson offered was not the aim. The notion of the artist as the objective viewer of both the material and spiritual world had been a position strongly developed from his early writings onwards. With the Vorticist theory of the image, Lewis proposed the artist needed to offer a snapshot-style objective and static representation to what was essentially understood as a liminal experience, one torn between the polarities of the metaphysical realm of a pure, abstract creativity, and the messy material world. Moreover, the physical world itself was understood as a realm being torn asunder by the ravages of modernization, and only the intuitive artist could develop a superior gaze to give meaning to this development. Vorticism was not merely trying to find a new visual approach to representing modernity in its many forms, but also sought to give it a new art, one that would reinvest a stale, bourgeois experience with a new spiritual significance. We can understand the ideas behind Vorticism more fully by looking at *Blast*, of which one edition was published before the war, and another during the conflict, in 1915.

Blast, 1914

In order to interpret the ideas behind Vorticism, and therefore Lewis's radical critiques of industrial modernity that he had developed by this time, we can turn in particular the various texts he contributed to the first edition of *Blast*. Its initial edition was published in July 1914, on the eve of the First World War. So these writings offer a key set of documents for assessing Lewis's carefully managed, and often aggressive, persona, and his modernist concerns, immediately before the outbreak of the war.

Indeed, even outwardly, on the shelves, the look of the journal was one designed to rouse shock and outrage. Unlike the bland print of other radical journals, such as *The New Age*, with *Blast* we see a diagonal single word, 'Blast', adorning a garish, pink cover. Inside, the opening essay, 'Long Live the Vortex', outlined much of what the new movement believed it was about. In particular, here we see the distinction between the superior perspective offered by the observing, detached artist, and the inferior viewpoint of the masses becoming more clearly defined: 'WE NEED THE UNCOSCIOUSNESS OF HUMANITY', it declared, 'their stupidity, animalism and dreams'. Meanwhile, it also announced opposition to other artistic trends of the period, asserting that: 'WE ONLY WANT THE WORLD TO LIVE, and to feel it's crude energy flowing through us.' Given its presentation of the artist's gaze as one offering a superior vantage of the world, imbued with a vital experience and intuitive understanding, the opening statement made further claims regarding the likely audience for this new aesthetic: 'Blast will be popular, essentially. It will not appeal to any particular class, but to the fundamental and popular instinct in every class and description of people, TO THE INDIVIDUAL.' In other words, the aim for such Vorticist-style enlightenment would be to circumvent traditional, bourgeois class hierarches. Yet implied here was the idea that Vorticism would generate its own, new elite of the attuned observer of the world. As such, one can clearly detect palingenetic themes of personal rebirth, and access to a transcendent awareness for the individual, as a central part of the vision. This was an idea exemplified by statements such as: 'The moment a man feels or realizes himself as an artist, he ceases to belong to any milieu or time.' The rest of the essay continued this theme, for example arguing that conventional education was at odds with a truly creative instinct, while stressing that the Vorticist viewpoint was neither crudely populist, aimed at 'gentlemen', nor simply a backward-looking folk art. Rather, Lewis stressed Vorticism represented a fundamentally new innovation for the individual instinct unleashed by the new age of modernity. It was also a perspective that implicitly sought a wider cultural revolution too. For example, it wanted: 'To make the rich of the community shed their education skin, to destroy politeness, standardization and academic, that is civilized, vision, is the task we have set ourselves.'[8] From such polemical stances, we see that the project, in its intellectual scope at least, was more than a just aesthetic, and rather sought a wider change in cultural sensibilities befitting a new age.

From its revolutionary opening shot, the magazine then veered quickly into its notorious bifurcation of things to be blasted and blessed, quite a typical strategy among such modernist messages at this time. Various themes were decried here, from the English weather, to the national sense of humour and love of sports, to the whole of the Victorian period. The 'BRITTANIC AESTHETE' was also decried for manifesting erroneous, bourgeois values. Typifying the radical break with the formalities of the English art world, the British Academy was also blasted by Lewis. Moreover, the earlier hero, Bergson, was decried, despite his considerable influence on Lewis's intellectual development. France was also subjected to some detailed 'blasts' here, typical of the critique of national identities that Lewis liked to set his analysis within. Moreover, the typically modernist, creative destructive device located within these early pages of *Blast* disclosed the aggressive tenor driving the aesthetic – a comportment that was even found in Lewis's own behaviour towards others at this time. While many things were blasted – some carefully chosen to evoke stuffy, bourgeois values, others selected seemingly at random – the section segued into positivity, 'blessing' in a similar manner various lists of phenomena to be endorsed by Vorticism. Here, the 'blessed' included the material aspects of modern England. Ports, and especially their machinery, were also blessed, as was an English identity that gravitated around seafaring traditions. Indeed, much of the blessing section attempted to evoke positive aspects of the national identity. English humour was blessed, despite it already having been blasted. Moreover, here the artistic heroes Shakespeare and Swift were positively referenced. Finally, France was blessed, primarily for its vitalistic qualities, despite again the country having been condemned earlier.[9] While this more notorious, contrary 'blast' / 'bless' section acted as a radical talking point, a second manifesto puts more flesh onto the bones set out in this first manifesto.

So in the second manifesto, 'Manifesto – II', we see opening statements setting out core antagonisms found within the Vorticist radical confrontation with a decadent modernity, for example, declaring: 'We are Primitive Mercenaries in the Modern Word.' It also developed such ideas through cryptic statements styling the aesthetic position as one defined by continual states of tension and discord: 'We fight on one side, then on the other, but always for the SAME cause, which is neither side or both sides and ours.' So, from such pronouncements we can see how antagonism for its own sake helped to define the movement . The second manifesto developed further Lewis's intriguing defence of aspects of an English identity, again with the stress on seafaring in particular. This was a national trait that, Lewis suggested, gave English artists a type of universality much lacking in continental figures. Moreover, critically, he stated that England offered an ideal location for the most advanced form of aesthetic modernism to emerge, because the nation truly lacked a refined and philosophical culture. As a nation bereft of a refined, intellectual legacy, England curiously presented a perfect realm within which the truly modern artist could work. According to the manifesto, the authentic modernist of the new era should be inspired by the industrial wreckage of the age, and nowhere was more marked by the unreflective embrace of modernity than England. So although lacking the artistic traditions of European countries, it was the 'Anglo-Saxon genius' that functioned as the taproot for Europe's entire experience of modernization. Indeed, from the development of trains to modern shipping, England's pioneering modernization of the world, described in terms of spirit and will, had established the 'external reality' of modernity. So a decadent modernity was the new muse for such 'modern artists', a point described by Lewis as follows: 'this enormous, jangling, journalistic, fairy desert of modern life' should be understood as a world that 'serves him [the artist] as Nature did more technically primitive man'.

Developing this theme further, elsewhere the manifesto Lewis praised modernity for producing 'steel trees' which offered such artists far greater intricacies to render into visual form than natural trees ever could. In other words, machines had taken over from nature as the focus for the modern artist, and in theory at least England would be able to become the hub of the new art that was inspired by the impact of modernity. Indeed, it was because the English had been so concerned with creating the modern world that, only in the present, were they starting to become aware that 'Art that is an organism of this new Order and Will of Man'. Finally, the discussion also made distinctions between 'northern' and 'southern' European temperaments, claiming the 'southern' inclination led to inferior modernist ideas such as Futurism, which were incompatible with the cooler, more self-aware, 'northern' temperament found in England. So again, we see Lewis distancing himself from Futurism in order to style his movement as a unique and district brand of modernist aesthetics.[10]

From these key statements in *Blast*, one can discern much of the bluster and general attitude that Lewis couched the movement within. A pioneer aesthetic, its manifestos came loaded with a radical, *futural* thrust that sought to give shape and form to what Lewis detected was a revolution occurring in human consciousness as a consequence of modernity's impact. Artists were the advanced guard, sensitive to the new conditions, while many within wider society would remain aloof to the full, cultural impact of modernity thus understood. Artists could educate those who wanted to be receptive, at least. The serious artist of the age needed to convey this fundamentally changing temperament, and at least awaken the minds of the individuals who did want to hear this message. Competitor figures such as the modernism of Marinetti, and the far less radical English movements such as the Omega Workshops, were actively condemned as a result: they were regarded as failures in the competition to express the new conditions of modernity. Yet however much Vorticism revelled in such antagonism, and contrary statements, the message was often not clear in the wider reception of the movement. The *Manchester Guardian* for one dismissed much of the rhetoric, and detected little new here: 'The truth is, these Vorticists have conceived a romantic and sentimental understanding of vortices (just as they have of "the future" and most other things), and they use the word "vortex" merely for a certain vague emphasis.'[11]

Yet despite remaining esoteric, in scope the ideas developed by Lewis's Vorticism were steeped in an original engagement with the major theories informing early aesthetic modernism. We have already discussed the critiques of Bergson found in the manifestos, but here it is important to stress that Lewis's major literary contribution to the first edition of *Blast* – the play 'The Enemy of the Stars' – was a text that developed further interest in, and critique of, the Bergsonian ideal of achieving a sense of pure transcendence from phenomenal world. Paul Edwards has developed the most sustained reading of Lewis's opaque play. According to Edwards, we should see 'The Enemy of the Stars' as a text operating as a philosophical fiction of the type developed in Nietzsche's writings, using a mythic narrative to develop allegorical commentary, rather than viewing the text as a play *per se*. To summarize the narrative, it recounted the story of a German student, Arghol, who came to the realization that any engagement he developed with other people alienated him from an original, 'true', self. By mixing with others, he became ever more detached from an authentic sense of being. To resolve this, Arghol sought solitude and travelled north to work for his uncle as a wheelwright, where he could live in near isolation. Yet here his uncle beat him, while Arghol also befriended the other worker in the yard, Hanp. In the course of the play Arghol revealed to Hanp his reasons for leaving Berlin. While recounting this story, Arghol became aware that, despite his new, ascetic existence, he had still failed to prevent his authentic self from being contaminated by others, and became angry with Hanp. They fought, and later Hanp stabbed Arghol. Having killed Arghol, Hanp then killed himself, in a mood of despondency.[12]

Edwards's reading of this complex text highlights its knotty philosophical roots, including Lewis developing Schopenhauer's notion of the Will, and Nietzsche's critique of the ascetic ideal set out in essay three of *The Genealogy of Morals*. To summarize Edwards's reading, one of the striking commentaries on the psychology necessary for the modern artist developed by the play was a critique of the idea that human consciousness could ever become able to achieve a pure sense of transcendence, of truly escaping into the ideal, higher realm proposed by Bergsonian intuition. Following the underlying message of the narrative, human consciousness was not pure or perfectible in the manner suggested by Bergson. From Lewis's viewpoint, all attempts to make it so would be futile and tragic, as befell Arghol. So a more limited interpretation of the human capacity to find modern, spiritual enlightenment was thus needed, one where romantic notions of the artist as having complete access to such higher realms was powerfully problematized rather than embraced. Indeed, one of the core points developed in 'The Enemy of the Stars' was that the modern artist could not become detached from the wider world, and escape into a pure realm of intuition. Rather he should see himself as a liminal figure, one inherently connected to the world's material qualities while painfully aware of its spiritual limitations.[13]

Lewis was not the only contributor to the journal, and so *Blast* continued with two pieces of short fiction, 'The Saddest Story' by Ford Madox Hueffer and 'Insoluble Matrimony' by Rebecca West, as well as some translated extracts from Kandinsky's *Ueber das Geistige in der Kurst* by Edward Wadsworth. A final section was called 'Vortices and Notes', and consisted of short essays, again written by Lewis. These shorter pieces comprised a further dozen statements setting out Lewis's clearly modernist confrontation with competitor aesthetic modernisms, and modernity more generally. To summarize some core points from these final writings: in 'Life is the Important Thing', Lewis critiqued the Impressionists for merely regurgitating nature in their images, which was a mark of an 'artists whose imagination is mean and feeble', for Lewis.[14] A longer piece, 'Futurism, Magic and Life', developed a wider, somewhat disjointed commentary on the changing role of the artist. The best art here was described as neither operating on the level of pure abstraction nor representing mere 'unorganized life'. Meanwhile, Picasso's 'revolution in the plastic arts' was provocatively blurring distinctions between the artist and the engineer.[15] Futurism was again dismissed as romantic and superficial in the essay 'The Melodrama of Modernity'.[16] The short statement 'Policeman and Artist' commented further on national identity themes, with England contrasted once again with France. Here, the English were presented as artless and unintelligent, refracted through unflattering commentary on artists such as William Blake.[17] Then the essay 'Fêng Shui and Contemporary Form' developed the intriguing theme that artists needed to develop a connection with a higher realm, in order to to determine the spiritual meaning of the orientation of the material world that surrounded them. This discussion again revealed Lewis's ambivalent attitude towards developing a modernist sense of the spiritual. The piece suggested that, just as Chinese geomancers were aware of a particular order for things, so too with the intuition of great artists: 'In a painting certain forms MUST be SO . . . Personal tricks and ceremonies of this description are casual examples of the same senses' activity.' Such anti-positivist, intuitive ideas informed the spiritual side of Vorticism, and so its artists needed to develop such an intuition for representing the material world in a spiritually satisfying manner. Although moving towards abstraction, artists should not try to divorce themselves from an intuitive engagement with the material world.[18] The next essay, again discussing Picasso, 'Relativism and Picasso's Latest Work' also picked up this theme. Commenting on Picasso's contemporaneous series of smaller pieces, crafted from zinc, string, glass and wood, for Lewis these works were too focused on the material, and so lacked the spiritual 'life' that the artist needed to evoke via his work. Through commenting on such experimentations with modern art, Lewis stressed that the 'mysterious machines of modern art are what they are TO BE ALIVE'.[19]

This discussion was followed by a more political piece, commenting on the new society artists needed to give visual form to, 'The New Egos'. Here, Lewis described a fragmented, disjointed vision of contemporary reality, one where unlike previous times, individual hero figures were not really part of the collective makeup of society anymore. Rather, in the contemporary period people were now thrown together into a mass society, forming fundamentally new bonds with each other, and interacting in a novel and intimate manner. Developing this analysis of the emergent, mass society, one that Lewis stressed ultimately dehumanized people, the essay argued that artists operating within this new realm could create a powerful new capacity to access a spiritual understanding of this novel world: 'One feels the immanence of some REALITY more than any former human beings can have felt it.'[20] Another of these short, notey pieces, 'The Improvement of Life', discussed the décor of an A. B. C. Tearoom as a phenomenon that provided greater inspiration to the modern artist than any major piece of architecture from an earlier era. Again, we see expression of the view that, because England had developed as an artless country, yet one powerfully marked by the impact of modernity, it offered the most fertile conditions for the modern artist. Just as Russia bred some of the world's most profound thinkers due to its inhospitable winters creating the perfect conditions for extended contemplation, Lewis stressed that England represented a 'Siberia of the mind' where a new art could emerge to offer new enlightenment to those individuals who want to become receptive to its inner meaning.[21] Finally, the essay 'Our Vortex' then gave further detail on the overall outlook of the movement, as an attempt to master the chaos and commotion of modern life. From the transcendent position of the artistic vortex, past and future could temporarily disappear, as such temporal categories were mere aspects of life not art. The art from the vortex itself was concerned with creating a 'New Living Abstraction' by locating itself outside such temporal categories, yet also the new art to be produced was described as non-life. Moreover, the Vorticist attitude was not superficially excitable, a characteristic used to discredit Futurism; rather it was ruthless in its depiction of modernity. Telling of Lewis's need to present this via an aggressive comportment, Vorticism thus understood was even predatory: 'We hunt machines, they are our favourite game'.[22] So here we again see the theme of Lewis's art adopting a superior, detached observer position, used to define the idea of the vortex at the heart of Vorticism.

So from a close examination of the contributions by Lewis to the first edition of *Blast* we find some striking examples of his ideas on the role of modernist art. Clearly, from his discussions on the modernization of Europe, England was understood as a pioneering, technological country. Meanwhile, via his ambivalent attitude towards the role of the spiritual and the purpose for abstraction we can see that the Vorticist aesthetic emerged as one steeped in themes evoking a radical confrontation with modernity viewed as decadence. Lewis, moreover, was a figure who sought to develop and provide new answers to the emergence of the chaos of modernity around him. Fellow 'competitor' modernists such as the Futurists were powerfully critiqued, seen as enemies with rival and inferior perspectives.

When we turn to one of the few remaining Vorticist paintings by Lewis, *The Crowd*, we can see many aspects of the movement's aesthetics expressed in this picture. The image is first of all striking for its semi-abstract depiction of the cityscape, presented as angular, imposing and dominating the individual figures portrayed within the painting, who themselves are rendered similarly semi-abstract in form. It is also a deeply political representation of modernity, and gravitates around a depiction of revolution being enacted. The ant-like, semi-abstract figures representing the crowd carry with them political flags, and appear to be attempting to liberate others in the image. Yet the painting is unclear in its treatment of such a revolution. It leaves open the question of whether it is offering endorsement of such a modern revolution, or operates as a reflection on its futility. The visual depiction of individuals becoming dehumanized by the overpowering forces of the modern industrial environment can be seen in even more extreme form in Lewis's wartime paintings, which we will come on to survey later in this chapter. But before examining his wartime painting, we need to understand how Lewis responded to the outbreak of the war.

Lewis and the Great War

In *Blasting and Bombardiering* Lewis claimed that, for him, 'War and Art in those days mingled, the features of the latter as stern as – if not sterner than – the former'.[23] So although the war was an important development for him, ultimately he kept his sights on what he claimed was the true stimulation of his intellect at this time, the revolution in art. Moreover, after 1914 we can see how Lewis came to view the war itself as an absurd development, a theme expressed in postwar writings such as *Blasting and Bombardiering*. When examining this wartime output itself, we see that, for Lewis, the nature of industrial warfare discredited any simplistic assumptions on the singularly beneficial impact of modernity found among the uncritical bourgeoisie. We can see this critique of conventional perspectives, and his promotion of modernist revolution, take on a number of forms in this wartime oeuvre.

Though we are not primarily concerned with biography here, helpfully Christine Hardegen has noted four phases to Lewis's war period. While the production of *Blast: War Number* was a key aspect of the first of these phases, lasting until early 1916 when Lewis signed up to fight, we can note that from March 1916 to May 1917, Lewis was in army training and developed some shorter fiction. This was followed by his front-line experiences, between June 1917 and November of that year. Finally, Lewis was able to explore these first-hand experiences of trench combat in his commissioned work as a war artist between December 1917 and 1919.[24]

To begin with the first of these stages, at the outbreak of war, we find that Lewis's championing of European trends in aesthetic modernism in England faced a new and pressing challenge: how could the aesthetic revolt retain relevance in a world overtaken by the stark, national dividing lines of the war? We have already seen that critiquing and praising national characteristics was a common aspect of the Lewis's modernist discourse, yet now the issue of taking sides loomed in a partisan way that was entirely unnecessary before August 1914. In an article published in *Outlook* in September 1914, 'A Later Arm than Barbarity', Lewis began to develop his new wartime critiques of Germany. These would be expanded upon in *Blast: War Number* as well as in his wartime revision and publication of his first novel, *Tarr*. In particular, in his *Outlook* article of 1914 Lewis stressed that Germany was locked into the mentality of a previous era, one essentially marked by a backward, romantic culture that needed now to be confronted by the Allies.[25] The twin causes of artistic modernism, and the political climate of the war, could thus find a level of compatibility for Lewis, though convincing his many detractors of this notion would be more difficult.

Following this early statement, when we turn to the final edition of *Blast*, the 'War Number' published in July 1915, we find a much more nuanced engagement with the changed realities within Lewis's once again substantial contributions to the volume. These texts allow us to see how Lewis combined his palingenetic longings for a new culture to supersede the dominant values of society, while his writings here also stress that the emergence of an industrialized war epitomized the mindless and destructive qualities that he had previously critiqued as core aspects of the impersonal, machine age. Meanwhile, a new problem for such radical figures was that, by this time, modernists had become a common, anti-patriotic target in the wider, nationalist discourses of wartime. As with adherents of Nietzschean views, and even the guild socialists, mainstream figures came to regard Lewis and others as synonymous with a more general state of degeneration within modern Britain.

So the war changed the nature of the confrontational modernist discourse available to journals such as *Blast*, and in response Lewis tried to recapture a sense of nationalism in his new strategy. The tone of *Blast: War Number* was set in part by its announcement of the death on 15 June 1915 of Henri Gaudier-Breska, an central figure within the movement. Moreover, Paul Peppis clearly identifies that, in Lewis's wartime edition of *Blast*, one can detect a transferal of the bogeymen within the Vorticist project.[26] Whereas the original *Blast* directed repeated blows on Marinetti, Futurism and the 'southern' European temperament, this sense of enmity towards an inferior cultural tendency was now squarely opposed to the 'romantic' Germany. This was a view that had been developed by Lewis from at least 1914, but given the subject matter of *Tarr* (discussed below) probably before this time too.

An aesthetic founded on the need for mobile antagonisms, it is perhaps unsurprising to find that the second and final edition of the Vorticist journal began with an editorial expanding on the broad attitude to the war in such a light. Here, Lewis set out how Germany had caused the war out of 'thwarted desires and ambitions', though it lacked any serious goals or objectives. Moreover, echoing the ideas of figures such as T. E. Hulme, he stressed that German nationalism was marked by a dangerous culture of romanticism, a hangover from a previous era, which now needed to be opposed by force. For the sake of the wider revolution underway in European culture, it had become necessary to resist this meaningless act of aggression by a backward, romantic culture. So opposing 'the Poetry of a former condition of life, no longer existing', Vorticism could position itself as a movement supporting the war effort, while also giving voice to 'the as yet unexpressed spirit of the present time, and of the new conditions of possibility'.[27] From such framing statements, we also see how the war period was conceived as a liminal time, one where the new artistic tendencies could develop, and where aspects of an old world could be eliminated through the destructive potential of warfare. Finally, Lewis was also keen to detach his criticisms of German nationalism from the 'unofficial Germany' that was part of the modernist revolution in the arts.

Lewis wrote many of the sections of *Blast: War Number*, which began with a series of five 'War Notes'. The first of these, 'The God of Sport and Blood', offered further examination of the new critique of German nationalism. In particular, Germany's leaders were presented as delusional figures, people who were descending into a 'democratic' state of weakness, and failed to function as true aristocratic politicians. Nietzsche, meanwhile, was strongly defended here, styed as not being a typical German susceptible to such degeneration of mind, according to Lewis. More typical of German leaders was the Kaiser, who was attacked in the opening lines of the essay as a figure who had declared war on Expressionism and Cubism. So this discussion again styled the war as one between tradition, and visions of the new, the former epitomized by German militarism, the latter evoked by figures such as Nietzsche.[28]

The next piece by Lewis, 'Constantinople Our Star', entered the more familiar territory of critiquing the artlessness of the English. It suggested that the war would not lead to England discovering passion for the arts, and rather stressed that, if victorious, the nation would remain content with empire, sports and humour. Intriguingly, the piece also sketched out a potential new cultural capital that could emerge should Russia acquire Constantinople, with the city becoming a hub of creativity to the benefit of all European artists, according to Lewis.[29] Indeed, as we saw with some of the commentaries in *The New Age*, such modernist figures were interested with how the war would affect the balance of power in Europe's cultural fields. The short piece 'Mr. Shaw's Effect on My Friend', meanwhile, criticized Shaw's notorious intervention, *Common Sense About the War*, for producing too crass a patriotic a spirit.[30]

'A Super-Krupp – Or War's End' followed, and developed further commentary on the role of the enlightened intellectual to the war. Again, we can note Lewis's trademark attempt at detachment when commenting on the crisis facing humanity that surrounded him. 'Do not let us, like Christian missionaries, spoil the savages all around us', the closing lines urged. Indeed, the writing here was typically hard, and wilfully detached from the situations it described. For example the text suggested that, as everyone would eventually die, it was merely a 'matter almost of taste' where to place such human tragedy, as if painting a picture. Meanwhile, the bulk of the essay argued that the artist could meaningfully speculate on the future as he was placed at a vantage point where he alone could see how what was probable in the coming period would connect with human desires. For Lewis in this seer mode, many popular political aspirations such as a war to end war, or the promotion of socialism, were matters for mere speculation. Yet ultimately, here at least he stressed that the idea of war was unlikely to end. Indeed, as a result of the rise of modernity, war would only become more impersonal and industrial in nature. He talked about on a state of perpetual war developing, while also elaborating on its new, industrial nature. Finally, Lewis again stressed the trope that he was the advanced intellect, while all around him he was surrounded by the erroneous thinking of an earlier period. He was 'ahead' of the war, and so was waiting for the rest of the world to catch up with his perspective, and understanding of modernity. As he put this: 'All art that matters is already so far ahead that it is beyond the sphere of these disturbances.' Such radical statements developing his temporal position with regard to wider cultural trends again demonstrate how Lewis conceived himself a man in advance of mainstream views and opinions.[31]

Lewis's final War Note, 'The European War and Great Communities' offered a further discussion on the sense of the destructive yet creative powers that the war possessed for modernists. Here, Lewis described the war as 'a primitive death struggle' that was tacitly accepted by many in Europe, who secretly felt revitalized by the experiences of the war. Indeed, this inner human thirst for war again suggested to Lewis that industrialized conflict would never go away, at least if civilization remained in its present form. The 'great communities' that Lewis discussed in the essay were essentially the great powers, and in contrast with the previous essay, Lewis offered a more detailed description of the future as he saw it unfolding. He argued that the 'great communities' would become modified to support the deep-seated human desire for war. However leaden with such pessimism, he pointed to something more darkly hopeful too. Lewis's gloomy projection of further wars in the future suggested that these communities would need modification to give coming conflicts meaning for those engaged in them. The current war appeared absurd because of the scale of the enemies, so smaller communities would be able to confer greater meaning onto warfare, and once again give soldiers a sense of gallantry. Though Lewis was not endorsing this projection as desirable, he set out reasons for its development. Finally, he once again integrated his own partisanship into the analysis, stressing Germany as the aggressor in the current war, with France and Belgium rightly defending themselves.[32]

To escape from a world of warfare, Lewis's idea of 'large communities' coming to an end in the future was extended in his essay 'The Art of the Great Race'. This was placed later into the volume, and set out an interpretation of the powers of the truly great artist figure. Reformulating ideas drawn from Nietzsche regarding the existence of a pan-European, nomadic man of great creative power, in 'The Art of the Great Race' Lewis developed his clearest description of the cultural significance of the war and of its revolutionary impact. Indeed, Paul Edwards stresses in particular how this essay 'offers and account of the First World War as the self-destruction of the nineteenth-century international system of bourgeois capitalism. It was "really" a stage in a revolution that would . . . restore true national cultures'.[33] So by examining 'The Art of the Great Race', we can clearly place Lewis's wartime message in a wider, palingenetic narrative, one where the renovation of European culture is at stake.

To summarize the thesis, Lewis argued that the truly great artistic figures, such as Shakespeare, were the product of the highest form of a national art. Moreover, when operating at their most refined point, such artists developed universal tendencies, and so could profoundly influence all Europeans. Only in certain periods could the standards of national art reach such heights, and more often than not internal divisions within national psyches hampered the harmony required for national cultures to truly excel. Such divisions within the nation also produced their own artistic movements, such as folk-art, music hall song or even Viennese Waltzes, yet these examples were all of a lower order than a truly 'ripe' national art. Given the state of Europe, national art in the present, for Lewis, was not balanced, and so could not develop a truly 'ripe' culture, yet: 'When all these vast communities have disintegrated; when economic conditions have adjusted themselves, and standards based on the necessities of the genius of the soil and the scope of life, have been fixed, there will be a period of balance again.' So the war might bring about some of the creative destruction that would lead to 'ripe' cultures developing in the future. Similarly, he concluded his later wartime essay, 'Inferior Religions' (discussed further below) with a call echoing this theme: 'It is obvious, though, that we should live a little more in small communities.'[34]

What was also striking about this vision for the future was its anti-democratic nature. Elsewhere, we have seen that democracy was a pejorative term for Lewis, for example he described German leaders as democratic, as opposed to the aristocratic Nietzsche. Here too we can note that the 'ripe' culture that Lewis identified with was an essentially hierarchical one, although Lewis did not elaborate on the detail of how this new hierarchy would ensure the freedom of the truly great cultural figures, and allow them to excel. Such wartime commentaries were developing themes well beyond a narrow aesthetic concern, and highlight the politically engaged nature of Lewis's wartime messages, once unpacked. They are predicated on a creative destructive dynamic reading of the war's significance, though with much speculation and obfuscation regarding his true wishes and desires for the war. In such statements, Lewis was not presenting himself simplistically as 'pro' or 'anti' war, but rather trying to examine the war's impact via the detached anthropologist voice he developed from his earliest writings onwards. Moreover, the subtext was always that he had access to a superior knowledge in order to make such reflections; he was a true member of the new elite that was being generated by modernity.

As we move further on through *Blast: War Number*, we find that Lewis added a cluster of four more essays extending his 'War Notes', which also help us piece together his perspective on the conflict. The first of these was 'Artists and the War'. Here Lewis again reiterated central themes already discussed. Germany was presented as the aggressor nation in the war, while limited praise was given to the British and French prosecution of their campaigns, described as professional and satisfactory. However, the main topic of the discussion was once again the impact of the war, especially for artists. Lewis suggested that the scenes of the war were highly important to the artistic imagination, and proposed they could successfully become incorporated into the emerging, modern aesthetic. For the English, Lewis again stressed that the war would not radially alter the consciousness of the masses; indeed only an unlikely defeat and loss of Empire could achieve this result. Meanwhile, defeat for Germany would have some limited impact, but again would not fundamentally change the national character in the way loss of Empire for England would. Moreover, the essay ended with Lewis stating the real question was whether more conventional artists would become interested in the latest trends in modern art – essentially a development he wanted to promote. To help achieve this, he boasted that after the war he would erect statues of Picasso and Van Gogh in London squares, to be followed by statues of other contemporary artist. Promoting the new art would help to redeem the world after the war.[35]

Meanwhile, in 'The Exploitation of Blood', Lewis became far more critical of journalists and critics who suggested that the war would cure English culture of any modernist tendencies towards revolutionary art, such as Vorticism. Likening such comments to looters seizing the opportunity to steal after an earthquake, Lewis here argued that those seizing on the blood of soldiers to criticize modernist developments in the arts were nothing better than blackguards. He also suggests that the war would have some impact on the consciousness of the masses, and that future art would be able to successfully respond to the new milieu. Yet those artists truly attuned to its impact would not be sentimental or reactive artists, but rather would be those who were at the forefront of art before the war broke out, such as himself.[36] The following essay, 'The Six Hundred, Verestchagin and Uccello', again defended the idea of using the war as subject matter. Curiously, Lewis suggested that censorship, and especially the problem of finding a way to give the immense scale of the war a clear sense of meaning, had militated against the emergence of a war literature or poetry: 'like the multitudes of drab and colorless uniforms . . . there is no room, in praising soldiers, for anything but an abstract hymn. These battles are more like ant-fights than anything we have done in this way up to now'.[37] He also criticized the public's attitude to 'war art' via further, critical discussion of the press. A shorter piece, 'Marinetti's Occupation' finished off the section, essentially suggesting that the war had overtaken Marinetti's boisterous personality. Though the Futurist would remain after the war, he would become a diminished, irrelevant figure.[38]

Other pieces by Lewis were scattered through *Blast: War Number*, such as 'A Review of Contemporary Art'. Here, the discussion did not develop the theme of the war, but rather extended further Lewis's analysis of Vorticism's unique place in the new movements in modern art. As we have seen, for Lewis, the progress of this cultural revolution was important to discuss in its own right, even as the war raged across Europe. Here, Cubism was once again critiqued for being too sterile, Futurism for being too superficial, Impressionism for lacking engagement with its subject matter and the Expressionism of Kandinsky for being too concerned with abstraction and spiritual matters alone. Moreover the discussion highlighted again the need to satisfactorily capture in the new art the urban and industrial scale of modernity, and so he concluded with several key arguments for developing the new aesthetic in the coming period. The essay stressed that the general standard of art in England was 'commercial, cheap, musical-comedy civilization . . . of the basest and most vitiated kind'. To achieve a fundamental renovation, English art needed to embrace a level of abstraction. More playfully, to promote this turn to radical artistic experimentation at all opportunities, Lewis even argued for a bill in parliament to be passed to prevent any conventionally recognizable images to be shown in public spaces. Moreover, he suggested that a Government Board was required to issue certificates to artists. Only with such a document could one include representations of human beings, trees, animals and other clearly recognizable images in art.[39] Such playful radicalism in terms of criticizing the English cultural milieu fitted clearly with Lewis's modernist tenor, yet also contrasted with his much less radical, more patriotic tone, developed in many places elsewhere in *Blast: War Number*.

Later essays included 'The London Group (March 1915)', a discussion on the London Group exhibition at the Groupil Gallery. In this essay, after reviewing some of the key works, Lewis's commentary again fell on press representations of artistic modernism in England during the war. Criticism of a review of the show published by the *Times*, titled 'Junkerism in Art', formed the core of Lewis's critique here. The *Times* review had derided the works of Lewis and others in the exhibition, claiming that they manifested an art that German Junkers would have likely engaged in if they were not fighting the war. It even suggested the rigidity of the Vorticist style acted as an aesthetic version of a goosestep. Lewis castigated the *Times*'s critic as merely a figure fearful of something he did not understand, while also suggesting that a good Junker would be far more interested in floral images, or sympathetic portraits of his mother, not Lewis's modernism.[40] The article from the *Times*, meanwhile, was unfailingly withering in its critique, not merely styling Lewis's movement as Germanic, but also a poor-quality variant of such Germanic tendencies.[41] Such commentary again highlights that, despite Lewis's turn to a level of patriotism in wartime, many critics of Vorticism believed that he had not been transformed by the war. For Lewis's part, his alienation was an essential and fundamental product of living during a transitional cultural era, and he would happily argue his position in the face of what he deemed mainstream philistinism.

Blast: War Number concluded with a fictional piece by Lewis, featuring a central character, Blenner, described later in *Blasting and Bombardiering* as loosely autobiographical. This fictional piece was written during the period of the events that it narrated, Lewis also later stressed. The story began in July 1914, with a description of crowds in London, while the backcloth to events was clearly the nation's preparations ahead of the outbreak of the war. This unified yet unthinking depiction of the modern masses was styled as a phenomenon that the individual could become lost in, providing something akin to a partial death, and as a consequence was anesthetizing the crowd from the full nature of the large-scale killing that was to follow. The central figure of the story, Blenner, was a 38-year-old retired 1st Lieutenant. The narrative followed him as he explored such crowds that were incapacitating individuality as the war broke out. The tension of the piece lay in Blenner's uncertain reaction to the crowds, intrigued by them, yet ultimately repulsed by the mass consciousness they were predicated upon. He instinctively wanted to retain his own identity, and to reject that of the crowd.

So in many ways, the broad concern of retaining individuality, and problematizing the masses, found earlier in 'The Enemy of the Stars', was engaged with again, although here the narrative was presented in a far more conventional, readable register. Moreover, Blenner was a more engaging central character given the wartime context: the good-natured patriotic soldier, though one who experienced the complex psychological interpretations of the war that Lewis himself appears to have lived through at the time. When Blenner learned that war had been declared on Russia by Germany from an article in the *Daily Mail*, he became viscerally excited and so travelled to London. On the way, he encountered a variety of people wrapped up in the excitement of the impending conflict. Yet he was particularly struck by a group of sailors, who alone seemed immune to the allure of the crowd. Such crowds were depicted in a broadly similar manner elsewhere in wartime fiction too, for example in May Sinclair's *Tree of Heaven*.[42] On his journeys, Blenner later met an American poet and author, Brown Bryan Multum, who was another striking figure immune to the allure of the crowd.

The story ended with Multum and Blenner becoming friends, and Blenner discussing Multum's book, which he had already read to try and make some sense of the outbreak of the war, *The Crowd Master*. This was itself a fictional analysis of modern crowds that presented English culture as dominated by a 'soft conservatism', a relic of its 'past-living'. So to oppose the backward-looking nature of modern England, Lewis deployed the American outsider figure, Multum, and stressed that his book praised the ideals of a mythic Walt Whitmanesque figure, one whose nature was purely invention, a feature necessary for the coming age. And so the narrative's commentary veered into a positive assessment, one reflecting encouragingly on the new nation of America in its later passages. Though lacking in spiritual refinement, it was stressed that America possessed a much-needed vitality, an idea that horrified yet also made sense, to the narrative's representative of England's need to discover a new identity, Blenner. So with 'The Crowd Master' we see an exploration of the passive masses, here styled as patriotic crowds that could anaesthetize Europeans into the mass death of warfare. Meanwhile, this also contextualized Britain and Europe in a wider process of the disruption of modernity leading to the reassessment of core values and, again, national identities, in particular by raising the theme of America as an embodiment of the future.[43] The liminal nature of the present, an era of transfer to something new and yet to be discovered, potentially offering a new order, were central themes within in this concluding textual piece to *Blast: War Number*. The story was presented as the first in a series, yet no further editions of *Blast* were published.

Although this was the final edition of the journal, Lewis remained productive throughout the war period, and we see further developments in his artistic voice during and immediately after the conflict. During the war, he both developed themes from Vorticism, and moved on from some of its more boisterous poses. Moreover, Vorticism was not the only hangover from the prewar period that found further elaboration in Lewis's wartime oeuvre. During the war he continued to develop his fictional writing too. In particular, before he left for the trenches, Lewis ensured that he competed his first serious novel, *Tarr*. This was a manuscript that he had begun in 1911, but by the outbreak of war had yet to complete. His looming, active participation on the front line imbued Lewis with the impetus to leave a finished novel before he joined the army, in order to leave a lasting example of his writing should he die in combat.

Tarr's central storyline lends itself to quick summary: satirizing the bohemian lifestyles of four central protagonists, the narrative is set in Paris ahead of the war. The central character, Tarr, was an artist who in many ways resembled the modern painter as a superman figure, and clearly Tarr was the character that we can most closely identify with Lewis's own views. The plot revolved around Tarr's relationships with two female characters, Bertha and Anastasia. The former was a female embodiment of the German, romantic ideal, while the latter a much more self-assured and confident figure. This structure allowed Lewis to develop the Tarr character as one setting out various opinions. In sum, he presented him as a figure who regularly pronounced on the distinctions between life and art through the text, and generally acted as an outlet for observations Lewis himself would broadly agree with. Finally, another now familiar theme was developed via a fourth character: a German student artist character, Kreisler, who was presented as the embodiment of the rotten core of the German, romantic ideal. Introduced as professional scrounger, Kreisler eventually descended into a state of deep despair, raped Bertha and then killed himself. Tarr, meanwhile, married Bertha in order to legitimize a child who was conceived from the rape, yet Tarr remained torn at the end of the novel between his affections for Anastasia and his relationship with Bertha, with the latter divorcing him a few years after the novel ended.

When published as a book in 1918, the anti-German Kreisler character was interpreted as a strong feature of the book, as the *Times Literary Supplement* put it:

> No-one, we think, has expressed the common German state of mind so clearly in an individual, or reduced it so finally to an absurdity. The secret of Kreisler is the desire for material power and his quarrel with the world because it will not take him seriously. He is utterly absurd and, at bottom, incompetent. He is without values except for himself; and knows, unconsciously, that there is nothing in himself to value.[44]

The novel was first serialized in the *Egoist* from April 1916, and here an accompanying epilogue linked the ideas expressed in the novel, which were largely conceived before the war, to the new context. In particular, Lewis described the Kreisler character as a 'very apposite' depiction of a German to publish during the war, and went on to assert: 'Germany's large leaden brain booms away in the centre of Europe. Her brain-waves and titanic orchestrations have broken us for too long not to have had their effect.' Aside from this theme of likening Germany to the romantic grotesque figure Kreisler, the Epilogue to the *Egoist* serialization developed a critique of Nietzsche too, for example, suggesting that his writings had 'made an Over-man of every vulgarly energetic grocer in Europe'. Finally, Lewis used this piece to call for artists and thinkers to be given greater latitude during the war conditions, in order to develop truly novel visions and ideas, rather than hiding behind a false English sense of humour that repressed more profound emotional responses to reality.[45]

These critiques of the stifling demeanour of the English bourgeoisie can be found in the wartime novel's text too. The opening chapter of part one, for example, saw Tarr discuss the key themes of distinctions between art and life with Alan Hobson, a figure broadly deployed to represent Roger Fry and others from the Bloomsbury circle. In Tarr's conversation with Hobson, we can find Lewis developing the theme that Tarr represented the superman figure, while Hobson was merely a symbol for the conventional, bourgeois mind-set. For example, Tarr declared in one such outburst: 'I am the new sort of pessimist. – I think I am the sort that will please! – I am the Panurgic-Pessimist, drunken with the laughter-gas of the Abyss. I gaze on squalor and idiocy, and the more I see it the more I like it.' Elsewhere in this opening exchange that framed Tarr's character as intellectually superior to conventional figures such as Hobson, we see him decry the English public school system as one producing a herd mentality, and suggesting that although Hobson believed himself to be an individual, he was really the creation of a crowd consciousness. Tarr on the other hand was closer to realizing true individuality.[46]

Other discussions, such as in the final section of *Tarr*, 'Swagger Sex', offered similar examples of Tarr as the embodiment of the artist as Lewis's problematic superman. For example, we find Tarr stating that true artists were able to connect to a higher vision, while ordinary people had to find such realization through sex. Indeed, it was even stressed that Kreisler raped Bertha because he was unable to achieve true greatness in art, and so needed to ventilate his pent-up frustrations. Moreover, in discussions with Anastasia, Tarr declared that art was an eternal power, while life was a transient phenomenon, always ultimately defined by its proximity to death. Yet despite such proclamations evocative of his superior perception, as with the novel's original epilogue, a critique of the Nietzschean ideal of the superman was implicit here too. Despite Tarr's representation as the true embodiment of the visionary artist, this does not mean he is entirely detached from the realities of the everyday world; he too is unable to transcend the more petty and complex situations presented by developing relationships with others. We see that superman is, to a degree, lampooned here, as he ends the narrative by taking on Kreisler's child as his own, and his future is briefly described as cycling through a number of other relationships. So Tarr was not presented as effortlessly achieving the superman ideal in all quarters of his life, despite his superior powers of perception and understanding of the modern human condition. Given Lewis's own background, again, there appears to be much biography in the Tarr character.

The novel went through further revisions, following its serialization in the *Egoist*. An American edition was published in June 1918, and later the Egoist Press published an English edition. The text of each of these versions has substantial differences, and these aspects of *Tarr* have been explored more fully elsewhere. The final, 1928 revision was based on the 1918 American version. Given our particular concern with analysing patterns of revolutionary thought, an ultimately deleted section of the Prologue to the Egoist version of the novel adds some further insight into the Tarr character as an exploration of the superior artist elite, and how this figure was a product of modernity:

> You are . . . introduced to an individual: an individual named Tarr. His own theory . . . is that an artist requires more energy than civilisation provides, or that the civilized mode of life implies: more *naïveté*, freshness and unconsciousness. So Nature agrees to force his sensibility and intelligence, on the one hand, to the upmost pitch, leaving him, on the other, an uncultivated and ungregarious tract where he can run wild and renew his forces and remain unspoilt. This is a type of Artist. Here . . . can be found a permanent opposition, of life outstripped, and art becoming lonely: and there is in the sex conflict a key to the definite duality of the artist to-day: a new machinery for the preservation of the Vision made for new conditions.[47]

This statement tersely sums up the Tarr character as a product of the new environment of modernity. He was a man flawed in his social dealings, especially regarding the opposite sex, but nevertheless a figure conceived as the embodiment of the genuine artist for the new age of modernity and uncertainty. So again we see this is no simple Nietzschean superman figure, yet is still clearly presented as an example of new elite of individuals capable of developing an aesthetic vision for the new age.

While the war only partially entered into the ideas found in *Tarr*, we find also that the traumatic impact of front line experiences was a quality explored in some of Lewis's shorter fiction that he published during the war, some of which are also worth examining here. One piece published in the *Egoist*, and written before Lewis fought at the front, was called 'The French Poodle'. Here, the lead character, an architect called Rob Cairn, was blown up by a shell yet survived severely traumatized, and returned to England suffering from neurasthenia. He discussed the meaning of the war with his professional partner, who concluded that 'This "great war" is the beginning of a period, far from being a war-that-will-end-war, take my word for it.' Cairn also reflected on the level of barbarity that the war was revealing, a dynamic that jarred with his earlier peacetime life, which had now been destroyed. He bought a dog to soothe his concerns, but became overly attached to the animal, and was jealous of its affections for others. Eventually he killed the dog, returned to the front and was then killed himself a fortnight later.[48] Geoff Gilbert notes how the mental scarring that the war was inflicting on people was explored here, though as an ambivalent development, perversely helping to give Cairn a more critical perspective on life than he had before the conflict.[49] In another of these shorter pieces, 'A Young Soldier', Lewis presented a youthful figure on the London Underground, re-energized by his new role as a warrior, described as essential to men as giving birth is to women.[50] These character studies again set out to objectively examine the impact of the war on the masses of humanity, and developed some curious nuances.

One of the most unsettling of these shorter accounts was 'Cantleman's Spring Mate', written while Lewis was training to become a gunner. The central protagonist of the short story, Cantleman, was a resentful soldier who seduced a village girl while training. He was also typically antagonistic towards an English middle-class sensibility. Indeed, Cantleman's aggression towards wider society came through strongly in the piece, for example reflecting on the theme of lack of beauty as follows: 'The newspapers were the things that stank most on earth, and human beings anywhere were the most ugly and offensive of the brutes because of the confusion caused by their consciousness.' Typically, the Cantleman character had hoped that the war would produce 'a new human chemistry', but had now become disillusioned with this prospect, and believed he was being sacrificed to nature as a result of the war, not to any higher human ideals. With this hostile attitude framing the narrative, Cantleman violently seduced and got pregnant a local village girl, Stella. The narrative stressed that Cantleman developed an uncaring, disconnected attitude towards Stella's plight, viewed as part of a misguided attempt to outwit nature. The ending of the story then linked Cantleman's killing of Germans in the trenches to his aggressive attitude towards Stella: both were examples of victories for nature over the limited abilities of the human consciousness. Rotting corpses in trenches provided opportunities for other life forms to exist, while the reproductive ability of women revealed another victory for nature's will to win over conscious human actions, the piece appears to suggest. A deeply misogynistic narrative, the text again presented the individuals afflicted by war as cynical and changed figures, in particular examining how they were being dehumanized through their experiences.[51]

Other pieces of wartime fiction also allowed Lewis to comment on the war. Some texts, such as 'The Soldier of Humour', reworked older writings and fitted them into a more relevant, wartime context. Others were much more directly connected with the war scenario itself, yet also were pieces that curiously offered ways for Lewis to develop his wider modernist message. For example, the series 'Imaginary Letters' published in the *Little Review* developed one of Lewis's most explicit statements setting out the Nietzschean theme of the artist as a higher being, yet one misunderstood by a decadent society. Overall, the 'Imaginary Letters' series detailed the fictional letters home of William Bland Burn who was based in St Petersburg. Subjects in these fictional letters ranged from Burn's son, Yorke; to anti-Semitism, especially when Burn discussed briefly the Russian Revolution; to an examination of a growing detachment between Burn and his wife, who ended the series with a desire to divorce Burn. The Burn character was not only misogynistic in these exchanges, but was also concerned with identifying what underpins great art. Set within this series is the essay 'The Code of a Herdsman', a set of rules for what he describes as the 'mountain people' that will ensure their distinction from 'the herd'. Once again we are in familiar Lewis territory here, with another evocation of Nietzsche-style elites looking down on the mass society.

So when we examine more Closely 'The Code of a Herdsman', interpolated within these fictional letters, we find that German romanticism was critiqued first and foremost. Here it is styled as a type of art too bound up with allegory to allow for any real clarity of thought. Careful use of language forms another of the set of rules, and superior mountain people were advised never to use clichés, and rather should develop their own, original epithets. Curiously, they were also told to become sensitive to their 'six' personalities, and so psychologically were styled as a collection of six men, not a single ego. 'Mountain people' were also instructed to disengage from any politics, as this was the activity of the herd. Rather, the superior realm of the 'mountain people' was styled as a meta-political elite, a point that emerged via the final statement:

> The terrible processions beneath are not of our making, and are without our pity. Our sacred hill is a volcanic heaven. But the result of its violence is peace.=The unfortunate surge below, even, has moments of peace.[52]

So once again we find in Lewis's wartime art the trope of presenting the artist as part of a self-aware elite observing the world, and in this case the world at war, in a radically detached manner. The elite is essentially unlike the masses, and connected to a higher realm. Yet though such themes clearly have a strong resonance with the Zarathustra mythology, Lewis wanted to eschew such direct linkages, and present himself as an original voice.

Another such fictive spokesperson for Lewis's views was developed in 1918 in the form of the character John Porter Kemp. Found in the short play published in the *Little Review*, 'The Ideal Giant', the Kemp character was a journalist given space to develop views on a number of issues related to Lewis's own worldview. Initially, Kemp outlined a range of superstitions he possessed, such as positioning pens next to inkpots, or laying out his clothes at night, small irrational rituals that he believed to be important. As a consequence, Kemp was acutely sensitive to things being, somehow, out of place. Throughout the play we find familiar themes being evoked: art is a higher force than reality, but needed to somehow reflect it; the notion of a 'pure' artists was nonsensical; gentlemanly, bourgeois values were erroneous; and Germany was exploiting the war situation. Moreover, there was discussion on the theme of what the 'ideal giant' was, and Kemp suggested that this was the brains of modern societies, the coming together of the intellectual elite. Scene II continued to critique contemporary society, with Kemp finding it 'maddening to live with such a profusion of action suddenly poured out, most wasted; at least not curing what requires that cure'. So via such statements we see again the themes of cure and redemption were examined as the play continued. Finally, scene III offered Kemp further space to comment on the war itself, and we again find the characterization of war as an event offering the opportunity for elemental renewal: 'We must contrive; find a new Exit. Any wildly subversive action should be welcomed. *We must escape from the machine in ourselves! Smash it up: renew ourselves*.'[53] The palingenetic thrust of Lewis's position came to the fore through such a character: the intellectual elite needs to cast aside decay in society, and forge a new path, in order to develop something fundamentally new.

The idea of the Kemp character as a figure marred by the need to perform rituals also links to a key wartime essay by Lewis, published in 1917, 'Inferior Religions'.[54] This essay was a central statement of Lewis's critique of wider humanity lacking the vision of the artist, a position that we have seen Lewis develop from his Breton writings before the war, and one he returned to again, for example with his discussions on the experiences of crowds during the war. Indeed, this theme seemed to underpin many of Lewis's criticisms of those he considered lacked the artist's superior sense of individuality and intuition. By this point in the war, the idea of a modern humanity thrown into its most primitive state as a result of the conflict was another central concern for Lewis, and came to underpin his wartime discussions critiquing the bourgeois myth of progress. We have already seen this theme developed in his wartime short fiction too, but to conclude this section it is also important to stress that we can identify this idea in his most famous wartime painting as well.

Indeed, in Lewis's final wartime phase as a commissioned war artist, we find his visual style presented the idea of industrialized warfare transforming front-line soldiers into dehumanized figures, atavistically turning modern men into people governed by their most base instincts. Tom Normand has offered some telling analysis of the major war painting by Lewis, *The Battery Shelled*, exploring its development of this theme. When we examine the painting, central to the overall image is soldiers under fire, figures whose responses are styled as intuitive, and representing 'the subconscious movement of figures who exist without individual will' as they react to the shelling, according to Normand. Their retreat from their battery, which is being attacked in the image, strips away their humanity, reducing them to either a base, natural state or to mechanized automatons. So these people made inferior are perhaps being rendered into hyper modern and robot-like dehumanized forms, or are in a primitive retreat to a most uncivilized state, but either way are certainly not experiencing the superior, self-aware gaze of the artist that Lewis promoted. Indeed, Normand stresses here the 'important point is that Lewis regarded war as degradation of civilisation, and that this was expressed in the release of animal and mechanical responses in the activities of warfare.[55] Finally, one can see a group of three figures to the left of the painting who are not caught up in the immediate crisis. These more distant observers watch as humanity is humiliated by modern war, while surrounded by a serrated, alien landscape. From such a reading of Lewis's visual representation of modern war in *The Batter Shelled,* we can see how the image epitomized his rejection of modernity as a force of progression for humanity. The image graphically depicts the degradation of the human experience by war, and the violent absurdity of modernity in its most extreme form.

The Caliph's Design and the *Tyro*

Lewis described in *Rude Assignment* how he viewed the immediate postwar period as one where he was thirsting after a new civilization. The immediate postwar milieu was understood as a new time, one which he felt he could help give form: 'It was more than just picture-making: one was manufacturing fresh eyes for people, and fresh souls to go with the eyes. That was the feeling.'[56] With this polemic attitude, Lewis sought to build on his role as the public face of the modernist movement in the arts after the war. Regarding the war paintings, such as *A Battery Shelled,* Lewis exhibited these in a show called 'Guns by Wyndham Lewis' in February 1919 at the Groupil Gallery. The response was mixed, with many critics commenting on the more representational style found in Lewis's war work when compared to his earlier Vorticism. Interestingly, the catalogue notes to the exhibition suggested that, for Lewis, this changed direction was only a temporary one. The particular style of these war paintings and sketches was helpful in order to express a more personal response to the war, but in itself would not mark the major trend in his postwar painting.[57]

So, in order to examine how Lewis responded to the postwar situation we can conclude this discussion by examining two key developments in Lewis's shifting voice in the aftermath of the war, the book *The Caliph's Design: Architects! Where is Your Vortex?* and the journal the *Tyro.* Both gravitated around the idea that the postwar culture needed to be seized by radical artists, who should become engaged with transforming wider society. In other words, the modernist artist should not restrict himself to mere aesthetic innovation and needed to become socially engaged. This drive to fundamentally reconfigure society through art was forcefully set out in Lewis's first major piece of postwar theorizing on art and culture, *The Caliph's Design.* Published in 1919, it marked a departure for the prewar concerns of Lewis, yet retained the core qualities of a radical confrontation with modernity, again essentially understood as in need of a palingenetic shift to a new and more satisfactory form of civilization. Interestingly, here Lewis was acting as a solo agent calling for revolutionary change, rather than developing a movement around himself. Toby Foshay has located in the thesis of *The Caliph's Design* a radical expansion of the entire cultural project that Lewis saw as vital to redeeming Western society by this time:

By 1919, Lewis had discovered the worm in the rose of his own revolutionary experimentation. The visual revolution, his own included, had not been conceived on a large enough scale. Not only panting but the whole environment needed to be redesigned in a new cannon: *Architects! Where is your Vortex?* For the sensibility of isolated *individuals* to become that of integrated *persons*, a new culture on a classical scale had to be conceived, one in which art defined social and economic relations, rather than vice versa.[58]

So although operating without a clearly defined movement, we can see that the new scope Lewis proposed in *The Caliph's Design* was far more visionary than his prewar concerns, and once again conform to the longing for a palingenetic shift in the social order.

To help set up his argument, in *The Caliph's Design* Lewis began by offering a parable spelling out this vision for elemental renovation, which ran as follows: a wealthy Caliph awoke one morning and rapidly sketched a design for a new street. He asked his chief architect and engineer, Mahmud and Hasan, to create his vision. Fearful of the Caliph's reaction should they fail, Mahmud and Hasan were given just one day to turn the Caliph's sketches into clear plans. They completed the plans, and within a month the city was transformed into a new and vibrant place, governed by the overarching vision intuitively realized by the Caliph in a moment of spontaneous brilliance. So this modernist parable developed the theme of not merely revolutionizing visual representation, as modernist artists were already achieving in art galleries, but rather here Lewis stressed that modernists needed to bring a whole new approach to the urban landscape through their aesthetic innovation. The visionary, guiding hand of the artist genius was needed to transform society into one governed by an overarching idea and sense of new order. As the Author's Preface stressed: '*You must get Painting, Sculpture, and Design out of the studio and into life somehow or another* if you are not going to see the new vitality dissected in a Pocket of inorganic experimentation.'[59] This theme was already implicit within Lewis's earlier, wartime critiques of Picasso for being too formal and lacking vitality, but were now writ large. There are further echoes of prewar concerns, and once again the problems with competing aesthetics among modernist artists were critiqued here. For example, according to Lewis modernists based in Paris were in danger of descending into a set of artists constrained by the walls of their studios, unable to make connections between their important aesthetic innovations and the wider public. Meanwhile, the Bloomsbury group in England was also targeted for Lewis's polemic. This time simply because he believed they were nothing more than a new incarnation of the amateurish dilettantism that had traditionally marred English art. He continued by warning:

The painter stands in this year in Europe like an actor without a stage. Russia is a chaos; whether a good one or a bad one remains to be seen. Writing in Paris has fallen among the lowest talents. Painting is plunged into a tired orgy of colour-matching. A tessaract broods over Cézanne's apples. A fatuous and bouffonne mandolin has been brought from Spain; an illusive guitarist twangs formal aires amid the debris. Germany has been stunned and changed; for the better, pious hopes says. But for the present art is not likely to revive there.

Having identified such elemental crisis in the wider world, and a lack of direction within the revolutionary attitude developing within the arts, Lewis stressed that the postwar world offered any aspiring artist merely 'the scepticism of a shallow, tired and uncertain time'. Moreover, he pronounced that 'there is no great communal or personal force in the Western World of to-day, unless some new political hegemony supply it, for art to build on and to which relate itself.'[60] He called for a wide array of painters to develop the new art that could help to develop such a regenerative force, and stressed that relying on a single group, and the energies of a single impresario, simply would not work.

Turning to the British context, Lewis also diagnosed the need for this project to be set within a radical rejection of, and conscious discontinuity with, the ideas developed in the Victorian age. Meanwhile, running through the text is a critique of both capitalists and of politicians, the figures who lacked the vision of the artist and who had allowed the urban space to degenerate in the first place. One paragraph from a short discussion on politicians is telling of the tenor of this diagnosis:

> A complete reform . . . of every notion or lack of notion on the significance of the appearance of the world should be instituted. A gusto, a consciousness should imbue the placing and the shaping of every brick. A central spectacle, as a street like Regent Street is, should be worked out in the smallest detail. It should not grow like a weed, without forethought, meaning, or any agency but the drifting of commerce. A great thoroughfare like Regent Street develops and sluggishly gets on its ill-articulated legs, and blankly looks as us with its silly face . . .
>
> Do politicians understand so little the influence of the Scene of Life, or the effect of Nature, that they can be so indifferent to the capital of a wealthy and powerful community?[61]

So with *The Caliph's Design* we find Lewis's presentation of his postwar vision as one characterized by calls for a general regeneration of society. The expansive new ideas set out in the text built on earlier concerns found in Vorticism. As we will see, he still proposed the superiority of the modernist artist after the war, but his sense of social responsibility was much more strongly expressed than in *Blast*.

Shortly after this intervention, Lewis developed a new theme to critique and satirize the shallowness he believed needed to be transcended in the postwar period. To conclude the analysis, it is worth reflecting at his first major postwar innovation in visual representation: the Tyro. The concept was launched in April 1921 at a major exhibition of his work, 'Tyros and Portraits'. Simultaneously, Lewis launched his first postwar cultural journal, also called the *Tyro*. The visual expression of the Tyro concept essentially was a grinning portrait. In his exhibited works on this theme, these pictures were painted to a high specification, revealing the seriousness with which he took the project. The Tyro images were designed to be strong critiques of the shallow and fractured culture he felt dominated the postwar society. In his new journal, the idea was described as follows:

> These partly religious explosions of laughing Elementals are at once satires, pictures, and stories. The action of a Tyro is necessarily very restricted; about that of

a puppet worked with deft fingers, with a screaming voice underneath. There is none of the pathos of Pagliacci in the story of the Tyro. It is the child in him that has risen in his laugh, and you get a perspective of his history.[62]

Clearly, there are powerful echoes of the themes of 'Inferior Religions' here. Yet this was combined with the idea that a new breed of suspect, untrustworthy and brash characters had been created by the traumas of warfare.

The Tyros were not much liked or appreciated when launched, and the *Times* concluded a review of the show as follows:

> There is not promise, we think, in the pictures which he calls Tyros. Tyro he defines as an elementary person. His tyros 'are immense novices who brandish their appetites in their faces.' He is trying, in fact, a new kind of caricature of types rather than of individuals; but in these there seems to be nothing but undifferentiated violence trying by mere energy to differentiate itself into works of art. They are expletives rather than impressions.[63]

Yet subsequent critical reflection has been kinder here. Paul Edwards places them in a longer tradition of English artistic, satirical images.[64] David Peter Corbett has also stressed the emergence of the Tyro as the culmination of a particular culture that came after the war, declaring that:

> the body's fragility is replaced with a fantasy of its impregnability, just as violence and ruination of the war are replaced in immediately post-war culture with a denial of that ruination and an assertion of normality and strength. Mourning is displaced by denial, acknowledgement of vulnerability is replaced by the fantasy of strength.[65]

This is a particularly interesting characterization, especially regarding those who would straightforwardly identify the interwar Lewis with fascism. The Tyro idea satirized a shallow hyper-masculinity drawn out by the war, yet such characteristics were soon taken up quite literally by many fascist ideologues searching for powerful forms that realized their visions of the fascist new man.

Turning to Lewis's writings on this Tyro theme, and the future for European art in the wake of the new, postwar crisis more generally, we find that the opening essay of the accompanying journal, the *Tyro*, was unequivocal on the theme of the war as a marking watershed moment for civilization. Titled 'The Children of the New Epoch', the clearly palingenetic qualities of the piece are evident in this heading alone. Characterizing the present as a period disconnected from the past was a central concern here, and Lewis declared that 'No time has ever been more carefully demarcated from the one it succeeds than the time we have entered on has been by the Great War of 1914–18.' So there could be no return to the cultures that existed before 1914, and the war stood as a barrier akin to a mountain range sealing off the past from the present. Building on themes already expressed in *The Caliph's Design*, this opening essay again styled the present a liminal period, yet to be given clear form. The trauma of the war still loomed large as a:

> . . . phenomenon we meet, and are bound to meet for some time, is the existence of a sort of No Man's Land atmosphere. The dead never rise up, and men will not return to the Past, whatever else they may do. But as yet there is Nothing, or rather the corpse of the past age, and the sprinkling of children of the new – There is no mature authority, outside of creative and active individual men, to support the new and delicate forces bursting forth everywhere to-day.[66]

So while devastation still dominated a shapeless age, the buds of new creative forms were also identifiable, and the world was in transition to something new. The rest of the publication built on this core diagnosis of postwar modernity.

To give an example of this mood of transition here, decrying the old, Lewis's following essay, 'Roger Fry's Role of Continental Mediator', continued to identify Bloomsbury with now-irrelevant ideas of a previous age. Fry's personality was central to the critique, and yet again he was presented as a figure hampering a new vitalism that needed to emerge within English art. The piece concluded by asserting that Fry was abusing his reputation for an expert knowledge of the European art milieu, and was stymying efforts to bring genuine new innovations to the awareness of those in Britain who turned to him as a guru.[67] Meanwhile, other essays in the first volume of the *Tyro* included contributions by T. S. Eliot and Herbert Read, as well as various illustrations of the Tyro character. There was also the beginning of a serial story by Lewis, 'Will Eccles' that explored the painter as an outsider figure. But this narrative was not continued in the second and final edition of the *Tyro* from 1922. In sum, the first edition of the journal set out Lewis's stall for the new era that was now much needed, and he used the volume as a platform to offer some clearer detail on the impact of the war for his project of cultural renewal.

Having diagnosed and examined the need for a new time following the war in this first edition of his postwar journal, we find that essays by Lewis in the second edition of the *Tyro* built on this core theme. For example, there was a short dialogue piece called 'Tyronic Dialogues – X. and F.' by Lewis, in which the attitudes of the grotesque Tyros were given some further definition through a fictional, verbal discourse. Again, the characterization is far from flattering. English society in the aftermath of the war was identified as holding a superficial quality, and social interaction lacked depth:

> Everyone is outwardly and for the world a charming fellow or woman, incapable of anything but the most generous and kind (always KIND, this is a key-word) behaviour. Everyone knows that in reality everybody is a shit, as much as he or she *dare* be. (And this 'courage' involved again endears the thoroughly dirty dog to his fellows. It supplies the tincture of romance.) The reticence and powers of hypocrisy of our English race enhance this situation.[68]

Meanwhile, echoing prewar Breton pieces, Lewis also offered another fictional piece, 'Bestre', alongside a lengthier essay theorizing the problems facing art in the postwar era, 'Essay on the Objective of Plastic Art in Our Time'.

With this major intellectual contribution to the final edition of the *Tyro*, Lewis presented a variety of themes to once again promote a modernist art that regarded itself as spiritually superior to the everyday world, yet was also concerned with representing material realm, rather than singularly delving into a visual world of pure abstraction. Typically, often the discussion here became quite esoteric, for example via some curious reflections on astronomy and the laws of science, we find Lewis expanding on the notion that artists should view the material world as if one was somehow above it, yet constructed from it, and needed to explore forms to become as close to them as was possible. As he put it, the new art needed to:

> . . . feel that our consciousness is bound up with this non-mechanical phenom-
> enon of life; that, although helpless in face of the material world, we are in some
> way superior to and independent of it; and that our mechanical imperfection is
> the symbol of that. In art we are in a sense playing at being what we designate as
> matter. We are entering the forms of the mighty phenomena around us, and seeing
> how near we can get to being a river or a star, without actually *becoming* that.

Finally, this quite dense discussion had a more novel, cosmic tenor to it in places, for example stressing: 'Our modern "impersonality" and "coldness" is . . . a constant playing with the fire; with solar fire, perhaps, and the chill of interstellar space.'

Such commentaries drawing on outer space were combined with an analysis of the artist's more earthly, temporal location. For example, in the section headed 'The Sense of the Future' we learn that, for Lewis, understanding the nature of time is crucial to discerning the genuine visionary artist. Reference points for artists may lie in the past, or in the future, but the true artist of the present age needed to radically connect to the future. As he put it:

> There are, however, some men who seem to contain the future as others contain
> the past. These are, in the profoundest sense, also our men of action, if you admire
> that term: for, as the hosts of the unlived thing, they are the impersonification of
> action. I think that every poet, painter or philosopher worth the name has in his
> composition a large proportion of *future* as well as of past. The more he has, the
> more prophetic intuition, and the more his energy appears to arrive from another
> direction to that of the majority of men (namely, the past), the better poet, painter
> or philosopher he will be.

The *futural*, palingenetic nature of this seemingly complex theory is self-explanatory. Mankind has a choice between either being backward looking or forward facing. Its best minds, to be found among the best of artists, would be those who could foresee the future, and it was these figures who could generate the new visions that would be able to truly reinvigorate the present. For those who could project forwards like this, the future had a 'history' too, and this needed to be identified and brought into existence by the heroic, visionary artist. Lewis concluded the section by stressing this point again: 'The future possesses its history as well as the past, indeed. All living art is the history of the future.'[69]

'Essay on the Objective of Plastic Art in Our Time' also expanded some wider points that Lewis had made on the possibilities of art reinvigorating postwar society that he had set out in his introduction to the second edition of the *Tyro*. Indeed, in this introduction Lewis was again careful to specifically identify the present as a time governed by two mentalities, one decaying, and another waiting to become fully realized. Any critics of the experimentations in art that were leading to the much-needed revolutionary new forms needed to be aware that:

> if you contrast it [forward looking tendencies] with the modes of expression that depend for their existence on the precarious remains of a past order of society and life, you will see that, depending as this other one does on a mentality in course of formation, whose roots, literally, are in the future, its chances of survival are better than its more immediately traditional rivals.

In other words, during a period of transition it was better to be on the side of the future, whatever this might become, than to be reliant on the false comforts of the past. More generally, Lewis also suggested here that the new innovators in art, such as Cubists and Vorticists, were already achieving a wider impact. For example, he pointed out that posters on advertising hoardings or on the tube had been influenced by the new directions in art. Here he also stressed that the 'result is newer (in art as in politics) the equivalent in intensity of the ideal implied in the work of the original mind. But great changes are produced, accompanied by their attendant human compromise.'[70] Here, we can see once again the postwar Lewis was concerned with an aesthetic project that could transform the visual representations found in wider society, even if the imitators he detected were unable to fully realize the vision of the true 'original minds', such as his own.

Finally, as we move through the 1920s, we see that Lewis continued his concern that artists needed to be sensitive to the notion that was to come would be radically different to that which came before. Though he did not know what form the new would take, especially in the realm of politics, his interwar career concerned with this sensitivity to the *futural* led him to develop radical, political and intellectual positions. *The Art of Being Ruled* called for an escape from the decadence of capitalist modernity, while *Time and Western Man* again attacked Bergson, and developed further his views on art being revitalized through continual antagonism. His embrace of visions for the future through conflict was even to be found in his hasty, though sustained, embrace of fascism in the 1930s. For example, in his book *Hitler* we find Lewis arguing that the antagonistic energies of Nazism, though not necessarily its Germanic form, needed to be somehow imported into England. So here he concluded that there needed to be a British '"extreme" party', one defined through its radical opposition to communism while embracing the fascist sense of dynamism, though not the actual politics, of Nazism.[71] He later even wrote for the British Union of Fascists, but rejected fascism before the outbreak of war in 1939, in his book *The Hitler Cult*.

So although Lewis in the interwar period was not a fully committed fascist ideologue, as with the guild socialists drawn to fascism, arguably his interest in the ideology stemmed from his emerging political modernist sympathies. In other words, fascism could appeal as it formed part of a search for an ideology that could radically oppose the ostensible decadence capitalist modernity, while also setting out a visionary set of ideals for a reborn future. So for a modernist intellectual such as Lewis, fascism's own palingenetic messages could become highly appealing. Much academic discussion on Wyndham Lewis has gravitated around his interest in fascism, and here Frederick Jameson is perhaps the most notorious reference point in the secondary literature, styling Lewis as a 'proto-fascist'.[72] Yet in doing so, Jameson adopts a very different idea of what comprises 'generic fascism' than is employed in this study, and does not regard the ideology as a form of revolutionary political modernism. Moreover, as we have seen, Lewis was a much more nuanced figure than a singular political characterization allows, and we should not be looking to identify him with one, essential ideological position. Rather, as with many modernists, Lewis's mind was pollinated by a wide variety of radical ideas, and only superficial analysis would reduce the nebulous Lewis to fascism alone. It is also important to stress that he was not struck by such ideas in the same way as his contemporary Ezra Pound, whose fulsome level of support for the Italian Fascist regime is only now fully coming to light.

Conclusions

So to conclude, with Wyndham Lewis we see that his various intellectual positions were consciously antagonistic towards what he called the mainstream's 'inferior religions'. Indeed he viewed the creative process as emerging from continued states of conflict. Moreover, we see the objective, superior gaze that Lewis believed only the true artist possessed formed a core component of the various critiques and commentaries that he developed as we have cycled through his prewar, wartime and postwar periods. To crystallize his wartime ideas, we can note that Lewis's major war painting *A Battery Shelled* epitomized his critique of war and modernity: industrialized killing was turning people into dehumanized animals driven only by instinct, watched over by other humans who themselves had a superior vantage point over the action, yet were still ultimately situated within the base, material realm. Meanwhile, some of Lewis's most powerful critiques of modernity were set out in the first edition of *Blast*, while his postwar writings reveal his sensitivity to the impact of the war, and its traumatic significance. For him, this had left European culture in desperate need of the revitalizing tendency that, he believed, modernist art had a unique role in providing. Establishing this position, we see that Lewis became ever more concerned with art's role and its interaction with the wider world, in particular its importance in bringing about a change in the urban landscape. This informed his critiques of competitor aesthetic modernisms. Indeed, his problems with Picasso's Cubism were based on its formal, inward-looking tendencies. Meanwhile, he felt that the equally modernist visual style of Kandinsky was far too concerned with the spiritual, so again failed to develop the right mix of material reality and superior spiritual intuition. Futurism was too caught up in the excitement of modernity to fully understand it. And finally the Bloomsbury set was too traditionally English to be able to provide a truly radical confrontation with modernity.

Furthermore, we can see echoes of the concerns expressed in *The New Age* when the intellectuals writing in its pages examined the postwar situation. Here, we saw that many figures identified a need for new radical ideas to shape the new era after the war, though there was little real scope for such cultural modernists to genuinely effect the wider change they presented as imperative. In the purer realm of aesthetics, Lewis was in a position to develop his new approaches, such as the Tyro theme, even if they were not well received. Yet in terms of effecting wider cultural change, as argued for in *The Caliph's Design*, Lewis too found this was a much more difficult enterprise. Indeed, Lewis stressed that the true intellectual had to be attuned to the future, not the past. But such a position ultimately led him to develop an interest in fascism, and even misread Hitler as a 'man of peace'. Yet this concern needs to be contextualized as part of Lewis's attempt in the interwar years to radically challenge the decadence of capitalism and modernity.

Moving to our final case study, H. G. Wells, here we find another figure who flirted with aspects of fascism by the 1930s, yet, unlike Lewis, Wells was a popular writer, and aesthetically speaking not a modernist figure. Nevertheless, via the cultural historical approach underpinning this study, we will be able to identify more similarities that one would first suspect to exist between Wells and the figures we have encountered so far.

H. G. Wells and the First World War

'This is the theology of a transition; and for that reason it has an intense dramatic interest', concluded the *Times Literary Supplement* in May 1917 when reviewing H. G. Wells's wartime religious tome *God the Invisible King*. 'The revolution has begun', it continued, 'but it is not, as Mr. Wells seems to think, ended, in his own mind or any other'.[1] Although the *Times Literary Supplement* review was largely critical when discussing the detail of Wells's proposition of a modernized religion for the masses, radically reconfiguring faith in God to fit the modern era, at the same time it suggested that exploration of such an idea by this juncture of the war was a valid area for enquiry. As this final chapter demonstrates, the notion of creating a new God for a radically new time – in so doing evoking the mythic qualities of youth and regeneration as an answer to the crisis of wartime modernity – offers us a further, intriguing example of modernist themes, though here configured to garner genuine mass appeal, a sort of 'populist modernism'. Indeed, the *Times Literary Supplement*'s description of his ideas as a 'theology of a transition' clearly reflects a concern in Wells to distil a new sense of higher order and purpose from the chaos of modernity; in other words, a radical confrontation with the decadence of modern times.

To explore Wells in this manner, the chapter will re-examine his considerable literary output in the era of the war. Here, we can explore how Wells developed his own interpretation of living through a profound rupture in historical time, combined with a programmatic vision of a new world emerging from a decaying one. This detailed reconsideration of Wells's wartime writings will place his ideas of a religious revival during the war centre state, a view he crystallized in *God the Invisible King*. Currently, analyses of Wells in this period tend to either skim over, or somehow diminish, the importance of his spiritually regenerative messages at this time. Frank Field's *British and French Writers of the First World War* is an excellent example of this lacuna.[2] Meanwhile, among the specialist studies of Wells's oeuvre, the best discussion of his vision of an alternate modernity is offered by W. Warren Wargar's *H. G. Wells and the World State*, though again this study does not engage with the religiosity that Wells developed during the war, skimming over the issue as a short-lived passing fad.[3] Successive biographers, including John Batchellor, Brian Murray, Michael Coren, Michael Foot, Vincent Brome and David C. Smith,[4] have also failed to grapple sufficiently with issues surrounding Wells's religious ideas.

As we will see, this was a theme that became central to his propaganda work and his fiction alike at this time. Moreover, the framework proposed here for understanding cultures of modernism allows us to see that that the development of a new sense of religious belief was a feature compatible with Wells's other radical and *futural* visions that he developed ahead of, during and after the war. Indeed, it is interesting to note that, by the 1930s, we find Wells critically assessing the new, totalitarian states. Communism was problematic but not to be rejected wholesale, while fascism was understood ambivalently as a 'good bad thing'. Both ultimately seemed to move some way to the political modernism he espoused. Yet before examining Wells's wartime writings and its relevance to this postwar set of interests, it is worth revisiting some key areas of his prewar biography and publications in order to establish how this fertile mind traversed the technological and ethical implications of modernity, from the *fin-de-siècle* period until 1914. A far more popular figure than the previous case studies, in this final chapter it will also be interesting to gauge the reception of Wells too, and so will examine the way Wells could connect to wider audiences and unsettle received views.

H. G. Wells's diagnosis of the crisis of the twentieth century

A class migrant, the young Wells escaped the potential restraints of his background and secured entry into London's Normal School of Science in 1884. In his first year, he thrived under the tuition of Thomas Huxley, but later realized that he was not suited to the rigours of in-depth, scientific study. Increasingly, he skipped classes to read historical texts and works of literature. After attending a meeting at William Morris's home in Hammersmith, Wells became interested in socialist ideas. From his early days, he was a figure fascinated by the revolutionary potential of science and technology, as well as the idea of a social revolution in the near future that would reorder human society in a more just system. So Wells found himself living in interesting times. Coming of age during the period developing the 'logic of abundance' and a 'revolt against positivism', while changes in the culture of time and space were epitomized by the discrediting of Newtonian laws of physics, awareness of such radical reconfigurations helped Wells's mind become a bountiful tool for imagining the future anew.

It is unsurprising that when we look at Wells's breakthrough novella, *The Time Machine*, we find the notion of time and the future for humanity being radically questioned. Essentially a reworking of the apocalyptic theme of the end of the world in a modern, more secular register, the Time Traveller's story reveals to the reader first the endgame of the human species, then the end of earthly time itself. Wells's narrative warned that the human race could descend into a decadent future if it failed to evolve dynamically to the ever-changing conditions of life. Without this *futural* drive to consciously re-assess itself and improve, humanity would wither into two categories, pleasure-seeking human cattle and cannibals.[5] With such a pessimistic idea of the future at its core, one way of understanding the novella's unexpected success was due to its resonance with Europe-wide trends eschewing the scientific certainties of positivism. Wells's articulation of a new sense of crisis for the future subverted conventional, liberal idea of a steady progress towards better worlds; this negative warning was something original for British literature. Reviews were often positive, presenting the piece as highly original and thought provoking. For example, claiming the new image of the end of the world was disturbing in its vivid plausibility, the *Pall Mall Gazette* stated it was 'not a reassuring picture that Mr Wells's remarkable fancy sketches for us, and yet one is puzzled to find a flaw in his logic'.[6] With this and subsequent novels, Wells successfully created a new literary genre, science fiction, which has subsequently allowed many writers to explore the antinomies of modernity, and their own concerns regarding 'the future'. In these later 'scientific romances' before the war, such as *War of the Worlds* and *In the Shadow of the Comet*, Wells continued to explore modern, secularized versions of the apocalypse myth. Importantly for our approach to cultures of modernism and palingenesis, we can see that the narrative structure of these novels too developed transitions from the past to the future through rearticulating rebirth myths: many of these books are structured by presenting a cataclysmic event ushering in a new, more spiritually aware, era for humanity.

By the turn of the century Wells had also begun to develop another new genre of writing, and published a series of high-profile books exploring the logical repercussions to society should the processes of modernization were to continue apace. Dubbed 'Human Ecology' and ostensibly following a 'scientific' rationale, Wells's analyses of the transition from present to future were highly speculative visions, works sketching out characteristically idealized alternate modernities in a highly plausible manner for his contemporary audiences. With much acclaim in both Britain and on the continent, the first of these texts, *Anticipations*, was published in 1901. As the *Economic Journal* put it: 'he confidently predicts the improvement which will be made by posterity, and by implication arraigns the mistakes that are made by contemporaries. Like the great prophets of old time, he not only announces the future, but denounces the present.'[7] Early chapters predicted rapid advancement in existing technologies of transportation, and the extension of cities into vast conurbations covering most of the countryside. After this, Wells arrived at the thorny issue of agency regarding humanity's transition to the new era. Eschewing the myth of progress, he deployed instead the idea of a cataclysmic war, a conflict emanating from a crisis in democracy, as a potential event that would cause the necessary elemental shift in world affairs ushering in his new era. As he poetically put this act of creative destruction, the 'grey confusion of Democracy' would 'pass away inevitably by its own inherent conditions, as the twilight passes, as the embryonic confusion of the cocoon creature passes, into the higher stage, into the higher organism, the world-state of the coming years'.[8] Aside from arguing war would ultimately lead to such social rebirth, Wells also began to sketch out the idea of a revolutionary elite who would lead humanity in the new era. This vanguard of 'New Republicans' comprised people who had become disillusioned with the *anomie* of capitalist modernity, and decided to form an 'open conspiracy' to steer the world towards a new world state. The themes of a new elite of conspirators peppered Wells's writings throughout his career. His final chapter, 'The Faith, Morals, and Public Policy of the New Republic' even sketched out the need for a new morality and a new religious sensibility to bind together the new era.

Wells followed *Anticipations* with two more texts setting out his Human Ecology, *Mankind in the Making* and *A Modern Utopia*, the latter probably remains the most well known of these writings. At the time, such works were seen as important interventions in debates on contemporary issues. 'Much of this we may not be ready to accept', declared the *Manchester Guardian* in 1905, 'but the picture remains in vital colour, more than interesting . . . its rational suggestiveness is a serious contribution to our sociology'.[9] Strikingly, in these utopias, Wells distinguished his vision from earlier idealized worlds, such as those forwarded by Plato, Moore, Campanella or even William Morris. He argued the utopias of these earlier figures were essentially 'static', whereas his approach was fully compatible with the new dynamics of modernity, and so operated on a forward-looking, 'kinetic' model of utopianism. This was ever-evolving vision of the future, and his own prophetic writings proposed the next of what would be an ongoing series of future modernities, a 'hopeful stage leading to a long ascent of stages', as he put it.[10] Ultimately, there was no final end point for history in Wells's future, just perpetual transition to new stages.

The emergence of a new elite was again developed in these writings. Select people becoming intuitively aware of the need for a new order was a strong theme developed by *A Modern Utopia*. In the parallel world Wells set the exploration within, he talked of how a 'Samurai' class had developed from a series of cataclysmic wars. These future wars were creatively destructive battles that ushered in 'new and more permanent relations, that swept aside obstructions, and abolished centres of decay'.[11] In such a utopian future, Wells divided humanity into four types – kinetic, poetic, dull and base. The leading Samurai class were made up of kinetic people, while the poetic would also have some input regarding the running of the world. Samurais all held key administrative positions in the World State, and formed a new 'voluntary nobility' who were committed to follow 'the Rule', described as a set of strict codes designed to 'keep all the Samurai in a state of moral and bodily health and efficiency'.[12] The Samurai class also possessed a sacred book, and were even forced to go alone on a pilgrimage once a year to keep their faith in the new moral system underpinning the World State. The idea of God that gripped the Samurai was not found in organized collective worship and theological dogma, but was simply a deeply personal relationship between man and his deity.[13] Wells's alternate modernity also foresaw the need to develop a eugenics policy and a powerful 'gardening state',[14] in order to weed out undesirable elements and encourage the strong to flourish.[15] Writing in this eugenic register, Wells argued that the idea of killing mentally ill and criminal adults was morally wrong. Instead, he advocated measures to prevent all types of people that he considered undesirable to society from procreating. Chiming with wider fears of degeneration, Wells argued that people in the 'descendent phase', needed to be destroyed. As he put it: 'the species must be engaged in eliminating them'.[16] With the exception of infants, this would not lead to mass executions: 'There would be no killing, no lethal chambers'. Rather, the exiles of utopia were to be housed on single sex islands, unable to breed. Yet the most vulnerable were not to be spared: 'Utopia will kill all deformed and monstrous and evilly diseased people at birth'.[17] These were powerful aspects of a unique strand of political modernist themes: a *futural* vision of an interventionist state reordering the world to fit a utopian scheme, run by a new elite.

The book ended with the narrator returning from his vision of utopia to the gloomier realities of Edwardian London. The secularized sense of faith in Wells's future came through strongly here too, revealed for example when the narrator was suddenly struck with a new sense of revolutionary consciousness while sitting on a bus 'lumbering up Cockspur Street'. He poetically described a sense of conversion thus:

Could one but realize an apocalyptic image and suppose an angel, such as was given to each of the seven churches of Asia, given for a space to the service of the

Greater Rule! I see him as a towering figure of flame and colour standing between earth and sky, with a trumpet in his hands, over there above the Haymarket against the October glow; and when he sounds, all the samurai, all who are samurai in Utopia, will know themselves and one another.[18]

Such ideas were taken seriously by educated society of the period. For example, on the importance of Wells's thesis the *Athenaeum* wrote: 'There has been no book of this importance published for the past thirty years; and it is possible and permissible to hope that some ideas sketched here will fructify in the future.'[19]

Aside from these texts revealing Wells's vision for an idea new type of state, he was deeply committed to a left-wing politics. He participated with the radical left debates, but only if he could remain a non-conformist voice. A member of the Fabian Society from 1903, as with the guild socialists, the radicalism that Wells promoted at this time yearned for a more poetic vision of societal renewal when compared to the austere, rational socialism that was developed under Fabianism. So by 1908 Wells resigned from the society, and in a last hurrah to convert younger Fabians to something more emotive and visionary he published *First and Last Things*. Epitomizing this rejection of a singularly rational approach to understanding the human condition, this series of lectures worked into a book was intended to be a candid appeal to the more radical Fabians. In this work, we again find criticism of the positivism of science, and the need to discover what he dubbed a 'kinetic' sense of life as opposed to 'static' logic.[20] Wells also reflected further on religion and faith. He championed belief in the universality of the human experience, describing how all had emerged from a common blood ancestry. By accepting this common origin, Wells claimed that one could come to realize the existence of an overarching, communal mind of humanity. By awakening this communal, supra-individual mindset, one could begin to find a new sense of religious salvation and even love, transcending the mere 'egoism' of individuality. As we will see, this secularized sense of transcendence was an important component of his wartime radical politics.

As a result of his successes as a novelist, alongside his Human Ecology works, by the outbreak of the war Wells had become a truly international figure, with a reputation spreading to America and, via numerous translations, across the continent too. By 1914, we can see a number of key themes developing within his influential voice. Responding to a sense of decadence in capitalist modernity, his ideas expressed the need to think beyond a steady sense of liberal-democratic progress towards a better world. Indeed, he championed radical change through the creative destruction of an apocalyptic cataclysm, and through the agency of a revolutionary, morally superior elite. Many of these central themes were articulated with another scientific romance predicting renewal though a calamitous war, *The World Set Free*, published just ahead of the war. Set in the 1950s, Wells here prophesized a war between the 'Central Powers', primarily Germany, and the 'Free Nations', including Britain and France. He even deployed the idea of the nuclear bomb as the futuristic device that would enact creative destruction on swathes of mainland Europe. Such devastation was ultimately necessary and positive as it allowed the great and good of the world to usher in a new era, one governed by a pacific World State, transcending the era of a destructive capitalism. Typically, alongside creative destruction introducing massive social change, a new spirit characterized the era after this nuclear war. This new spirit unifying society was religious, though not Christian, altruistic not egotistical, morally regenerated and awakened to a new collective consciousness. As we will see below, such ideas came to frame his attitude to the war.

The war that will end war

Despite Wells's repeated descriptions of a European war in texts like *The World Set Free*, the outbreak of conflict in 1914 came as a genuine shock. 'I let my imagination play about it', he claimed in later years, 'but at the bottom of my heart I could not feel and believe it would really be let happen'.[21] It was a life-changing event for European society, as was made clear in his later autobiography: 'no intelligent brain that passed through the experience of the Great War emerged without being profoundly changed. Our vision of life was revised in outline and detail alike . . . it was the revelation of the profound instability of the social order'. Developing the theme of war as a method for moving beyond flaws in European society, he also stated that it revealed the 'possibilities of fundamental reorganisation' and a weakness in the 'collective mentality' of mankind.[22] Following the outbreak of the war, Wells argued that a new, global system of governance was needed, a reconfigured map of Europe was required, and even a new way of conceiving of God was essential, all in order for a new age to emerge from the carnage unfolding in Europe. Such a vast project for European regeneration in the wake of industrialized destruction represented Wells's own political modernism at its most hubristically imaginative.

A powerful mood of war fever was evident early on. Wells's first book was probably his most excitable of the war, and was clearly caught up in the wider culture of exhilaration endemic among European intellectuals in August 1914. Articulating the need for elemental change, it comprised a series of essays written at the outbreak of war for the *Daily Chronicle*, the *Nation*, the *Daily News* and the *War Illustrated*. Titled *The War that Will End War*, the book coined one of the key slogans of the era. The theme of creative destruction, of war representing the end of one era and the emergence of a new, peaceful one, was clearly embodied by this catchy phrase. From *The War that Will End War* we also see how Wells regarded the fighting as 'the vastest war in history', one that was 'a war not of nations, but of mankind. It is a war to exorcise a world-madness and end an age'.[23] Moreover, Wells believed that every 'fighter who fights against Germany now is a crusader against war. This, the greatest of all wars, is not just another war – it is the last war!'[24] Topics discussed ranged from the origins of the fighting, to the distribution of food in Britain under the new conditions, to the differing geopolitical threats of a modernized Russia against the aggression of Germany, to calls for American intervention. Moreover, he demanded an end to the private trade in arms: 'That is the real enemy', he stated, 'the evil thing at the very centre of this trouble'.[25]

We also gain from these early war writings an outline of the move towards a world state that Wells, even at this very early stage, hoped would shape the future peace. The mood music of living through a time of fundamental transition was central to the emergence of a new era: 'Never did any time carry so swift a burden of change as this time', he declared, and also asserted that it 'is manifest that in a year or so the world of men is going to alter more than it has altered in the last century and a half, more indeed than it ever altered before these last centuries since history began'.[26] From this emphasis on living during elemental change, Wells continued that the stable national borders of Europe before the war now 'waver under one's eyes', and ideas 'that have ruled life as though they were divine truths are being chased and slaughtered in the streets'.[27] Property and individualism had become concepts of a previous age, promoting an acceptance of a new era of social ownership: 'The state takes over flour mills and food supply, not merely for military purposes, but for the general welfare of the community . . . There is not even a letter to the *Times* to object.'[28] Anticipating Wilson's 14 points, another chapter titled 'The Need of a New Map of Europe' claimed the continent could 'begin a new period of history'[29] by reconfiguring national borders in a more 'just' division. To give the details here: France would recover Lorraine, and Alsace could either become linked with France or the Swiss Confederation. Trieste, Trent and possibly Pola should be returned to Italy, the Austrian Empire could be disbanded and a new confederation, similar to Switzerland, would be constructed to unite the Slavic peoples. Bulgaria should gain lost land from Serbia, and Romania could be given Transylvania. Finally, Poland would become a united country, although it would retain the Tzar as its head of state. The need for this new map was vital, for failure to fundamentally recast the very idea of Europe would lead to 'a new set of ugly complications and prepare a still more colossal Armageddon than this that is now going on'.[30] So the tension between opportunity and crisis was also clear: if the decadent era that had created the war was not transcended, even greater calamities would befall the continent. Only a true world conference could decide the terms of the peace, and so this was why Wells called for a Peace League to 'control the globe'.

In short, the war announced to Wells that Europe was experiencing an elemental breakdown of its social structure, fundamentally subverting institutions and social conventions. As he put it, these 'crumble about us, and release unprecedented power to the two sorts of rebel that ordinary times suppress, will and ideas'. Indeed, Wells believed that it would be 'will' and 'ideas' that would 'take a larger part in this *swirl-ahead* than they have even taken in any previous collapse'; and the 'desire for a new world of definite character' would become 'a guiding force' for 'shaping the new time'.[31] From such statements, we can see that a powerful rhetoric of radically embracing the new was central to his wartime publicism. The key questions were: was 'the new world' to be 'shaped by the philosophers or the Huns'? And 'shall we be able in this vast collapse or re-birth of the world, to produce ideas that will rule?'[32] The final of these early essays, 'The War of the Mind', also discussed the importance of intellectuals such as himself, vital for a successful outcome he felt. For Wells, governments tended to be uncreative institutions that would only ever 'follow necessity'. Echoing themes of an emergent guiding elite, he stated that, in order to develop a new vision, it rested 'with us who, outside all formal government, represent the national will and intention, to take this work into our hands . . . we have to create a wide common conception of a re-mapped and pacified Europe, released from the dangers of a private trade in armaments, largely disarmed and pledged to mutual protection'.[33] The propaganda war would be vital to ushering in the new. He concluded the chapter with a discussion on the failure of Christianity to prevent war, to offer moral leadership and to provide a rationale towards a new peace. While such traditional leadership had failed, the gap needed to be filled by radical modernizers.

In order to spread his message, Wells published many pamphlets during the war designed to promulgate his unique message of radical renewal. Many of these contain further details on how he conceived the war crisis leading to a new era in world affairs. For example, the 1916 pamphlet *The Peace of the World* discussed the contradiction that the war was creating in the hearts of the combatant nations. As he put it, 'every man is divided against himself' because, on the one hand, everyone wanted peace, yet, on the other, there was something grimly appealing and even voyeuristic about the war:

> a sensation of greatness, a beautiful tremendousness, in many of the crude facts of war, they excite in one a kind of vigorous exultation; we have this destructive streak in us, and it is no good pretending that we have not; the first thing we must do for the peace of the world is to control that.[34]

The destruction of war excited human instincts; so harnessing this for good was an important role of the intellectual. Again, here Wells underpinned his demand for a 'World Congress' after the war, and discussed the need for America to become central to this new forum. Another pamphlet of the era, *The Elements of Reconstruction*, continued Wells's propaganda effort. Here, he argued for the need to use the profound crisis of the war as a catalyst to transcend what he described here as the 'Selfish Age', a period that had been characterized by piecemeal reforms and the pursuit of narrow profit by capitalists. Wells developed these themes by sketching out how Britain's agricultural and industrial economies could be controlled by national trusts, while frictions in labour relations could be eliminated.

Aside from pamphlets, Wells continued to publish propaganda books too. To present the war as the time for fundamental reordering, Wells even reprised his Human Ecology in a book called *What is Coming? A Forecast of Things after the War*. Here, he began by setting out an argument for greater professionalism in the drive towards a permanent peace, while also predicting that the war would end not through some final breakthrough and total defeat of one side, but rather due to a slow process of exhaustion. Via his projections, it would be Germany and her allies who would fail, and then peace would be negotiated between three major world power groups, the pan-Americans, Germany and her allies and the anti-German allies of Britain and France. Yet by uniting these groupings under a common agenda, a World State could emerge. Postwar Britain would be regenerated too. Essentially, Wells believed that the wartime conditions were acting as a catalyst for a new ethos and spirit among the youth of Europe, who would act in opposition to 'our ostensible rulers and leaders [that] have been falling behind the times'. This new spirit, he continued, would save Britain and other European countries from the stilted nature of political leadership that had characterized the prewar era. He defined this new mood as 'the creative spirit as distinguished from the legal spirit'. Moreover, 'it is the spirit of courage to make and not the spirit that waits and sees and claims; it is the spirit that looks to the future and not to the past'. For Wells, this attitude even had religious qualities in the form of a 'thinking back to oneself from greater standards and realities'.[35] As with many radical intellectuals across Europe, including the guild socialists, Wells thought the trenches themselves would ferment a new type of positive, creative mindset. For at least two decades following the war, Wells prediction stated that British life would be impregnated with these wartime 'new men', who he described thus: 'he is young and he is uniformed in khaki, and he brings with him a new spirit into British life, the spirit of the new soldier, the spirit of subordination to a common purpose'.[36]

Meanwhile, Wells also praised the move towards a more powerful state via the increased collectivization of the national economy. Indeed, big state solutions to the chaos of modernity were to be welcomed: 'There is a new economic Great Britain to-day, emergency made, jerry-built no doubt, a gawky, weedy giant who may fill out to such dimensions as the German national system has never attained. Behind it is an *idea*, a new idea, an idea of the nation as one great economic system working together'.[37] According to this speculation, though the Europe of 1930 would still see much of the capitalist system in place, key areas of the economy, such as shipping, railways, coal, metal industries, large quantities of engineering and the majority of the agricultural sector would already have come 'more or less completely under collective ownership, and certainly very completely under collective control'.[38] Moreover, this transition was all to be welcomed as part of the wider move to a new era of peace.

Wells's previous works on Human Ecology had also argued for a new elite to emerge to redeem the world. Unsurprisingly, he also used *The Peace of the World* to set out this idea as a central aspect of the war experience. He felt that, in wartime, moods of 'intense religiosity, of devotion and of endeavour are let loose', and so, in the near future 'there will be much more likelihood that we may presently find, what is impossible to find now, a number of devoted men and women ready to give their whole lives, with quasi-religious enthusiasm, to this great task of peace establishment'.[39] In other words, the new Samurai class, imbued with their new religion, were now generating themselves, finding consciousness, in the wartime crisis of modernity. We can map Wells's promotion of this emergent religious consciousness by looking at some of his clearest statements on such metaphysical issues, as developed in the books *War and the Future* and *God the Invisible King*.

War and modern religion

Wells quickly followed *What Is Coming?* with another, more general statement on the significance of the conflict, *War and the Future*. Published in 1917, it consisted of new material alongside essays from *Cassell's Magazine*, the *Daily Chronicle* and the *Daily News* printed in late 1916. Reviews were less than fully positive, and often misunderstood the book's now more prominent religious tenor. The *English Review* felt Wells was 'invariably interesting', though noted that 'he seems to have been converted to some idea of a People's God, quite forgetting that so long as nations have boundaries and flags and patriotism no God or any manner of Gods will abolish war'.[40] However, Wells was clear that he was no defender of national boundaries in the long term, and did not really see them as compatible with his new faith. Meanwhile, the *Times Literary*

Supplement described Wells's conversion in a more barbed fashion, as 'interesting rather as coming from a man who has given so much thought to the development of mechanical appliances than for its bearing on the complexities of the moment'.[41] Yet such criticism, suggesting that his interest in faith was suspect as it was coming from a figure previously interested in solely technocratic maters, was somewhat inaccurate. As we have seen, Wells's concern with the impact of modernization and the need for renewed religious faith was on-going. This was a strand of thought he had already developed embryonically, especially in texts such as *A Modern Utopia* and *First and Last Things*.

Though much of *War and the Future* comprised reportage of his journeys in Europe during August and September 1916, including the war in Italy and in France, it also developed far more clearly his understanding of the spiritual dimension of the war, again presenting the transition to the future as representing a profound break with the past. For example, the opening chapter, 'The Passing of the Effigy', critiqued the worship of what he dubbed 'effigies', individual heroes figures and singular, supposedly great leaders, such as the Kaiser. He even dismissed Nietzsche as over-hyped, an old-fashioned mystic who worshipped his own dated version of the 'effigy', the superman. With the outbreak of the war, Wells argued that it 'seems that the twilight of the half gods must have come, that we have reached the end of the age when men needed a Personal Figure around whom they could rally'.[42] He also claimed that 'mankind is still as it were collectively dreaming and hardly more awakened to reality than a very young child'. Countering the critique developed by the *English Review*, he stressed that nationalism was one characteristic feature of this passing dream state, allegiances that would fall away in the future, as would its various associated effigies. The 'time draws near', Wells summarized, 'when mankind will awake and the dreams will fade away, and then there will be no nationality in all the world but humanity, and no king, no emperor, no leader but one God of mankind'.[43] The palingenetic qualities of such statements are quite clear.

Regarding the more mundane issue of the mechanics of modern war, Wells characterized the actual fighting in more depressing, unheroic tones. Modern warfare was based on experimentation and a series of blunders, armies lost battles rather than won them. What is more, while the nature of warfare had undergone a significant transformation over the previous 24 years, many of the military leaders had failed to adjust to these new conditions and technologies. Again, the existing elite were presented as figures out of step with their times. Given the necessity of huge economic resources to be able to sustain fighting, modern, industrialized warfare had suddenly become an option available to only to a handful of countries, Britain, France, Germany and the USA. A second rung, Japan, Italy, Russia and Austria, were also capable of sustaining limited modern warfare. Consequently, the future of all warfare was now in the hands of these few powers. Future conflicts would either be fought by them, or with the backing of one or more of these states.[44] By uniting these central nations, Wells claimed that a future organization could be created that would act as the custodian of a world peace. The duties of this League of Peace would include limiting all arms production to help prevent warfare, and hosting an International Tribunal for settling international disputes. Demonstrating his disapproval for national sovereignty, the Tribunal would also have powers to intervene in national governments' tariffs and other legislation affecting international relations and 'commercial warfare' in order to maintain the peace.[45] Further, an International Boundary Commission would seize on the opportunity 'such as the world may never have again of tracing out the "natural map" of mankind'. All this was part of the longer transition to the new world order. It was the responsibility of America to step forward and offer its backing to such international institutions, and Wells claimed that this step would potentially be 'a world settlement made primarily to establish a new phase in the history of mankind'.[46] So though Wells is deeply associated with the call for the League of Nations, it is important to recognize the visionary ideals he invested in these calls. For him, the institution needed to cement the transition to a radically different world. Once the actual League of Nations was created, he was deeply critical of the institution, as we will see below.

Wells also reflected here on the wider repercussions of the conflagration on the British and European psyche, and how new institutions were needed to allow people to grapple with the emergent new age. For the most part, Europeans had failed to grasp the overarching implications of the war. People were often simply overwhelmed by the new spectacle of battle, such as exploding shells or burning zeppelins. Therefore, they were yet to see the event in its historical, epic context. Further, running throughout *War and the Future*, and especially in these final chapters, was a strong critique of organized religion and its moral leadership, alongside the hope for a new model for religion to emerge from the war. Wells's opposition to the institutionalization of faith was out in a chapter titled 'The Religious Revival'. 'Organisation is the life of material and the death of spiritual processes,'[47] he claimed, while stating that real sins were being committed by members of organized religions. Reiterating an earlier wartime assertion, this was because they preached the national cause over the universal ideal of religion: 'the sin of national egotism and the devotion of men to loyalties, ambitions, sects, churches, feuds, aggressions, and divisions', he argued, 'are an outrage upon God's universal kingdom'.[48] Wells also asserted that the new international arrangements, which he believed would emerge from the war, needed to offer people a sense of a greater order, giving them 'a leadership and reference outside themselves'. Visionary politics and a new religion were being combined in this text. This need for a sacred dimension to the coming era, for Wells, was 'why I assert so confidently that there is a real deep religious movement afoot in the world'.[49] He concluded the book by claiming that the future needed to manifest 'the Kingdom of God over a world-wide system of republican states' because this was 'the only possible formula under which we may hope to unify and save mankind'.[50] So from such discussions in *War and the Future*, we get a glimpse of Wells's emergent ideas on faith and a new world theocracy, but for their fullest expression of this vision we have to turn to his next book.

Wells's *God the Invisible King* was central to this wartime discourse of new religions to redeem a decadent, capitalist world. Devoted to an in-depth discussion on the nature of the modernist religion that he imagined would supersede all previous religious structures, here Wells set out how and why he believed a new faith was emerging spontaneously during the war. Many academic analyses tend to be dismissive of this aspect of Wells's oeuvre. For example, in his *Shadow of the Future: H. G. Wells, Science Fiction and Prophecy* Patrick Parinder describes this aspect of Wells's writings as 'wayward' and 'spurious'. After the War, Wells distanced himself from many of its ideas, yet this dismissive approach does miss the point that such ideas furnished

Wells with a clear vision during the war itself. At the height of the conflict, Wells's new religion offered him an important metaphysical framework for interpreting the deeper significance of the crisis of the war.

Interesting, we can note that *God the Invisible King* was itself a development influenced by the ideas of others, as well as one that built on Wells's own, earlier concerns regarding radical faith. He developed the book through conversations with friends of the era, such as Gilbert Murray and Joseph McCabe,[51] meanwhile, its ideas even impacted on pro-war American Christians in 1917.[52] Its transatlantic reach was also demonstrated by the *New York Times* review, which summarized the text thus: '... it shows Mr Wells at his best. . . . He believes, very sincerely apparently, that the book is a compact, comprehensive account of a widely spreading new religion.'[53] In Britain, the implications of the book were also widely discussed. For example, the *Review of Reviews* described its thesis as 'inspiring and beautiful', stressing that 'he tells of the "modern religion", gives us much food for thought, and will be of help to many.'[54] The *Athenaeum*, meanwhile, praised Wells's idealism, characterizing the book as 'poor theology . . . but it is real religion.'[55] The theatre critic William Archer even offered his own response to the text, critiquing the thrust of the ideas, yet supportive of some of Wells's overarching aims.[56] After the war Wells's vision was still resonating with some: the vicar of Christ Church, Plymouth felt it necessary to offer a more fulsome critique,[57] again demonstrating that the book had genuine impact.

Wells's preface made clear that he was not interested in simply reworking Christianity, but rather his vision was one concerned with 'a profound belief in a personal and intimate God'.[58] The radically modernizing imperative running through Wells's theology sought to clear previous religions 'out of the way at this present time of exceptional religious need'. To achieve this clearing away of the old, Wells took special issue with the Christian notion of the Trinity, arguing that this had little to do with the teachings of Jesus *per se*, rather, it was merely an *ex post facto* human construct arising from the later First Council of Nicaea. This body had forwarded a conception of God that suited the needs of creating an organized Church, in so doing had effectively stymied true religious knowledge. In tone, he defined the book as 'missionary', and claimed that he was 'zealous to liberate' and was 'impatient with a reverence that stands between man and God'.[59] The underlying modernist thrust of radical renewal is therefore already clear from such framing discussions.

At its core, Wells's modern theology was founded on a distinction between what he called 'God the Creator' and 'God the Redeemer'. The former was a 'Veiled Being' a figure who created the universe and was unknowable to the mind of mankind. However, the latter, 'the God in our hearts', was the metaphysical entity that Wells's new faith was primarily concerned with. 'God the Redeemer' Wells described as a finite God, a being that 'exists or strives to exist in every human soul'; and 'he has an aim and that means he has a past and a future; he is within time and not outside it'.[60] Wells's conception of 'God the Redeemer' offered a spiritual bridge between eternal spiritual truths, as manifest in his ultimate 'God the Creator', and the finite, temporal realm of everyday human consciousness. This focus freed Wells from having to make speculative statements on the ultimate origins of the universe, concentrating his new creed on what was described as the essentials of a religious temperament.[61]

Echoing the critique of 'effigies' he had been developing in *War and the Future*, in the opening chapter Wells stressed that the 'renascent religion that is now taking shape, it seems, has no founder' and rather than gravitating around a symbolic person he simply stressed '. . . it is the Truth, its believers declare'.[62] Later, Wells claimed that the sense of transcendence, the connection with a 'higher' realm, underpinning this modernist religion had been described most accurately in the work of William James. With James as his guide, for Wells the experience of a conversion to his God ran as follows. After what was called 'an initial state of distress with the aimlessness and cruelties of life, and particularly with the futility of the individual life . . . [an] inability to form any satisfactory plan of living' (or in other words after experiencing a profound sense of modern, 'nomic' calamity) an existential crisis begins to find resolution when 'in some way the idea of God comes into the distressed mind, at first simply as an idea, without substance or belief'. Faith in Wells's God, then, essentially developed from a confrontation with the disturbing, unsettled existence found in the modern world, from a chaotic reading of modernity. For Wells, this embryonic recognition of God through confrontation with a decadent reading modernity was often initially resisted. Indeed, echoing his own ideas before the war on the idea of a racial collective consciousness in *First and Last Things*, the initial stages of conversion to God as an 'invisible king' according to Wells continued in the following manner: to begin with, 'he is spoken of preferably by such phrases as the Purpose in Things, as the Racial Consciousness, as the Collective Mind'. Indeed, Wells claimed that *God the Invisible King* was a continuation of this earlier work. As this new sense of faith was worked over, such naïve concepts that groped towards God, but failed to comprehend his presence accurately, could be overcome. In so doing, Wells's 'God the Redeemer' would soon become a self-evident presence. Revelation of the new faith felt as if 'one was touched at every point by a being akin to oneself, sympathetic, beyond measure wiser, steadfast and pure in aim'. One realized that 'God is with us and there is no more doubt in God'.[63]

Throughout the book, Wells's approach syncretized many religions into his modernist sense of the transcendent; for example, arguing that, like Buddhism, his modern religion was not concerned with offering immortality, but rather was conceived simply as an 'escape from the self-centred life and over-individuation'.[64] In the chapter 'Heresies', we are given some details on what Wells's vision of God was not. Religion was limited. It was essential not to be over speculative, and people must not use the religious temperament to exaggerate God's powers. For example, faith in God did not allow for the belief in magic, a point Wells highlighted by critiquing claims of some within the Anglican clergy that God was able to influence the weather in order to help the British Army defeat Germans. Wells condemned such claims as profoundly un-religious. Another quality that God did not possess was providence, rather his religion promoted the self to action. Though God would always be 'with' his believers, Wells stated that 'God does not guide our feet'. Wells's God actively discouraged quietist attitudes and inaction. The 'finding of God is the beginning of service', the text asserted, 'it is the release of life and action from the prison of the mortal self . . . [the] peace of God comes not by thinking about it but by forgetting oneself in him'.[65] Wells's God was also not a fear-inducing deity, and so the book critiqued Christian theologians who attempted to use the terror of God's anger as a means to convert children. Autobiography enters the picture here: this was an experience from his own youth that, the text stated, had prevented Wells from believing in God for many years. Finally, God was not concerned with enforcing a particular sexual morality, the 'detailed interpretation of that "right" is for the dispassionate consideration of the human intelligence'.[66] Such statements demonstrate the distance between Wells's religion and the established Christian churches in Britain.

To counterpoint this list of what God was not, the chapter 'The Likeness of God' gave detailed insights into God's nature. Primarily, 'God is Courage', Wells emphasized – a statement that he often repeated in his war fiction. Moreover, Wells claimed that 'God is a person who can be known as one knows a friend, who can be served and receive service, who partakes of our nature; who is, like us, a being in conflict with the unknown and the limitless and the forces of death'. The modern God was thus a beneficial presence for His believers, and valued 'much that we value and is against much that we are pitted against. He is our king to whom we must be loyal; he is our captain, and to know him is to have direction in our lives'.[67] The new God was also, essentially, defined by love, and here Wells even used the trenches to evoke the 'higher' type of adoration that characterized God. He distinguished between one's love for the deity and romantic love thus: 'There is a strange and beautiful love that men tell of that will spring up on battlefields between sorely wounded men . . . There is often a pure exaltation of feeling between those who stand side by side manfully in any great stress', and so it followed that 'God must love his followers as a great captain loves his men'.[68] Meanwhile, though God was humanized, He lacked a physical body. Using another wartime analogy to help express this point, for Wells God was as 'real as a bayonet thrust or an embrace'.[69] Moreover, just as a person is made up of cells but is fundamentally something more than an assemblage of parts, so God was something more than the assemblage of human minds past, present and future, yet he existed only through them.

Significantly for a new deity for new times, Wells's radically modernized God was essentially youthful in nature, emerging from the death of old religions and into new life. It is worth citing some text at length here to convey the tone of Wells's idea of rebirth:

> [The] God of this new age, we repeat, looks not to our past but to our future, and if a figure may represent him it must be the figure of a beautiful youth, already brave and wise, but hardly come to his strength. He should stand lightly on his feet in the morning time, eager to go forward, as though he had but newly arisen to a day that was still but a promise; he should bear a sword, that clean, discriminating weapon, his eyes should be as bright as swords; his lips should fall apart with eagerness for the great adventure before him, and he should be in very fresh and golden harness, reflecting the rising sun. Death should still hang like mists and cloud banks and shadows in the valleys of the wide landscape about him.[70]

The association between Wells's new God and the energy of youth is clear from this description. Such evocations of spiritual renewal were central to the vibrancy of the text, as was commented on in numerous reviews. One of the most revealing chapters was called 'The Invisible King', which gave further descriptions of life after finding the new God. Under the heading 'Modern Religion a Political Religion', Wells argued that the Christian idea separating the realms of God and Caesar no longer applied. Rather, the new faith's 'implicit command to all its adherents is to make plain the way to the world theocracy'.[71] Indeed, Wells's political religion was expressly counter-hegemonic, it sought revolt: 'Our God is, we feel, like Prometheus, a rebel'.[72] In order to signify action over the passivity of ordinary politics and religion, the crucifix of the new faith 'would show God with a hand or a foot already torn away from its nail, and with eyes not downcast but resolute against the sky; a face without pain, pain lost and forgotten in the surprising glory of the struggle and the inflexible will to live and prevail'.[73]

With this new attitude, the 'idea of God as the Invisible King of the whole world means not merely that God is to be made and declared the head of the world, but that the kingdom of God is to be present throughout the whole fabric of the world'.[74] Consequently, in Wells's re-sacralized vision for the coming, alternate modernity, people would turn their minds to fulfilling the will of God, and would 'begin to develop the latent citizen of this world-state within himself'. These converts would then 'fall in with the idea of the world-wide sanities of this new order being drawn over the warring outlines of the present, and of men falling out of relationship with the old order and into relationship with the new'.[75] Elsewhere, we even learn that the wealthy would cede their private property to the new order, and businesses would be run by managers acting in the public interest. Further, the law would be re-directed to 'adjust the differing views of men as to the manner of their service to God'.[76] Wells's modern religion did not lack an ambitious vision of change.

In the final chapters, Wells discussed the transition from the present to the future in more detail. The new religion, while currently at an embryonic stage, exhibited 'many signs that the revival is coming very swiftly'.[77] In the 'last few decades', the analysis declared, 'the Western mind has slipped loose from this absolutist conception of God that has dominated Christendom, at least, for many centuries'.[78] Thus offering a sea-change in decadent religious attitudes, wartime was 'not an age of despair but an age of hope'.[79] The future would be revitalized as a 'wave of religious revival and religious clarification' would also 'most certainly bring with it a great revival of art, religious art, music, songs, and writings of all sorts, drama, the making of shrines, praying places, temples and retreats, the creation of pictures and sculptures'.[80] Further, the future would not have an organized structure or priesthood of any kind, although *ad hoc* religious organization would flourish for those who needed such outlets in order to reconnect with a sense of the transcendent. Ultimately for Wells, the emergence of new religion needed to be expressed lyrically: it was 'like a diamond', arising 'bright, definite, and pure out of a dark matrix of structureless confusion'. Or, 'it is a Mountain of Light, growing and increasing. It is an all-pervading lucidity, a brightness and clearness. It has no head to smite, no body you can destroy; it overleaps all barriers; it breaks out in despite of every enclosure. It will compel all things to orient themselves to it . . . It is the Kingdom of God at hand'.[81] Such poetic impressions of the renewal of the world under a new faith clearly chime with the modernist paradigm developed by this study, critiquing extant modernity and presenting an alternate, utopian one in its place. However, Wells's widely read non-fiction was not the only vehicle for promulgating these ideas. His equally popular fiction also developed themes promoting the radical modernization of religion. So how were religious themes developed in these texts?

The new religion and wartime fiction

It has already been highlighted that *The World Set Free* offered a striking example of how Wells's fiction revelled in the theme of war leading to political and spiritual revolution. Another prewar novel, *The Research Magnificent*, eventually published in 1915, again shows Wells working on these themes fictionally. The plot centred around a journey of intellectual discovery, embarked upon by its central character, William Porphyry Benham, who journeyed around the world on a quest to discover a new sense of 'the aristocratic life' and the 'Noble Society'. Eventually, Benham discovered a new ideal of God, and concluded that this figure provided a sense of unity for the new elite, which itself was the 'new knighthood, the new aristocracy'. Other familiar themes were also worked on. Not only would conversion to the new 'Prince' create an 'open conspiracy' that would be opposed to the domination of the world by democratic governments, but also the new faith would be dedicated to the establishment of a new republic that would cover the whole world.[82] Such ideas were interesting to a wider readership. To cite just one reception, the *English Review* praised the book, noting a change in the tone of Wells's wartime voice, which 'now calls for an aristocracy; to lead, to assume responsibility, to enforce efficiency to govern. This is certainly a change to the Wells of our peace-time illusions'.[83]

Another work commenced before the war yet published during it was *Boon*, a book that Wells began working on in 1905 and had revised intermittently. Indeed, Samuel Hynes deemed it to be the first important novel of the war.[84] For the most part, *Boon* discussed how a sense of decadence characterized the contemporary literary imagination. Taking Henry James as its primary target, Wells juxtaposed examples of the people and tendencies that he believed were wrong within the contemporary literary milieu. To achieve this, he developed a fictive, prolific modern author, George Boon. This character developed a speculative thesis on the 'Mind of the Race', yet died before this modernist social philosophy was completed. The novel itself was narrated by another fictional author, Reginald Bliss, who pieced together aspects of the 'Mind of the Race' idea from fragments of Boon's writings and conversations. In the light of *God the Invisible King*, we can see the concept of the 'Mind of the Race' as another, early articulation of Wells's idea of a new collective consciousness, one far more altruistic than the egoistic individual created by modern capitalism, and characterized by a distinct, spiritual experience. Meanwhile, showing Wells's wider significance, readers at the time were reluctant to characterize the work as simply as light fiction. In its commendation of the book, the *Athenaeum* review described how Wells 'wanders around the arena unrestricted by the limits of the novel or the essay', while describing the book's final short story, its only truly fictitious content, as 'a satire so audacious, yet so perfect, as to give the book a permanent repute'.[85]

This 'unfinished' story, 'The Last Trump', reflected once more on a modern version of Judgement Day. Discovering an old trumpet in a brick-a-brack store, some car mechanics blew into it and inadvertently activated the Last Judgement. For an instant the dead lived, and people across the whole world felt somehow profoundly affected and moved, before once again normality resumed. The story then followed one West End preacher, Mr Parchester, who tried to discuss his awareness of this revelation of the apocalypse with people around him, yet they seemed entirely unaffected by the immanence of the Last Judgement. Even when he discussed the matter with his boss, Bishop Wampach, Parchester was dismissed as being ridiculous. As the story concluded: 'If a thing is sufficiently strange and great', Boon's narration lamented, 'no one will perceive it', or in other words, the modern age had lost awareness of truly great things.[86] Reflecting on the pessimistic tone of this story, the Bliss character then continued to extend the underlying message that Boon had tried to articulate in 'The Last Trump' by relating it directly to the significance of the war. He argues that Europe's descent into conflict had temporarily destroyed Boon's faith in the 'Mind of the Race', and that, if Boon had lived, he would have returned to a more optimistic outlook and realized that 'this multitudinous individual unhappiness is still compatible with a great progressive movement in the general mind'. Further, the 'tremendous present disaster of Europe may not be, after all, a disaster of mankind . . . We must see these things from the standpoint of the Race Life, whose days are hundreds of years'.[87] As is quite clear, Wells's wartime religious convictions were emerging in these well-received books, allowing him to interpret the war as creative destruction.

While *The Research Magnificent* and *Boon* were significant developments in Wells's religiosity, his next work quickly became a central text in the war's literature, again in no small part due to its religious message. 'For the first time we have a novel which touches the life of the last two years without impertinence',[88] heralded the *Times Literary Supplement* when reviewing the first of Wells's fictions that grappled with the war as its central theme: *Mr Britling Sees it Through*. This was one of Wells's most successful novels, selling 13 print runs by the end of 1916 alone. His old friend Maxim Gorky even claimed it to be 'the best, boldest, veracious and human book written in Europe in this accursed war!'[89] The plot revolved around a conversion story: Mr Britling discovered God through his exposure to the war. This narrative even became a popular reference point in sermons across the country, at least until Wells clarified the distinctly non-Christian nature of his religious views in *God the Invisible King* a year later. The central Mr Britling character was clearly autobiographical, and the book followed the story of the family and acquaintances of a successful author and commentator both before and during the war. The book featured Britling's ranging discussions on world politics and religion, which repeatedly echoed Wells's own ideals of radical renewal in the wake of a creatively destructive war. Also living with the Britling family before the war was a German tutor, Heinrich, whose subsequent death at the front line became a central aspect of the novel's conclusion. Following August 1914, the novel's main concern was a documentation of Wells's own changing ideas of the meaning of the war through the fictional Britling. Initially, he was greatly excited by the potential change in values that would, he believes, inevitably occur as a result of the war, and wrote an essay titled 'And Now War Ends', reprising Wells's own war to end war ideal.

Moreover, the world became liminal for Britling: 'Now everything becomes fluid', he explained to his family at one point, continuing: 'Now suddenly we face an epoch. This is an epoch. The world is plastic for men to do what they will with it. This is the end and the beginning of an age. This is something far greater than the French Revolution or the Reformation . . . And we live in it.'[90] After comprehending that the war represented an epochal shift, Britling came to see the necessity for the development of a world congress following the fighting, alongside the need for a new League of Nations. Furthermore, he discovered within himself a hatred for Germans that confused him, especially after reading about atrocities committed and reports of the death of civilians in zeppelin raids. After all, before the war he had known 'decent' Germans, so why not now? Increasingly, Britling could not regard the war as the heroic crusade that he felt had characterized its first months. Politicians continued to prove themselves ineffective at creating a grand vision for change and renewal, while the level of cruelty that the world could descend into became profoundly disturbing to sensibilities constructed in the far calmer, prewar era. Thus war became a 'monstrous absurdity',[91] a struggle without a point.[92] To add to the horror, shortly after these depressing realizations, Britling learned of his son's death at the front line.

Having experienced these depressing blows, Britling realized that no-one was safe until all potential causes of wars had been eliminated, and so began planning in earnest what he called 'a real map of the world', a new future.[93] In what are now very familiar themes, he began writing a new essay on the war, 'The Better Government of the World', after experiencing a new religious consciousness, a new sense of God. The book's conclusion then depicted Britling writing a letter to Heinrich's parents after receiving news of his death. Some belongings had to be returned to Heinrich's family, and Britling felt that he should write an accompanying note, which he penned alongside his latest war essay. While composing this letter, Britling suddenly experienced a new and more profound connection with God, described as 'a Presence so close to him that it was behind his eyes and in his brain and hands . . . It was the Master, the Captain of Mankind, it was God, there present with him, and he knew that it was God'.[94] After several failed drafts, Britling decided that his note to Heinrich's parents should convey his new sense of religiosity, thereby offering a vision of hope emerging from the divisions and horrors of war:

> Religion is the first thing and the last thing, and until a man has found God and been found by God, he begins at no beginning, he works to no end . . . And before the coming of the true King, the inevitable King, the King who is present whenever just men forgather, this blood-stained rubbish of the ancient world, these puny kings and tawdry emperors, these wily politicians and artful lawyers, these men who claim and grab and trick and compel, these war-makers and oppressors, will presently shrivel and pass – like paper thrust into a flame.

After a short pause he then said to himself 'Our sons who have shown us God'.[95] These final sentences, and therefore the lasting message that Wells enshrined in this highly popular book, clearly offered a palingenetic reading of war. They sketched out the rediscovery of a sense of religion that allowed for Britling to move away from a modernity that had become self-destructive. War revealed the decadence of the present order, and pointed the way towards a new, better world to come. Reflecting its international appeal, even American reviewers picked up on the powerful novelty of a wartime religion developed by this closing letter. The *North American Review* concluded that Wells 'is able to conceive of a God who is not responsible for all the ills of humanity, of a God who is close and real . . . It seems to embody the meaning that the war has for the personal life'.[96]

However, the theme of traditional religious sensibilities being reconfigured to fit a modernized sense of religiosity was most clearly articulated in his 1917 novel, *The Soul of a Bishop*. Having already picked up on Wells's emergent religious perspective, *North American Review* offered clear commentary on the links between Wells's major works at this time: 'In *God the Invisible King* he made a rhapsodic tract out of the essential philosophy of *Mr. Britling Sees It Through*. Now he has dramatized the tract, and, in *The Soul of a Bishop*, offers us *God the Invisible King* in the shape of a fable addressed to the capacities of those who may have found the earlier exposition too unremittingly theological for comfortable digestion.'[97] As such, the narrative here can be seen as an attempt to begin to popularize his new religion, with a plot that is set both before and during the war, following the spiritual travails of the fictional Bishop of Princhester. The bishop begins the novel expressing doubts about his belief in God, and especially in the notion of the Trinity. Meanwhile, the contemporary world was changing all around him. Not only had the death of Queen Victoria closed 'an epoch of tremendous stabilities',[98] but the subsequent prewar years were marked by an 'upheaval', altogether different from Victorian radicalism, that was predicated upon 'impatience and unreason'.[99] In addition to the social and spiritual problems of Edwardian modernity, the bishop's daughter, Eleanor, saw her father as an inherently dated figure, his morality unsuitable for this new era of change and novelty. The realization that she may have a point only accentuated the bishop's uneasy attitude, and so through this predicament prewar Britain was presented as in dire need of fundamental change. By the spring of 1914, the whole mood of the country 'was like the uneasiness sensitive people experience before a thunderstorm. The moral atmosphere was sullen and close'.[100] With the outbreak of a creatively destructive war, people suddenly 'realized the epic quality of history and their own relationship to the destinies of the race'.[101] Old elites were also strongly criticized. The failure of the church to offer any sort of moral leadership further disturbed the bishop, and he developed signs of nervous tensions, such as smoking cigarettes, to ease his anxiety. Eventually, he confessed his various spiritual concerns to a figure epitomizing the bohemian socialite, Lady Sunderbund, portrayed as a somewhat ridiculous figure by Wells.

To try to solve his depression, the bishop visited his doctor, and was prescribed a mysterious drug by an enigmatic locum. This shadowy figure claimed he could lift the bishop out of his current reality, defined by the doctor merely as a set of 'working illusions', and into a new one. By taking this drug, the bishop was elevated into a higher sense of consciousness, the Kingdom of Heaven, three times. The first of these encounters revealed to him the Angel of God. Faced with this possibility, the bishop asked the Angel to tell him the truth about God, yet the angel explained to him that the human mind could not comprehend this ultimate truth. However, echoing *God the Invisible King*, the angel did claim that God 'is courage, he is adventure, he is the King, he fights for you and against death'.[102] Following this vision, the bishop realized that his teachings of God to date were wayward, and he returned to earthly consciousness. After confessing this revelation to Lady Sunderbund, she immediately supported his newfound religiosity – the only character that did. After taking the drug a second time, he asked the angel how he could serve God during the war. From this discussion, the bishop realized that true religion is yet to come, and so again we see redemption lying in the future. God was not yet fully manifest in human reality, so 'Mankind is like a smouldering fire that will presently, in quite a little time, burst out into flames.'[103] Moreover, the war was not the will of God but rather the epitome of the blindness of mankind to God. Nowhere, the bishop realized, were religious leaders preaching the new gospel of mankind, of the world unified and pacific under one God. Rather, Christian leaders were all ultimately talking in nationalistic tones. If God was to rule on earth, then the teachings of the various established churches needed to be transcended.

Following the second vision of the Angel of God, the bishop delivered his revelations in a sermon. Here, he again developed a radically *futural* message and told his congregation of the 'unexampled dawn' to come, claiming that: 'It is your privilege' and 'your grave and terrible position, that you have been born at the very end and collapse of a negligent age, of an age of sham kingship, sham freedom, relaxation, evasion, greed, waste, falsehood, and sinister preparation. Your lives open out in the midst of the breakdown for which that age prepared.'[104] The creative destructive possibilities of wartime were thus made patently clear. As he gave this sermon, the bishop was energized by a sensation that God was close to him because he sensed a 'divine figure militant, armed, and serene'[105] standing with him during his delivery. Following what was seen as a shocking sermon, the bishop lost his post in the church, and moved to London. Eventually his family, especially Eleanor, supported him in a new, much poorer life. He also turned down an offer from the wealthy Lady Sunderbund to establish a gaudy new church in the capital. The bishop had a final vision, this time without the aid of the drug, where he envisaged the coming of a world state, and, having seen God without the aid of the drug, became fully convinced of his new path. 'There is no doubt', concluded the *Review of Reviews* 'that Mr Wells has voiced . . . thoughts and doubts which are surging in the brains of many to-day.'[106] The *Times Literary Supplement* broadly concurred: 'the book is interesting; and in nothing perhaps more interesting than in its showing of the difference that has been made by the war and its implied forecast of the social and religious life that is to follow the war.'[107] When promoting his sense of religious rebirth through fiction, Wells was clearly finding a receptive audience.

Following this success, the lengthiest of Wells's novels during the war was *Joan and Peter*, conceived as a partner novel to *Mr Britling*. It told the story of the education of two orphans, Joan and Peter, unrelated but brought up as brother and sister. By developing narratives describing their travails at school, Wells used these central characters to develop a further critique of contemporary society, here focusing on the nation's educational institutions. Again, a sense of how people related their lives to time and history was important to Wells. His sensitivity to an inability to put the war into a historic frame of reference among many who were living through it was blamed on a lack of historical understanding in the educational system of the day: 'Between the latest history they [Joan and Peter] had read and the things that happened about them . . . was a gap of a hundred years or more.'[108] Essentially, history was represented as impotent if not connected to the contemporary world, an idea Wells took up again after the war. Joan and Peter's ward, Oswald Sydenham, believed primarily that the current conflict was a product of a deficient culture. In particular, the 'war was an educational breakdown', and in Peter's adolescent years Sydenham even found Peter's consciousness of the past based on reading radical socialist literature less despair inducing than the history on offer in nation's schools. A lifelong supporter of the empire, Sydenham himself believed socialism to be ideologically wrong, but appreciated that the ideology provided a much-needed schema for understanding connections between historical, social and economic realms. In schools, on the other hand, a stifling conservatism prevailed: pupils learned to obey the rules of the game, the best became prize-boys, then scholars, then fellows, then dons, and finally pedagogues, and so the decadent cycle continued.[109] This critique of education also caused an impact among reviewers, with the *Saturday Review of Politics, Literature, Science and Art* dubbing its criticism a 'Hymn of Hate',[110] while the *Athenaeum* praised the novel for highlighting a fundamental problem in wartime Britain, 'that our educators are not educated'.[111] With his more liberated historical awareness, the precocious Peter soon developed an interest in the creative destructive qualities of socialism, and his early adulthood advocated a style of state collectivism reminiscent of Wells's own embrace of the radical left.

Regarding the theme of destruction leading to renewal, when discussing social and political affairs with Oswald, Peter was clear that 'one *must* break up old things before one can hope for new' and that 'we could recover from a very considerable amount of smashing. I'm pro-smash. We have to smash'.[112] The younger generation, then, were represented as intuitively aware of the need for modernist style palingenetic change even ahead of the war. After its outbreak, Wells's narration again framed war as an event holding the potential for regeneration. England was portrayed initially as a nation 'awakening', described thus: 'The whole Empire was lifted; a flush of unwonted splendour suffused British affairs'. However, this 'clear flame of enthusiasm' was soon subverted by 'disillusionment as that general bickering that was British public life revived again'. This shift could be detected in the poetry of the war as 'glowing young heroes', such as Rupert Brooke, 'shine with a faith undiminished'. He and his ilk 'sing and die in what they believe to be a splendid cause and for a splendid end'. After three years, Siegfried Sassoon had shifted the tone and developed a 'cry of anger at the old men who have led the world to destruction . . . dull, ignorant men . . . men who have lost the freshness and simplicity but none of the greed and egoism of youth'. Now youth asked their elders '*What is this to which you have brought us? What have you done with our lives?*'[113]

With this narrative of the war's significance as a backcloth, the creatively destructive Peter enlisted first as a private, in order to experience the discipline of war, before becoming a pilot. Empowered by the latest technology, he experienced the romanticism of the air, then the horrors of a dogfight in which he was badly injured. He also underwent *futural* epiphanies while flying, and felt that 'he droned his liquid way towards a new sort of life altogether, towards a greater civilisation, a worldwide life for men with no boundaries in it at all except the emptiness of outer space, a life of freedom and exultation and tremendous achievement'.[114] After he was shot down, he also experienced a vision of God, a figure somewhat distinct from the youthful image given in *God the Invisible King*. Located in a messy office, the Lord God now 'had the likeness of a lean, tired, intelligent looking oldish man, with an air of futile friendliness masking a futile indifference'. When Peter enquired as to why the war continued and why He did not stop it, God replied that it was for the likes of Peter to change things, not him, stating that 'If you have no will to change it, you have no right to criticise it', and arguing 'You asked me why I didn't exert myself. Well – why don't *you* exert yourself?'[115] Wells's God of action was still an authoritative figure in the book. Similarly, the novel's concluding messages also ran along now familiar lines, invoking the need for elemental change to characterize the coming peace. Oswald, was converted to the need for a League of Free Nations,[116] and told Joan and Peter to create the world anew: 'you have to reach back and touch the England of Shakespeare, Milton, Raleigh, and Blake – and that means you have to go forward . . . you have to create. Now. You, with your fresh vision, with the lessons you have learned still bright in your minds, you have to remake the world'.[117] So, world conflict as the scenario for creative destruction concluded the book's representation of the war.

Wells's modernized religion and education was also the central to a final work written during the war, again a critically well-received novel, *The Undying Fire*. For example, the *English Review* stressed 'There is a vast amount of intellectual brilliancy in this work' and concluded by stressing 'we see the artist as the spiritual force in the modern world. This is at once homily and scientific essay: big stuff bubbling over with creative thought and fancy, worth all the sermons of the Church put together for the past three years'.[118] Set during the final year of the war, showing Wells's syncretic approach to developing his religious messages the novel was essentially a modernized version of the Book of Job. With a critique of education as a central theme, the novel was dedicated: 'To all the schoolmasters and schoolmistresses and every teacher in the word'. The biblical Job is replaced by Job Huss, a headmaster at a 'great modern public school at Woldingstanton',[119] where he employed 'new methods in the teaching of history and politics' alongside modern languages and a rigorous, scientific curriculum. The downfall of Huss's world began when he believed that he had lost his only son in the war, and then developed a tumour requiring a serious operation. Meanwhile, two of the school governors, Sir Eliphaz Burrows and Mr William Dad, alongside the school's utilitarian and ambitious head of chemistry, Mr Farr, decided that, given Huss's poor health alongside a recent fire at the school that they attributed to Huss, he should be removed from his position. Facing replacement with the more business-minded Mr Farr, and echoing the Book of Job, the three men then went to Huss's bedside before the operation. The four figures were soon embroiled in a theological discussion on the nature of God, and how religion affected the educational direction of the school. Here, Huss railed against the notion of education serving primarily commercial ends. He also adumbrated his idea of mankind holding within itself an 'undying fire', essentially a reiteration under a different name of Wells's previous ideas of a collective connection with a deity that was both deeply personal as well as an expression of community with the entire human race, past, present and future. The three visitors were horrified by these statements and called for him to repent what were, to them, heretical views.

Undeterred, Huss continued to argue that, although God showed no sign of his existence, he was a clear presence to all those who have been able to transcend egoistical forms of consciousness.[120] Further, God was a figure who inspired rebellion for Huss, bringing future salvation from the war and his own crises: 'I am the servant of a rebellious and adventurous God', who for Huss is a deity 'who may yet bring order into this cruel and frightful chaos in which we seem to be driven hither and thither like leaves before the wind, a God who, in spite of all appearances, may yet rule over it and at last mould it to his will'.[121] Huss then reiterated Wells's now standard *futural* vision, claiming that the new God needed to form the foundation of any League of Nations.[122] Again, salvation essentially lay in enough people transcending ego-led individualism, epitomized by the technical and commercial mind, and discovering their common 'undying fire' within their inner souls. Only this formula would prevent modern man from descending into cul-de-sacs of individualism. Thus, God is 'crying out in our hearts to save us from these blind allies of selfishness, darkness, cruelty, and pain in which our race must die', and Huss argued that 'he is crying for the high road which is salvation, he is commanding the organised unity of mankind'.[123]

As in *God the Invisible King*, above all God is styled here as courage. This Huss discovered while undergoing his operation, when he experienced an intuitive connection with God and Satan. Under anaesthesia, Huss learned that life was ultimately predicated upon uncertainty regarding the future; so as in his earlier utopias, here the future represented a realm of continual struggle. God justified this point thus: 'Why should you struggle if the end is assured? How can you rise if there is no depth into which you can fall?'[124] And He appealed to Huss to develop the will to struggle and change the injustices and horrors of the world. Following his operation and this revelation, Huss's life was entirely regenerated. The surgeon discovered that Huss's tumour was not cancerous, and his recovery was the most successful he ever witnessed. Meanwhile, the remaining governors of Woldingstanton decided to stand by Huss, and he soon started to plan how the new school will be reformed to meet the needs of the postwar reconstruction. Emphasizing the veracity of the educational ideals that he had expounded in his theological debates, an ex-pupil also wrote a letter expressing how Huss's brand of education had evoked in him the necessary creative spirit needed to make '*a real world state, a world civilisation and a new order of things*' after the war.[125] Completing his path to redemption, Huss's son sent a telegram explaining that he had been captured, held as an enemy prisoner of war and would be returning home in due course.

So from these diverse wartime novels, we can see that the argument that Wells articulated in his political writings – asserting the need for faith in a new conception of God, a figure unifying the transition to a new world state – was also a well developed theme in his fictional writings too. These texts demonstrate a sustained attempt to develop a radical, confrontational message in wartime Britain, calling for cultural rebirth and a new sacral era to follow the creative destruction of war. These were concerns that Wells continued to develop in the immediate postwar period, and are worth examining briefly too.

War, history and the future

To get a sense of continuity and change in Wells's political messages, we can turn to his final non-fiction book on the war, *In the Fourth Year: Anticipations of a World Peace*. Here, he wrote in a far more pragmatic register than in 1914, and focused on the need for what he was now calling a 'League of Free Nations' to emerge from the war. His first chapter reasserted his claim that a peaceful future lay with the four major powers capable of maintaining industrial warfare: Britain, France, Germany and the USA. He also argued for the need to create a League of Allied Nations before the war ended. The establishment of the league would also eventually see the end of the empire in its current form, and its creation would initiate the transfer of sovereignty from individual nation-states to the new league. Wells grounded the need for this vision in a new critique of the ways in which modern technology was subverting the concept of the nation-state. For example, when air transport became commercially viable, he questioned how one would manage the logistics of a nation-state's air space. Further, aerial bombing campaigns would become far more advanced than the current systems in a future war, as would submarine warfare, thereby extending battle zones far beyond the front line. As a result, 'Existing states have become impossible as absolutely independent sovereigns' and the 'new conditions bring them so close together and give them such extravagant powers of mutual injury that they must either sink national pride and dynastic ambitions in subordination to the common welfare of mankind or else utterly shatter one another'. Consequently, it 'becomes more and more plainly a choice between the League of Free Nations and a famished race of men looting in search of non-existent food in the smouldering ruins of civilisation'.[126] Wells's *futural* speculation again pointed him in the direction of a world state redeeming a decadent society.

Regarding the role intellectuals and his new religion, the most revealing discussion came in the final chapter, 'The Study and Propaganda of Democracy'. The duty of 'every school teacher, every tutor, every religious teacher, every writer, every lecturer, every parent, every trusted friend throughout the world' was to create the 'greatest of all propagandas' and 'become a teacher and missionary' for a new world. Wells also claimed that at 'the word "God" passions bristle. The word "God" does not unite men, it angers them. But I doubt if God cares greatly whether we call Him God or no. His service is the service of man'.[127] So despite his new faith set out in *God the Invisible King*, Wells had come to realize by 1918 that the term 'God' was not such a useful tool for propaganda. His nebulous conception of the modern deity did not necessarily require His name to be articulated though. The new God's underlying values were impregnated into Wells's vision of a new League of Free Nations, so he felt happy enough for the institution to be established first, then refine the religious sentiments it would enshrine later. Nevertheless, he concluded by asserting his continued need for his modern religion thus:

> never have I been so sure that there is a divinity in man and that a great order of human life, a reign of justice and world-wide happiness, of plenty, power, hope, and gigantic creative effort, lies close at hand. Even now we have the science and the ability available for a universal welfare, though it is scattered about the world like a handful of money dropped by a child; even now there exists all the knowledge that is needed to make mankind universally free and human life sweet and noble. We need but the faith for it, and it is at hand.[128]

In the aftermath of the war, Wells remained profoundly moved by the modern crisis the war had created. He became actively engaged in the League of Free Nations Association, alongside Leonard Woolf, J. A. Spender, J. L. Garvin, Wickham Steed and Gilbert Murray. In the wake of the war, he published *Russia in the Shadows* – a book comprising reportage writings of his travels through Soviet Russia in the autumn of

1920. Here, he was far from complementary as regards the state of the country. Typical of the damning critique, his chapter on the state of Petersburg pulled no punches when describing the chaos into which Soviet Russia was descending: 'Our dominant impression of things Russian is an impression of a vast irreparable breakdown . . . Never in all history has there been so great a *débâcle* before'.[129] More worryingly, he argued, the chaos in the region carried with it implications for all of Europe: 'The dominant fact for the Western reader, the threatening and disconcerting fact, is that a social and economic system very like our own and intimately connected with our own has collapsed'.[130] His final chapter argued for the need for Western powers to support Russia, not because Bolshevism was the ideal solution for the on-going crisis of capitalist modernity, but because it was the only solution for Russia, other than total chaos. Further, if Bolshevism failed and the country descended into such chaos, this societal decadence would only spread further into Europe. Should such an eventuality occur, he warned, 'all modern civilisation will tumble' into a similar fate.[131] By the 1930s, Wells would later take a more positive assessment of the Soviet Union, though he never came to regard the state as the ideal future form for society. In *Russia in the Shadows*, his underlying concern was to stress the continued need for sensitivity to Western civilization teetering on the verge of total collapse after the war.

This concern was again articulated in another non-fiction work from 1921, *The Salvaging of Civilisation*, which offered a more general critique of the postwar world. Of the importance of the book, the *English Review* stated that it should be read in every school, concluding with the point: 'The world's problem today is: Shall we build a new world, or shall we just wait and see? This will be the new religion, and Mr Wells has stated it with a fine gesture of enthusiasm'.[132] There was still an audience in Britain for Wells's vision of radical renewal. According to Wells's new analysis, the 'new phase of disorder, conflict, and social unravelling upon which we have entered' would last until a new, overarching ideal governed the world. Even if 'for a time the decadence seems to be arrested', what was only an illusion of peace would not last because, without elemental change, 'a fresh war-storm sufficiently destructive and disorganising' would 'restore the decadent process'.[133] Wells also proposed the need for a new form of patriotism to be developed in the chapter 'The Enlargement of Patriotism to a World State', claiming that the 'world perished for want of a common political idea'.[134] Extending this idea, the heart of the book comprised of two chapters on the topic of the 'Bible of Civilisation', a modernized form of the holy book. 'I think that during the last century', Wells opined, 'the Bible has lost much of its former hold. It no longer grips the community'.[135] Highlighting his concerns over the break-up of the social fabric under modernity, he railed: '*our modern communities are no longer cemented*, they lack organized solidarity, they are not prepared to stand shocks and strains, they have become dangerously loose mentally and morally . . . We need to get back to a cement. We want a Bible'.[136] This new version of a unifying holy book would tell the story of the development of the earth, the growth of life from the oceans to the emergence of animals and finally tell the story of the evolution of the human race to the present day. Further, 'it will still point our lives to a common future which will be the reward and judgement of our present lives'.[137] As in *Joan and Peter*, modern society had 'lost touch with history', for Wells, therefore it had 'ceased to see human affairs as one great epic unfolding.'[138] By renovating the idea of a unifying holy book, 'We shall be living again in a plan', he claimed, 'Our lives will be shaped by certain definite ends. We shall fall into place in a greater scheme of activities. We shall recover again some or all of the steadfastness and dignity of the old religious life.'[139]

His interest in modernizing religiosity to glue together a new age thus continued into the interwar period. We can finish the analysis by highlighting the fact that Wells had by this point even developed his own prototype of this new text, his new history of the world. This is a text that in its aims and aspirations can be understood as conforming to the embracing understanding of Wells's 'populist modernist' ideals: it radically confronted aspect of the present, and sought to carve out the cultural space for new ideas, and a new era, to emerge in the future.

Turning finally to this epic work, Wells gave a summary of its central thesis regarding the future of the world in an interview for the *Observer*. Paraphrasing, the paper noted 'What the world will be in a million years Mr Wells declined to speculate. But, taking the next hundred years, he declared that there must be either one wide and peaceful federal government dominating the world or decadence.'[140] In giving a 'new plan' to humanity, the first of its two volumes began with a history of the planet's position in space, and then discussed the evolution of life on earth before finally turning to the history of human existence, rooting the emergence of human experience in secularized time. Regarding the character of mankind revealed by this history, we can see a number of partisan points underpinning Wells's political views, now set in a comprehensive historical narrative of the world. For example, he clearly stated that early man was bereft of warfare, and that war 'has not been in the world for more than 20,000 years'.[141] In other words, war was not an essential characteristic of human existence. Echoing his religious writings, he also claimed that people needed a point of reference outside themselves to guide them through life, lifting them out of an egotistical individualism. Indeed, he asserted that his history was 'strictly in accordance with the teachings of Buddha', and that there is 'no social order, no security, no peace or happiness, no righteous kingship or leadership, unless men loose themselves in something greater than themselves'.[142]

The *Times Literary Supplement* was keen to highlight that Wells's history was politically motivated. Its review stressed how the book argued that 'Individualism has been the mother of all misery. Nationalism – nations counting as individuals – has come to take the room of absolutism, with increased ravage. Nationalism, like the tribal gods, should be relegated to limbo.' In its place, Wells typically argued for the unification of humankind, so 'history for him is the record of whatsoever has furthered or hampered progress to this aim'. Because of this political thrust, the *Times Literary Supplement* concluded that Wells 'enthusiastically welcomes teleology into the sphere of history'.[143] So this was not read as a neutral text by serious commentators at the time, but rather was recognized as one that allowed Wells to ground some of his speculation regarding the need for religion and the future of mankind. Moreover, the sense of how historical change occurred was central to the text. For example, in his analysis of modern history, Wells argued that French Revolution had marked a watershed moment in historical time, and that this was merely the 'opening outbreak of a great cycle of political and social storms that still continue' and this storm would last until 'every vestige of nationalist monarchy has been swept out of the world and the skies clear again for the great peace of the federation of mankind'.[144] Indeed, for Wells history moved in fits and starts: 'periods of revolution are periods of action', he stressed, 'in them men reap the harvests of ideas that have grown during the phases of interlude, and they leave the fields clear for a new season of growth'.[145]

As for the very recent history of the First World War, Wells argued that it had emerged from modern imperialism, and, pointing the finger of blame, argued that the most 'megalomaniac' instance of this trend could be found in Germany. Typically, the only possible alternative to Imperialist ideology on the world stage was for new, international and democratic institutions to emerge, replacing the divisive style of diplomacy epitomized by embassies and foreign offices.[146] Discussing postwar Europe, he underscored his sensitivity to the decadence of the era, arguing that Europe had become like 'a man who has had some vital surgical operation very roughly performed, and who is not yet sure whether he can now go on living or whether he has been so profoundly shocked and injured that he will presently fall down and die'.[147] As for the League of Nations, this was 'not a league of people at all; it was a league of "states, dominions, or colonies"... a league of "representatives" of foreign offices' that had failed even to 'abolish the nonsense of embassies at every capital'.[148] So at the core of this critique of the present was the assertion that his vision of a world government that he had developed throughout the war as an essential outcome was still a far off reality. As with Lewis, Orage and many others, the postwar situation was one requiring a new spark of inspiration.

Counterpointing this profound despair at the present, the final chapter, 'The Possible Unification of the World into One Community of Knowledge and Will', offered a *futural* sketch of an alternate modernity. Synthesizing political and scientific speculation, mythic notions of death and rebirth, a paean to the creativity of youth, an appeal to rediscover the epic, Wells concluded his book in typically prophetic tenor, stating that:

> Men will unify only to intensify the search for knowledge and power, and live as ever for new occasions . . . Life begins perpetually. Gathered together at last under the leadership of man, the student-teacher of the universe, unified, disciplined, armed with the secret powers of the atom and with knowledge as yet beyond dreaming, Life, forever dying to be born afresh, forever young and eager, will presently stand upon this earth as upon a footstool, and stretch out its realm amid the stars.[149]

How convincing this meta-narrative linking past, present and future was to his readers by this time is a mute point. Undoubtedly, he still had many followers. However, though the *Athenaeum*'s review of Wells's history was positive overall, it began with a critique of this vision for the future. This was because it found nothing convincing in Wells's faith in God, central to the vision of regeneration sketched out in the volume, which it dismissed as merely 'an italicising of his own emotions; he despises mysticism; he regards Buddha and Christ as mere social revolutionaries, and the Neo-Platonists as nothing; his Invisible King is consequently a Broken Spectre who can never have a place of his own'.[150] Such comments show how Wells's attempts to map redemption onto historical time was a central theme of how the book was interpreted by its critics. Others reviewers, meanwhile, were far more positive. For example, the *English Review* praised the abridged version of the text, *A Short History of the World*, thus: 'This is Wells at his best . . . out of it we shall get a new meaning of history, a new attitude, and a totally new method of estimating the past, present and future.'[151] Indeed, for better or worse, it was this radical thrust to his postwar history writings that interested his audience.

As stated in the opening section of this chapter, later in the interwar period Wells continued to critique the liberal-democratic structures that he believed to be outmoded. Indeed, as Phillip Coupland has highlighted, during this period Wells critically assessed both communism and fascism as potential contenders for the new ideology of the coming era.[152] However, he ultimately distrusted Stalinism, and although interested in aspects of fascism, especially in Italy, rejected its potent ultra-nationalism, and snubbed early BUF attempts to win him over. This was despite being initially courted by Mosley as he tried to establish fascism as a mass movement in Britain. Though Wells was sympathetic to the general concerns of such political modernisms, ultimately his technocratic ideals for utopia were not compatible with either of these politics. As with Lewis, at bottom it was the search for the radically new politics that allowed for transition to an alternate modernity that framed such interests.

Conclusions

By re-examining Wells's war writings a number of points can be made. First, we see radical modernization combined with religious renewal as a central component of Wells's wartime thinking. This included novel innovations, such as the division between a finite 'God the Redeemer' and an infinite 'God the Creator', as well as linking a modernized theology to political concerns. Indeed, this new faith formed the ontological base upon which his political modernism could be developed. As in his prewar fiction, this re-sacralized new era presented the citizens of a futuristic world state as figures spiritually reborn and socially unified, bringing peace and prosperity to the twentieth century. Second, Wells clearly regarded the war as a fundamental rupture in the flow of historical time, a war to end war and for the world to begin anew. This articulation of the wartime modernist hope that interpreted the conflict as the end of one era and the beginning of a new one was central to all his wartime writings. Finally, we can see that, even before the war, many of the themes – such as developing a modernized faith, a synergy between the utopianism of his fictional and non-fictional writings, a rejection of piecemeal change, the sense of crisis in temporal categories, calling for a revolutionary elite, the idea of a world state and so forth – were already well developed. So the war provided Wells with an event filled with the necessary destructive and creative qualities that allowed him to weave these strands of thought into a coherent, and often convincing, tapestry that promoted secularized redemption for humanity. In sum, Wells's 'populist modernism' at this time regarded modernity in general and the war in particular as a period when humanity was experiencing elemental confusion. Radically confronting this alleged decadence of modernity, his cultural production articulated a countervailing vision of renewal.

Conclusion

'The morning freshness of the world-to-be intoxicated us', declared T. E. Lawrence when reflecting on his war experiences. 'We lived many lives in those whirling campaigns, never sparing ourselves: yet when we achieved and the new world dawned, the old men came out again and took our victory to re-make in the likeness of the former world they knew. Youth could win, but had not learned to keep: and was pitiably weak against age. We stammered that we had worked for a new heaven and a new earth, and they thanked us and made their peace.'[1] Such a statement, typical of the tenor of *Seven Pillars of Wisdom*, evoked two key themes that we have extensively explored in the case studies above: the desire to escape from an old world, and the failure of the palingenetic hope to satisfactorily generate a new reality. Many intellectual figures experienced the First World War through this lens.

Writing in a radically different manner to Lawrence, Bertrand Russell, for example, also believed war represented a profound sense of rupture in European history, and that it pointed urgently to the need for a new social and political reality to be built upon the remains of a decaying civilization. When we turn to the final chapter of his wartime examination of the coming period, *Principles of Social Reconstruction*, we see that Russell set out his own vision for the future. Echoing many of the themes we have thus far encountered, he again stressed the need for a new era, one where life would be characterized by co-operation, not competition, and by a new sense of community, both within and between nations. The fundamental change would be characterized by a shift to an entirely new social philosophy, one capable of restoring a vital quality to the lives of Europeans. As Russell put it, the 'world has need of a philosophy or a religion, which will promote life', while also stressing that if 'life is to be fully human it must serve some end which seems, in some sense, outside human life, some end which is impersonal and above mankind, such as god or truth or beauty'. Nothing less than a new sense of the eternal was needed to guide mankind out of its present crisis, and so it was acutely necessary for Europeans:

> to create a new hope, to build up by our thought a better world than the one which is hurling itself into ruin. Because the times are bad, more is required of us than would be required in normal times. Only a supreme fire of thought and spirit can save future generations from the death that has befallen the generation which we knew and loved.[2]

And again, operating in a radically different tenor to Russell, a further example of this broad trend of war as fundamental transition was the Irish Nationalist Patrick Pearse.

He claimed in 1915 that the 'last sixteen months have been the most glorious in the history of Europe . . . The old heart of the earth needed to be warmed by the red wine of the battlefields. Such august homage was never being offered to God as this, the homage of millions of lives gladly offered for love of country'. Moreover, such sacrifice was important for his own revolutionary consciousness. Indeed, Pearse conceived his blood sacrifice following the Easter Rising as a part of a wider cultural war against the British, and was aware that the Easter Rising itself was doomed to failure. Nevertheless, he believed his martyrdom would inspire others by setting out a new heroic ideal that would keep alive Irish nationalism.[3] Indeed, we can tour around many areas of wartime culture in Britain, and find further examples of this nexus between war, sacrifice and renewal. Rupert Brooke's war poetry and elevation to national hero status after his death epitomizes the crystallization of war through the lens of sacrifice and regeneration.

So identifying this broad trend takes us back to model of modernism sketched out in the opening chapter, which drew, in particular, on Modris Eksteins's work that grounds an understanding of modernism via the conceptual metaphor of *rites de passage*. Wartime cultures of modernism thus conceived can be understood as myriad, highly radical confrontations with modernity that seek to redeem protagonists from a decadent world and give form to the idea of a regenerated one. Moreover, we also noted that Eric J. Leed has founded an analysis of these wartime cultures as unsuccessful *rites de passage*, as they failed to usher in a new, regenerated reality. To conclude the examination of this trend, what follows will briefly build on these concerns by speculatively developing two related conceptual approaches: Victor Turner's model of *communitas* and Anthony Wallace's model of mazeway re-synthesis. Both are figures promoted by Roger Griffin's approach to scrutinising modernist cultures, and their models for interpreting radical cultural change allow us to add further depth to the conceptualization of cultures of modernism as palingenetic responses to decadent readings of modernity.

To start with *communitas*, here the anthropologist Victor Turner outlines a paradigm for understanding how all cultures, from tribal communities to modern urban societies, have structured their rationalizations of fundamental transitions. In particular, Turner's work emphasizes the importance of a mental state of living through profound transition, which he calls 'liminality'. This culture of transition located between two more fixed ideas of a cultural identity is not a feature restricted to premodern societies, and can be found in modern contexts too. It can be discovered in particular among cultural producers who view themselves as existing between two distinct eras, such as modernists. Turner argues that a liminal mentality also takes a communal form, and that cultures that are generated by people who believe themselves to exist during a period of fundamental change are typically marked by a renewed sense of the sacred, increased emotive connections between individuals, and the need for a renewed sense of community. These become key features expressed between fellow 'liminal people'. Turner dubs this type of community calling for fundamental renewal '*communitas*', a form of counter-culture that becomes radically opposed to mainstream 'structured society'.

Tensions between a world experienced as stability and order, and radical community marked by *communitas* can be seen, to greater or lesser extents, in all societies. Moreover, people marked by this sense of *communitas* perceive themselves as 'outsiders' who instinctively need to develop alternate visions articulating radically the new forms that mainstream society needs to take, and so often enthusiastically seek to realize novel sets of cultural and societal norms in order to 'revitalize' their community. Consequently, Turner's approach argues people marked by liminality and *communitas* believe themselves to be 'reduced or ground down to a uniform condition to be fashioned anew and endowed with additional powers to enable them to cope with their new station in life'.[4] Moreover, those manifesting sensitivity to a liminal state of mind often feel a more profound and subjective sense of the sacred, and seek a reconnection with an allegedly 'purer' understanding of the transcendent. Ultimately, according to Turner, the cultures created by such movements offer 'a symbolic milieu that represents both a grave and a womb', and consequently tropes of death and birth become elided in myriad powerful and emotive ways of thinking that are marked by senses of profound destruction and visions of creation.[5] Such observations strongly resonate with the various explorations of cultures of modernism developed by this study, which were further radicalized by exposure to war. The case studies of the guild socialists, the wider contributors to *The New Age*, as well as Lewis and Wells, all conform to such tendencies, and so can be seen as diverse examples of Turner's counter-cultures marked by *communitas* developing during the war.

Augmenting Turner's suggestive conceptual framework, we can also turn to the ideas of Anthony Wallace. Here we find another anthropologist whose conceptual model for interpreting change helps us understand the roots of radical forms of cultural change. Like Turner, Wallace is acutely sensitive to the psychological problems created by living during period of rapid transition and sudden traumas. One key theme underpinning Wallace's conceptual framework is his examination of the 'mazeway', a term he uses in a broadly synonymous way to an ideology or worldview.[6] Wallace elaborates this concept by asserting the mazeway is a mental construct that is in constant need of active calibration with the wider world. This is necessary in order to maintain correspondence between the outside realm and the internal mazeway that makes sense of the world. Any significant failure to maintain something approaching a credible relationship between the mazeway and outside reality results in increased states of stress, alongside feelings of alienation. Moreover, one potential consequence of rapid alterations and traumatic experiences in the material realm is to spark a specific phenomenon whereby people attempt to radically alter their mazeway via a single, radical jump, rather than through the more common processes of piecemeal updating and alteration. This radical attempt to recalibrate mazeways is a process that Wallace calls 'mazeway re-synthesis', and is a concept cognate with what this study has called palingenesis. Again he presents a communal variant of this phenomenon. The variegated cultural trends that attempt mazeway re-synthesis for entire cultures and societies are called 'revitalization movements' in Wallace's anthropology. Such revitalization movements are marked by the projection of a vision of total change into the near future. So what are more often considered to be long-term and gradual shifts in cultural and political arrangements are styled by revitalization movements as needing to occur in one decisive, revolutionary switch. Often, the trope of identifying societal 'sickness' in the present and its 'health' in their alternate vision for its future, alongside renewed senses of the sacred, are central aspects of the cultures developed by such revitalization movements. Again, we can see this tension between societal sickness, and a new need for social health, in the case studies of cultures of modernism examined in this volume.

So with these anthropological concepts in mind, when we turn again to our case studies, and indeed cultures of modernism more generally, we can see the great relevance of these themes for contextualizing the trope of regeneration among such modernists during the Great War. Modernity, and especially the experiences of total war, could easily be interpreted by intellectuals as phenomena opening up a liminal reality. The impact of these forces caused myriad, radical counter-cultural movements, marked by *communitas* and pioneering attempts at 'mazeway resynthesis', to develop from within Europe's complex cultural dynamics. So by drawing on this anthropology, the idiosyncratic readings of the war that we have surveyed over the course of this study can each be characterized as ideas framing the conflagration as a period of transition between two eras. They tended to experience the outbreak of war as a form of spontaneous *communitas*; if not already, they were quickly entrenched in states of rebellion against bourgeois 'structured society'; they then sought fundamental societal and cultural change from the horrors of the conflict; and finally believed that the postwar world needed to be defined by a revitalized sense of community. However, as Leed reminds us, although prewar reality was largely destroyed, we also see that the tendency was for the postwar era to fail to match the heightened expectations for change. Hopes for revolutionizing European culture and society generated by modernist intellectuals in 1914 remained largely unrealized. So by 1918, for many intellectual figures, such as those this study has examined, European culture and society seemed closer to death than new life; as Wells put it, after the war Europe was akin to a patient recovering from major surgery. Instead of revelling in the new order, the very survival of the continent was even more profoundly in question by the war's end, a fear leading to the creation of works articulating this crisis and the potential of the continued decline of Europe. In Britain, aesthetic modernists tapped into this deep-seated sense of decline, a cultural milieu that became far more pessimistic regarding a transfer to a new world than had previously existed. More generally, many political modernists after the war were thrown into a new crisis, with some programmatically reaching out for a new epoch. The rise of fascism and communism in the interwar period epitomized this radicalization of politics.

So to conclude with a note on implications for future study, the methodology for mapping this cultural crisis – set out here merely to focus on a select range of British-based intellectuals – clearly also lends itself to further and wider exploration. Indeed, it is hoped that the theme of exploring cultures of modernism as radical confrontations with decadent readings of modernity can be used to continue reconfiguring our understanding of such milieus in their widest sense. The examination of cultures of modernism in politics and philosophy, as well as the arts, helps to open us up to a much richer understanding of 'modernism' than merely using it as a term for literary criticism. It becomes of far greater relevance to a wider range of cultural and intellectual historians too. It has expanded the concept into a comparative term for interdisciplinary analysis, study rooted in re-examining the interconnections between art, radical philosophy and politics, found within revolutionary thought during the early twentieth century in Britain and across Europe.

Notes

Introduction

1 Robert Scholes and Clifford Wulfman, *Modernism in the Magazines: An Introduction* (New Haven: Yale University Press, 2010). Also see Mark S. Morrison, *The Public Face of Modernism: Little Magazines, Audiences and Reception 1905–1920* (Madison: University of Wisconsin Press, 2001) and Peter Brooker and Andrew Thacker, *The Oxford Critical and Cultural History of Modernist Magazines: Volume I: Britain and Ireland 1880–1955* (Oxford: Oxford University Press, 2009).
2 Roger Griffin, *Modernism and Fascism: The Sense of a Beginning under Mussolini and Hitler* (London: Palgrave, 2007).
3 Dan Stone, *Breeding Superman: Nietzsche, Race and Eugenics in Edwardian and Interwar Britain* (Liverpool: Liverpool University Press, 2002), p. 10.
4 Robert Wohl, 'Heart of Darkness: Modernism and Its Historians', *The Journal of Modern History,* vol. 74, no. 3 (September 2002), pp. 573–621.
5 Modris Eksteins, *Rites of Spring: The Great War and the Birth of the Modern Age* (London: Papermac, 2000), p. 211.
6 Ibid., p. xvi.
7 According to Eksteins, the idea that Britain displayed 'comparatively little interest in the manifestations of modern culture does not require extensive documentation', ibid., p. 117.

Chapter 1

1 Peter Nichols, *Modernisms: A Literary Guide* (Basingstoke: MacMillan, 1995), ch. 8.
2 Jay Winter, *Sites of Memory, Sites of Mourning: The Great War in European Cultural History* (Cambridge: Cambridge University Press, 1995).
3 This approach is most clearly associated with Griffin's recent re-reading of modernism as key theme for analysing interwar fascisms. Indeed, his expansive discussions on the term and its cultural history in *Modernism and Fascism* underpin the methodology outlined in this opening chapter. Roger Griffin, *Modernism and Fascism: The Sense of a Beginning under Mussolini and Hitler* (London: Palgrave, 2007).
4 Anthony Giddens, *Modernity and Self-Identity: Self and Society in the Late Modern Age* (Stanford, CA: Stanford University Press, 1991).
5 Marshall Berman, *All that is Solid Melts into Air. The Experience of Modernity* (London: Verso, 1982), esp. pp. 15–36.
6 Zygmunt Bauman, *Modernity and Ambivalence*, p. 5.
7 Steven Kern, *The Culture of Time and Space, 1880–1918* (Cambridge: Harvard University Press, 2000).
8 See David Harvey, *The Condition of Postmodernity: An Enquiry into the Origins of Cultural Change* (Oxford: Blackwell, 1990), esp. ch. 2.

9 H. Stuart Hughes, *Consciousness and Society: The Reformation of European Social Thought 1890–1930* (Brighton: The Harvester Press, 1979), p. 37.

10 Similarly, Louise Blakeney Williams, has also emphasized this point, arguing that cyclical interpretations of historical change allowed 'Modernists to accept change confidently because it ensured a permanence and stability underlying the flux, and because it inspired the conviction that the past was always present and would soon return'. See: Louise Blakeney Williams, *Modernism and the Ideology of History: Literature, Politics, and the Past* (Cambridge: Cambridge University Press, 2002), p. 208.

11 Kermode played on the 'tick tock' sound of clocks when articulating his model of plots, 'ticks' represent genesis and beginnings, whereas 'tocks' signify apocalypses and endings. Between the 'tick' and the 'tock', he continued, lay a comforting sense of stability and order, whereas between the 'tock' and a subsequent tick lay an interregnum, an apocalyptic moment waiting for a new tick to create a sense of renewal and order. Modernist thought, through this lens, was characterized by a sense of time between a 'tock' and a 'tick'. In other words, it was marked by a sense of an ending that was expecting a new beginning. See Frank Kermode, *The Sense of an Ending: Studies in the Theory of Fiction* (Oxford: Oxford University Press, 2000).

12 Ronald Schleifer, *Modernism and Time. The Logic of Abundance in Literature, Science, and Culture* (Cambridge: Cambridge University Press, 2000), p. 9.

13 Ibid., p. 10.

14 Peter Osborne, *The Politics of Time: Modernity and the Avant-Garde* (London: Verso, 1995), p. 164.

15 Peter Osborne, *Philosophy in Cultural Theory* (London: Routledge, 2000), ch. 4.

16 The term is derived from the Greek 'palin' again, and 'genesis' birth. In philosophical discourses, the term has been used to signify the rebirth of the soul in a new body.

17 Roger Griffin has used the term to signify the myth of national rebirth that was central to fascist political discourses, which claimed that they alone held the potential to renew the nation's organic 'soul'. See Roger Griffin, *The Nature of Fascism* (London: Routledge, 1993).

18 Ernest Jones, 'War and Individual Psychology', *The Sociological Review,* vol. 8, no. 3, July 1916, pp. 167–80.

19 James Joll, *The Origins of the First World War,* Second Edition (London: Longman, 1992), p. 229.

20 Eric Hobsbawm, *The Age of Empire, 1875–1914* (London: Abacus, 1994), p. 326.

21 Robert Wohl, *The Generation of 1914* (London: Weidenfeld and Nicolson, 1980), p. 212.

22 Ibid., p. 217.

23 Ibid., p. 235.

24 Roland N. Stromberg, *Redemption by War: The Intellectuals and 1914* (Kansas: Regents Press of Kansas, 1982), p. 187.

25 Ibid., p. 189.

26 Ibid., p. 198.

27 Eric J. Leed, *No Man's Land: Combat and Identity in World War I* (New York: Cambridge University Press, 1981), p. 44.

28 Ibid., p. 213.

Chapter 2

1 Samuel Hynes, *Edwardian Occasions: Essays on English Writing in the Early Twentieth Century* (London: Routledge and Kegan Paul, 1972), pp. 39–40.

2 See Gary Taylor, *Orage and The New Age* (Sheffield: Sheffield Hallam University Press, 2000), p. 4.

3 David S. Thatcher, *Nietzsche in England, 1890–1914* (Toronto: University of Toronto Press, 1970), p. 226. For a study exploring the history of Orage's activities while based in Leeds, see Tom Steel, *Alfred Orage and the Leeds Arts Club, 1893–1923* (Aldershot: Scolar, 1990).

4 A. R. Orage, *Friedrich Nietzsche, the Dionysian Spirit of the Age* (London: no publisher, 1906), p. 20.

5 Here, Orage also explained that the Nietzschean view of the world was, in the final analysis, a mystical one; it was this mysticism which Orage found most common ground with his philosophy – a mysticism that he likened to William Blake, especially in the latter's 'Marriage Between Heaven and Hell'.

6 A. R. Orage, *Consciousness: Animal, Human and Superhuman* (London: no publisher, 1907), p. 83.

7 In his final book on Nietzsche, Orage offered a far more detailed analysis of the core ideas of his philosophy. For more on Orage's key role in the introduction of Nietzsche to English audiences, see Thatcher, *Nietzsche in England*, p. 261.

8 Tom Steele, *Alfred Orage and the Leeds Art Club 1893–1923* (Mitcham: The Orage Press, 2009), p. 56.

9 G. D. H. Cole in Steele, *Alfred Orage and the Leeds Art Club*, p. 124.

10 Steele, *Alfred Orage and the Leeds Art Club*, p. 133.

11 Wallace Martin, *The New Age Under Orage: Chapters in English Cultural History* (Manchester: Manchester University Press, 1967), pp. 109–10.

12 Thatcher, *Nietzsche in England*, p. 248.

13 Taylor, *Orage and The New Age*, pp. 35–6.

14 *The New Age*, vol. 15, no. 14 (1914), p. 315.

15 Ibid., vol. 15, no. 17 (1914), p. 386.

16 Ibid., vol. 16, no. 1 (1914), p. 2.

17 Ibid., vol. 18, no. 11 (1916), p. 244.

18 Ibid., vol. 19, no. 5 (1916), pp. 97–8.

19 These columns were unsigned and published sporadically. Essentially, they were written up versions of various discussions Orage had with his contributors on philosophical and political matters of the day.

20 *The New Age*, vol. 15, no. 17 (1914), p. 396.

21 Ibid., vol. 18, no. 26 (1916), p. 605.

22 Ibid., vol. 18, no. 19 (1916), pp. 438–9.

23 Ibid., vol. 18, no. 22 (1916), p. 510.

24 Ibid., vol. 18, no. 23 (1916), p. 535.

25 Ibid., vol. 18, no. 21 (1916), pp. 485–6.

26 Ibid., vol. 20, no. 24 (1917), p. 554.

27 Ibid., vol. 20, no. 21 (1917), p. 481.

28 Ibid., vol. 20, no. 22 (1917), p. 506.

29 Ibid., vol. 21, no. 3 (1917), p. 50.

30 Ibid., vol. 22, no. 3 (1917), p. 43.

31 Ibid., vol. 22, no. 10 (1918), pp. 182–3.
32 Ibid., vol. 22, no. 19 (1918), pp. 365–6.
33 Ibid., vol. 19, no. 19 (1916), p. 435.
34 Ibid., vol. 17, no. 10 (1915), p. 218.
35 Ibid., vol. 20, no. 1 (1916), p. 1.
36 Ibid., vol. 19, no. 21 (1916), p. 481.
37 Ibid., vol. 17, no. 8 (1915), p. 171.
38 Ibid., vol. 16, no. 16 (1915), p. 498.
39 Ibid., vol. 17, no. 18 (1915), p. 418.
40 Ibid., vol. 22, no. 15 (1918), p. 282.
41 Ibid., vol. 16, no. 17 (1915), p. 442.
42 Ibid., p. 147.
43 Ibid., vol. 16, no. 3 (1914), p. 58.
44 Ibid., vol. 20, no. 7 (1916), p. 148.
45 Ibid., vol. 17, no. 21 (1915), p. 489.
46 Ibid., vol. 16, no .4 (1914), pp. 81–4.
47 Ibid., vol. 16, no. 10 (1915), p. 235.
48 Ibid., vol. 23, no. 11 (1918), p. 163; and ibid., vol. 23, no. 15 (1918), p. 230.
49 Ibid., vol. 23, no. 18 (1918), p. 279.
50 Ibid., vol. 23, no. 24 (1918), p. 375.
51 Ibid., vol. 23, no. 4 (1918), p. 50.
52 Ibid., vol. 23, no. 25 (1918), p. 391.
53 Ibid., vol. 25, no. 9 (1919), p. 141.
54 Ibid., p. 142.
55 For a summary of the ideas of Social Credit, see Taylor, *Orage and The New* Age, pp.
    99–124; see also two essays by Douglas: 'Economic Democracy' and 'Credit Power and
    Democracy', both published in *The New Age*. 'Economic Democracy' ran between June and
    August 1919, and 'Credit Power and Democracy' ran between February and August 1920.
56 For more on Orage's turn to mysticism, see Louise Welch, *Orage with Gurdjieff in
    America* (London: Routledge, 1982).
57 *The New Age*, vol. 38, no. 22 (1926), p. 258.

Chapter 3

1 'The Ferment of Revolution. I. A Growing Movement. Old Theories and Present Facts',
   the *Times*, 25 September 1917, p. 9.
2 'The New Revolution', the *Manchester Guardian*, 6 October 1917, p. 6.
3 Ann J. Ardis, *Modernism and Cultural Conflict, 1880–1922* (Cambridge: Cambridge
   University Press, 2002), ch. 5.
4 Tom Villis, *Reaction and the Avant-Garde: The Revolt Against Liberal Democracy in
   Early Twentieth-Century Britain* (London: Tauris Academic Studies, 2006).
5 A. J. Penty, *The Restoration of the Gild System* (London: Swan Sonnenschein and Co.,
   Ltd, 1906), pp. 55–6.
6 Ibid., p. 94.
7 *Times Literary Supplement*, 28 May 1914, p. 254.
8 Brown, 'Geography and Human Grouping, I', *The New Age*, vol. 15, no. 23 (1914),
   pp. 545–6.
9 Brown, 'Geography and Human Grouping, II', ibid., vol. 15, no. 24 (1914), pp. 569–70.

10 Brown, 'Geography and Human Grouping, IV', ibid., vol. 15, no. 26 (1914), p. 620.

11 Brown, 'Nationalism and the Guilds, I', ibid., vol. 16, no. 11 (1915), pp. 274–5.

12 Brown, 'Nationalism and the Guilds, II', ibid., vol. 16, no. 12 (1915), pp. 305–6.

13 Brown, 'Aspects of the Guild Idea, I', ibid., vol. 17, no. 1 (1915), p. 7.

14 Brown, 'Aspects of the Guild Idea, II', ibid., vol. 17, no. 2 (1915), p. 31.

15 One example identified here was their embrace of rigid class structures, which would be eschewed in the alternate modernity of guild socialism. Brown, 'Aspects of the Guild Idea, V', ibid., vol. 17, no. 5 (1915), p. 102.

16 Brown, 'Aspects of the Guild Idea, VI', ibid., vol. 17, no. 6 (1915), p. 126.

17 Brown, 'Aspects of the Guild Idea, IX', ibid., vol. 17, no. 9 (1915), p. 198.

18 Brown, 'Aspects of the Guild Idea, X', ibid., vol. 17, no. 10 (1915), p. 221.

19 Brown, 'Guilders of the Chains, No. 1 – Sir Joseph Lyons', ibid., vol. 17, no. 20 (1915), p. 470.

20 Brown, 'Guilders of the Chains, No. 2 – Charlie Chaplin', ibid., vol. 17, no. 21 (1915), pp. 494–5.

21 Brown, 'Guilders of the Chains, No. 3 – Charles Garvice', ibid., vol. 17, no. 22 (1915), p. 518.

22 Ewer, 'The State and the Guilds, 1 – Leviathan', *The New Age*, vol. 18, no. 1 (1915), p. 8.

23 Ewer, 'The State and the Guilds, 3 – Destruction of the Guilds', ibid., vol. 18, no. 6 (1915), pp. 126–7.

24 Ewer, 'The State and the Guilds', ibid., vol. 18, no. 21 (1916), pp. 490–1.

25 A. J. Penty, *Old Worlds for New: A Study of the Post-Industrial State* (London: George Allen and Unwin, Ltd, 1917), pp. 9–10.

26 Penty, 'After the War', *The New Age*, vol. 20, no. 11 (1917), pp. 246–8.

27 Penty, 'The Function of the State', *The New Age*, vol. 22, no. 9 (1917), pp. 165–6.

28 Penty, 'National Guilds v. the Class War', ibid., vol. 23, no. 16 (1918), pp. 250–3.

29 Penty, 'On the Class War Again', ibid., vol. 23, no. 21 (1918), pp. 330–1.

30 For further details, see John S. Peart-Binns, *Maurice B. Reckitt: A Life* (Basingstoke: Bowerdean and Marshall Pickering, 1988).

31 *The New Age*, vol. 17, no. 19, p. 445.

32 Ibid., vol. 17, no. 21, p. 494.

33 Ibid., vol. 17, no. 22, pp. 517–18.

34 Maurice B. Reckitt and C. E. Bechhofer, *The Meaning of National Guilds* (London: Cecil Palmer and Hayward, 1918), p. 11.

35 Cole, *Labour in Wartime* (London: G. Bell and Sons, Ltd, 1915) p. 289.

36 Cole, *The World of Labour: A Discussion of the Present and Future of Trade Unionism* (London: G. Bell and Sons, Ltd, 1917), pp. vii–xvii.

37 Cole, 'Reflections on the Wage System. II – Labour and the Labourer', *The New Age*, vol. 20, no. 21 (1917), pp. 487–8.

38 Cole, 'Reflections on the Wage System. IV – The Control of Production', ibid., vol. 20, no. 23 (1917), pp. 534–5.

39 Cole, 'Reflections on the Wage System. V – The Control of the Product', ibid., vol. 20, no. 24 (1917), pp. 557–8.

40 Cole, 'Reflections on the Wage System. VI – Purchase, Sale and Investment', ibid., vol. 20, no. 25 (1917), pp. 581–2.

41 Hobson, 'Guild Principles and the War', *The New Age*, vol. 16, no. 3 (1914), p. 67.

42 Hobson, 'The Permanent Hypothesis. A Critique of Reconstruction. II – Quo Vadis?', ibid., vol. 20, no. 2 (1916), pp. 30–1.

43 Hobson, 'The Permanent Hypothesis. A Critique of Reconstruction. III – The New Social Contract', ibid., vol. 20, no. 3 (1916), pp. 54–6.

44 Hobson, 'The Permanent Hypothesis. A Critique of Reconstruction. IV – Outlines',
     ibid., vol. 20, no. 4 (1916), pp. 78–80.

45 Hobson, 'The Permanent Hypothesis. A Critique of Reconstruction. VII – In War',
     ibid., vol. 20, no. 10 (1917), pp. 223–5.

46 Hobson, 'The Criteria for Peace', ibid., vol. 23, no. 8 (1918), p. 118.

47 Hobson, 'Chapters on Transition – I – Signs of Change', ibid., vol. 23, no. 10 (1918),
     pp. 148–9.

48 Hobson, 'Chapters on Transition – I – Signs of Change (continued)', ibid., vol. 23,
     no. 13 (1918), pp. 198–9.

49 Hobson, 'Chapters on Transition – I – Signs of Change (continued)', ibid., vol. 23,
     no. 14 (1918), pp. 214–15.

50 Hobson, 'The Workshop. III – Collective Contract, *The New Age,* vol. 23, no. 18
     (1918), pp. 283–4.

51 Hobson, 'The Workshop. IV – The New Shop Steward Movement', ibid., vol. 23, no. 19
     (1918), pp. 298–300.

52 Hobson, 'The Workshop. V – War Conditions and the New Shop Stewards', ibid.,
     vol. 23, no. 21 (1918), pp. 331–3.

53 Hobson, 'The Workshop. VI – The Industrial Unit and the New Shop Steward', ibid.,
     vol. 23, no. 22 (1918), pp. 346–7.

54 Hobson, 'The Workshop. VIII – Wage Inequalities and Trade Union Personnel', ibid.,
     vol. 23, no. 24 (1918), pp. 378–9.

55 Hobson, 'The Workshop. XI – Some Implications of Control', ibid., vol. 23, no. 25
     (1918), pp. 394–5.

56 Hobson, 'The Influence of the Wart upon Labour. Being a Second Chapter on
     Transition. 1 – A General Survey', ibid., vol. 24, no. 2 (1918), pp. 21–3.

57 S. G. Hobson, *Pilgrim to the Left: Memoirs of a Modern Revolutionist* (London: Edward
     Arnold & Co., 1938).

58 Leon Surette, *Pound in Purgatory: From Economic Radicalism to Anti-Semitism*
     (Urbana: University of Illinois Press, 1999), p. 84.

59 Por, 'War and After', *The New Age,* vol. 15, no. 20 (1914), p. 475.

60 For more on Por's interest in transferring the guild socialist system to Italy, see Odon
     Por, *Guilds and Co-operatives in Italy* (London: Labour Publishing Company, 1923);
     and on the impact of Fascism on Por's thinking see Odon Por, *Fascism* (London:
     Labour Publishing Company, 1923).

61 Stephen Dorril, *Blackshirt: Sir Oswald Mosley and British Fascism* (London: Penguin
     Books, 2006), pp. 69–80.

Chapter 4

1 Samuel Hynes, *A War Imagined: The First World War and English Culture* (New York:
    Atheneum, 1990), p. 63.

2 Romney, 'Military Notes', *The New Age,* vol. 15, no. 15 (1914), p. 341.

3 Alice Morning, 'Impressions of Paris', ibid., vol. 15, no. 16 (1914), p. 371.

4 German in origin, Oscar Levy settled in London in 1894, and spent much of his time
    subsequently championing Nietzsche's philosophy in Britain. For more on Levy's
    critique of Western culture, see Dan Stone, *Breeding Superman: Nietzsche, Race and
    Eugenics in Edwardian and Interwar Britain* (Liverpool: Liverpool University Press,

2002), ch. 1; and David S. Thatcher, *Nietzsche in England, 1890–1914* (Toronto: University of Toronto Press, 1970), esp. pp. 40–9.

5 Dan Stone, *Breeding Superman: Nietzsche, Race and Eugenics in Edwardian and Interwar Britain* (Liverpool: Liverpool University Press, 2002), pp. 17–18.

6 Levy, 'Nietzsche and This War', *The New Age,* vol. 15, no. 17 (1914), p. 393.

7 A. E. R., actually A. E. Randall, was one of the first writers in England to draw upon the theories of Freud in analysing literature. He also took the pseudonym John Hope Francis when writing the weekly 'Drama' column for the journal. For more details, see Wallace Martin, *The New Age Under Orage: Chapters in English Cultural History* (Manchester: Manchester University Press, 1967), p. 125 and p. 140.

8 A. E. R., 'Views and Reviews', *The New Age,* vol. 15, no. 18 (1914), p. 424.

9 A. E. R., 'Views and Reviews', ibid., vol. 15, no. 23 (1914), p. 552.

10 'Thou art a God too, / O Galilean! / And thus singled-handed / Unto the combat, / Gauntlet or Gospel, / Here I defy thee!' ibid., pp. 551–2.

11 A. E. R., 'Views and Reviews', ibid., vol. 15, no. 24 (1914), p. 576.

12 An Oxford Indian, 'The Significance of India's Loyalty', ibid., vol. 15, no. 22 (1914), p. 526.

13 For more see Roger Lipsey's two volumes of edited works, and especially his third volume of biography: *Coomaraswamy 3: His Life and Works* (New Jersey: Princeton University Press, 1977).

14 Coomaraswamy, 'A World Policy for India', *The New Age,* vol. 16, no. 8 (1914), pp. 192–3.

15 Indeed, during the war he published a book based on his articles for *The New Age*, see Ramiro de Maeztu, *Authority, Liberty and Function in the Light of the War* (London: George Allen and Unwin, 1916).

16 Ibid, p. 123.

17 Ibid., p. 13.

18 Ibid., p. 101.

19 Ibid., p. 119.

20 Pound, 'Affirmations. VI. Analysis of this Decade', *The New Age,* vol. 16, no. 15 (1915), pp. 409–11.

21 Levy, 'Nietzsche and the Jews, II', ibid., vol. 16, no. 8 (1914), pp. 193–5.

22 Levy, 'Nietzsche and the Jews, I', ibid., vol. 16, no. 7 (1914), p. 171.

23 Levy, 'The German and the European. A Dialogue', ibid., vol. 17, no. 8 (1915), pp. 176–9.

24 Levy, 'The German and the European. A Dialogue, II', ibid., vol. 17, no. 12 (1915), pp. 270–2.

25 Levy, 'The German and the European. A Dialogue, III', ibid., vol. 17, no. 17 (1915), pp. 399–401.

26 Levy, 'The German and the European. A Dialogue, IV', ibid., vol. 17, no. 23 (1915), pp. 541–4.

27 Levy, 'The German and the European. A Dialogue, V', ibid., vol. 17, no. 26 (1915), pp. 614–17.

28 T. E. Hulme, *Selected Writings* (Manchester: Carcanet, 1998), p. 209.

29 Ibid., p. 214.

30 North Staffs., 'War Notes', *The New Age,* vol. 18, no. 5 (1915), pp. 101–2.

31 North Staffs., 'War Notes', ibid., vol. 18, no. 2 (1915), pp. 29–30.

32 North Staffs., 'War Notes', ibid., vol. 18, no. 8 (1915) pp. 173–4.

33 See Michael Roberts *T. E. Hulme* (Manchester: Carcanet New Press Ltd, 1982); Leslie
    Susser, 'Right Wings over Britain: T. E. Hulme and the Intellectual Revolt against
    Democracy', Z. Sternhell (ed.), *The Intellectual Revolt Against Liberal Democracy,*
    1870–1945 (Jerusalem: Israel Academy of Sciences and Humanities, 1996),
    pp. 356–76; and Richard Schusterman, 'Remembering Hulme: A Neglected
    Philosopher-Critic-Poet', in *Journal of the History of Ideas,* vol. 46, no. 4 (1985), pp.
    559–76. For his collected writings, see Karen Csengeri (ed.), *The Collected Writings of*
    T. E. Hulme (Oxford: Clarendon Press, 1994).

34 North Staffs., 'War Notes', *The New Age,* vol. 18, no. 8, pp. 173–4.

35 T. E. Hulme, 'Translator's Preface', in Georges Sorel, *Reflections on Violence* (London:
    Allan and Unwin, 1916), p. xi.

36 Herbert Read, 'Sorel, Marx and the War', *The New Age,* vol. 19, no. 6 (1916), pp. 128–9.

37 Edwin Muir, *An Autobiography* (Edinburgh: Cannongate Classics, 2000).

38 Edward Moore, 'We Moderns', *The New Age,* vol. 20, no. 12 (1917), pp. 280–2.

39 Ibid.

40 Edward Moore, 'We Moderns', ibid., vol. 20, no. 17 (1917), pp. 401–2.

41 Edward Moore, 'We Moderns', ibid., vol. 21, no. 18 (1917), pp. 388–9.

42 Edward Moore, 'We Moderns', ibid., vol. 20, no. 20 (1917), pp. 470–1.

43 Edward Moore, 'We Moderns', ibid., vol. 20, no. 25 (1917), pp. 592–3.

44 Edward Moore, 'We Moderns', ibid., vol. 20, no. 7 (1916), pp. 160–1.

45 Edward Moore, 'We Moderns', ibid., vol. 21, no. 1 (1917), pp. 14–15.

46 Edward Moore, 'We Moderns', ibid., vol. 21, no. 3 (1917), pp. 63–4.

47 Edward Moore, 'We Moderns', ibid., vol. 20, no. 3 (1916), pp. 63–5.

48 Kosmopolites, 'War and its Makers, IV', ibid., vol. 19, no. 15 (1916), p. 342.

49 For more on Æ, see: Henry Summerfield, *That Myriad-Minded Man: A Biography of*
    George William Russell 'A.E''' (Gerrards Cross: Colin Smythe, 1975).

50 Æ, 'New Ireland', *The New Age,* vol. 22, no. 10 (1918), pp. 187–9.

51 For more on Vran-Gavran see Martin, *The New Age Under Orage,* p. 284.

52 Vran-Gavran, 'Ideas and Methods', *The New Age,* vol. 22, no. 22 (1918), p. 433.

53 Vran-Gavran, 'Ideas and Methods, II', ibid., vol. 22, no. 23 (1918), p. 455.

54 Vran-Gavran, 'Modernism and Antiquism', ibid., vol. 22, no. 25 (1918), p. 487.

55 Vran-Gavran, 'Jesus the Carpenter', ibid., vol. 23, no. 1 (1918), pp. 11–12.

56 Vran-Gavran, 'Communism of the Saints', ibid., vol. 23, no. 5 (1918), pp. 71–2.

57 Lavrin was a prolific literary critic who was especially productive during the
    interwar period. His books addressed themes such as Russian literature, Nietzsche,
    Ibsen and modernism. For more on Lavrin's thinking on Nietzsche, see Janko
    Lavrin, *Nietzsche and Modern Consciousness* (London: W. Collins Sons and Co.,
    1922).

58 Lavrin, 'The Tragic Individual', *The New Age,* vol. 22, no. 26 (1918), p. 503.

59 Levy, 'The Idolatry of Words, I', ibid., vol. 24, no. 10 (1919), pp. 160–1.

60 Levy, 'The Idolatry of Words, III', ibid., vol. 24, no. 14 (1919), pp. 223–5.

61 Levy, 'The Idolatry of Words, Concluded', ibid., vol. 24, no. 16 (1919), pp. 260–1.

62 Major C. H. Douglas, 'A Mechanical View of Economics', ibid., vol. 24, no. 9 (1919),
    pp. 136–7.

63 Major C. H. Douglas, 'The Control of Production', ibid., vol. 25, no. 1 (1919), p. 4.

64 Major C. H. Douglas, 'Economic Democracy (Chapters I and II)', ibid., vol. 25, no. 6
    (1919), pp. 97–9.

65 Major C. H. Douglas, 'Economic Democracy (Chapter III)', ibid., vol. 25, no. 7 (1919),
    pp. 113–15.

66 Major C. H. Douglas, 'Economic Democracy (Chapter VII)', ibid., vol. 25, no. 11 (1919), pp. 177–9.
67 Major C. H. Douglas, 'Economic Democracy (Chapter VIII)', ibid., vol. 25, no. 12 (1919), pp. 195–8.
68 Major C. H. Douglas, 'Economic Democracy (Chapter VII)', ibid., vol. 25, no. 11 (1919), pp. 177–9.
69 Major C. H. Douglas, 'Economic Democracy (Chapter V)', ibid., vol. 25, no. 9 (1919), pp. 146–8.
70 Major C. H. Douglas, 'Economic Democracy (Chapter XI and XII) (*concluded*)', ibid., vol. 25, no. 15 (1919), pp. 243–4.
71 Richard Thurlow, The Return of Jeremiah: The Rejected Knowledge of Sir Oswald Mosley in the 1930s', in Lunn, K. and Thurlow, R. eds, *British Fascism: Essays on the Radical Right in Inter-War Britain* (Oxford: Billig and Sons, Ltd, 1980), pp. 100–13.

Chapter 5

1 Alan Munton, 'Wyndham Lewis: From Proudhon to Hitler (and back): the Strange Political Journey of Wyndham Lewis', *E-rea*, vol. 4, no. 2 (2006).
2 The most comprehensive biographical account of Lewis's life is: Paul O'Keeffe, *Some Sort of Genius: A Life of Wyndham Lewis* (London: Pimlico, 2001). Meanwhile, the most comprehensive analysis of Lewis's life and work is Paul Edwards, *Wyndham Lewis: Painter and Writer* (New Haven: Yale University Press, 2000).
3 Wyndham Lewis, 'The "Pole"', the *English Review*, vol. 2, no. 6 (1909), pp. 255–65.
4 Wyndham Lewis, 'Some Innkeepers and Bestre', ibid., vol. 2, no. 7 (1909), pp. 471–84.
5 Wyndham Lewis, 'Our Wild Body', *The New Age*, vol. 7, no. 1 (1910), pp. 8–10.
6 O'Keeffe, *Some Sort of Genius*.
7 For more on this painting, also see Lisa Tickner, 'The Popular Culture of Kermesse: Lewis, Painting, and Performance 1912–13', *Modernism/modernity*, vol. 4, no. 2 (1997), pp. 67–120.
8 'Long Live the Vortex', *Blast*, no. 1 (1914), pp. 7–8.
9 'Manifesto – I', ibid., no. 1 (1914), pp. 11–28.
10 Wyndham Lewis, 'Manifesto – II', ibid., no. 1 (1914), pp. 30–43.
11 *Manchester Guardian*, 17 July 1914, p. 7.
12 Wyndham Lewis, 'The Enemy of the Stars', *Blast*, no. 1 (1914), pp. 51–85.
13 Edwards, *Wyndham Lewis*, pp. 139–65.
14 Wyndham Lewis, 'Life is the Important Thing', *Blast*, no. 1 (1914), pp. 129–31.
15 Wyndham Lewis, 'Futurism, Magic and Life', ibid., no. 1 (1914), pp. 132–5.
16 Wyndham Lewis, 'The Melodrama of Modernity', ibid., no. 1 (1914), pp. 143–4.
17 Wyndham Lewis, 'Policeman and Artist', ibid., no. 1 (1914), p. 137.
18 Wyndham Lewis, 'Fêng Shui and Contemporary Form', ibid., no. 1 (1914), p. 138.
19 Wyndham Lewis, 'Relativism and Picasso's Latest Work', ibid., no. 1 (1914), pp. 139–40.
20 Wyndham Lewis, 'The New Egos', ibid., no. 1 (1914), p. 141.
21 Wyndham Lewis, 'The Improvement of Life', ibid., no. 1 (1914), p. 146.
22 Wyndham Lewis, 'Our Vortex', ibid., no. 1 (1914), pp. 147–9.
23 Wyndham Lewis, *Blasting and Bombardiering: An Autobiography (1914–1926)* (London: John Calder, 1982), p. 63.

24 Christine Hardegen, 'Actors and Spectators in the Theatre of War: Wyndham Lewis's First World War Art and Literature' in Corbett, ed., *Wyndham Lewis and the Art of Modern War* (Cambridge: Cambridge University Press, 1988), pp. 58–77.

25 Wyndham Lewis, 'A Later Arm than Barbarity', *Outlook*, 5 September 1914, p. 299.

26 Paul Peppis, '"Surrounded by a Multitude of Other Blasts": Vorticism and the Great War', *Modernism/Modernity*, vol. 4, no. 2 (1997), pp. 39– 6.

27 'Editorial', *Blast*, no. 2, pp. 5–6.

28 Wyndham Lewis, 'The God of Sport and Blood', ibid., no. 2, pp. 9–10.

29 Wyndham Lewis, 'Constantinople Our Star', ibid., no. 2, p. 11.

30 Wyndham Lewis, 'Mr. Shaw's Effect on My Friend', ibid., no. 2, p. 12.

31 Wyndham Lewis, 'A Super-Krupp – Or War's End', ibid., no. 2, pp. 13–14.

32 Wyndham Lewis, 'The European War and Great Communities', ibid., no. 2, pp. 15–16.

33 Edwards, *Wyndham Lewis*, p. 190.

34 Wyndham Lewis, ' Inferior Religions', the *Little Review*, vol. 4, no. 5 (1917), pp. 3–8.

35 Wyndham Lewis, 'Artists and the War', *Blast*, no. 2, pp. 23–4.

36 Wyndham Lewis, 'The Exploitation of Blood', ibid., no. 2, p. 24.

37 Wyndham Lewis, 'The Six Hundred, Verestchagin and Uccello', ibid., no. 2, pp. 25–6.

38 Wyndham Lewis, 'Marinetti's Occupation', ibid., no. 2, p. 26.

39 Wyndham Lewis, 'A Review of Contemporary Art', ibid., no. 2, pp. 38–47.

40 Wyndham Lewis, 'The London Group 1915 (March)', ibid., no. 2, pp. 77–9.

41 The *Times*, 10 March 1915, p. 8.

42 Paul Jackson, '"The Exquisite Moment": May Sinclair's Vision of a New Spiritual Reality Forged through War', Paul Jackson, *Minerva: Women and War*, vol. 1, no. 2 (2007), pp. 77–90.

43 Wyndham Lewis, 'The Crowd Master (First Part)', *Blast*, no. 2, pp. 94–100.

44 'A Scientific Experiment. *Tarr* by Lewis, Percy Wyndham', the *Times Literary Supplement*, 11 July 1918, p. 322.

45 Wyndham Lewis, 'Tarr – Part VII (Swagger Sex), Chapter VI, and Epilogue', the *Egoist*, vol. 4, no. 10, pp. 152–3.

46 Wyndham Lewis, 'Tarr – Part I, Chapters I-III', ibid., vol. 3, no. 4 (1916), pp. 54–63.

47 O'Keeffe, ed., Wyndham Lewis, *Tarr: The 1918 Version* (Santa Rosa: Black Sparrow Press, 1990), p. 360.

48 Wyndham Lewis, 'The French Poodle', the *Egoist*, vol. 3, no. 3, pp. 39–41.

49 Geoff Gilbert, 'Shell-Shock, anti-Semitism, and the Agency of the Avant-Garde', in Corbett, ed., *Wyndham Lewis and the Art of Modern War*, p. 79.

50 Wyndham Lewis, 'A Young Soldier', the *Egoist*, vol. 3, no. 3, p. 46.

51 Wyndham Lewis, 'Cantleman's Spring Mate', the *Little Review*, vol. 4, no. 6 (1917), pp. 8–14.

52 Wyndham Lewis, 'Imaginary Letters: Six Letters of William Bland Burn to His Wife – III: The Code of a Herdsman', ibid., vol. 4, no. 3 (1917), pp. 3–7.

53 Wyndham Lewis, 'The Ideal Giant', ibid., vol. 5, no. 1 (1918), pp. 1–18.

54 Lewis, 'Inferior Religions'.

55 Tom Normand, 'Wyndham Lewis, the Anti-War Artist', in Corbett, ed., *Wyndham Lewis and the Art of Modern War*, pp. 25–7.

56 Wyndham Lewis, *Rude Assignment: A Narrative of my Career Up-to-date* (London: Hutchinson, 1950), p. 129.

57 For further discussion on this point, see David Peter Corbett, '"Grief With a Yard Wide Grin": War and Wyndham Lewis's Tyros', in Corbett, ed., *Wyndham Lewis and the Art of Modern War*, pp. 106–7.

58 Toby Foshay, *Wyndham Lewis and the Avant-Garde: The Politics of the Intellect*, p. 12.
59 Wyndham Lewis, *The Caliph's Design: Architects! Where is Your Vortex?* (Santa Barbara: Black Sparrow Press, 1986), p. 12.
60 Ibid., p. 120.
61 Ibid., p. 28.
62 Wyndham Lewis, 'Note on Tyros', the *Tyro*, no. 1, p. 2.
63 The *Times*, 14 April 1921, p. 8.
64 Edwards, *Wyndham Lewis*, p. 256.
65 Corbett, 'Grief With a Yard Wide Grin', p. 119.
66 Wyndham Lewis, 'The Children of the New Epoch', the *Tyro*, no. 1, p. 3.
67 Wyndham Lewis, 'Roger Fry's Role of Continental Mediator', ibid., no. 1, p. 3.
68 Wyndham Lewis, 'Tyronic Dialogues – X. and F', ibid., no. 2, pp. 46–9.
69 Wyndham Lewis, 'Essay on the Objective of Plastic Art in Our Time', ibid., no. 2, pp. 21–37.
70 'Editorial', ibid., no. 2, pp. 3–10.
71 Wyndham Lewis, *Hitler* (London: Chatto and Windus, 1931), pp. 191–202.
72 Frederick Jameson, *Fables of Aggression: Wyndham Lewis, the Modernist as Fascist* (Berkeley: University of California Press, 1979).

Chapter 6

1 *Times Literary Supplement*, 17 May 1917, p. 230.
2 See Frank Field, *British and French Writers of the First World War: Comparative Studies in Cultural History* (Cambridge: Cambridge University Press, 1991), esp. pp. 123–41.
3 W. Warren Warger, *H. G. Wells and the World State* (New Haven: Yale University Press, 1961).
4 David C. Smith, *H. G. Wells: Desperately Mortal* (New Haven: Yale University Press, 1986). Smith's biography offers one of the most sympathetic appreciations of Wells's wartime religious thought. See pp. 230–2.
5 For a detailed discussion of how Wells articulated a 'static' utopia in *The Time Machine* see John S. Partington, '*The Time Machine* and *A Modern Utopia*: The Static and Kinetic Utopias of the Early H. G. Wells's in *Journal of Utopian Studies*, vol. 13, no. 1 (2002), pp. 57–68.
6 The *Pall Mall Gazette*, 10 September 1895, p. 4.
7 The *Economic Journal*, vol. 12, no. 45 (1902), pp. 90–2.
8 H. G. Wells, *Anticipations of the Reaction of Mechanical and Scientific Progress upon Human Life and Thought* (London: Chapman and Hall, 1914), p. 175.
9 *Manchester Guardian*, 25 April 1905, p. 5.
10 H. G. Wells, *A Modern Utopia* (London: Penguin Books Ltd, 2005), p. 11.
11 Wells, *A Modern Utopia*, p. 176.
12 Ibid., p. 188.
13 Ibid., pp. 201–2.
14 The allusion is to Zygmunt Bauman's concept of the 'gardening state', a common theme of political modernism. John S. Partington has argued that scholars have sometimes over-emphasized his interest in the negative aspects of eugenics and euthanasia, taking the ideas expressed in *Anticipations* as Wells's final word on this topic, rather than seeking to understand how these ideas developed throughout his

lifetime. See John S. Partington 'The Death of the Static: H. G. Wells and the Kinetic Utopia', *Utopian Studies*, vol. 11, no. 2 (2000), pp. 96–111, and John S. Partington, 'H. G. Wells's Eugenic Thinking of the 1930s and 1940s', *Utopian Studies*, vol. 14, no. 1 (2003), pp. 74–81.

15 Wells later compared his idea of a revolutionary vanguard to Lenin's Communist Party, claiming that both possessed an 'arrangement whereby a man or woman could be a militant member of the organization and then drop out of its obligations and privileges', both imposed 'special disciplines and restrictions on the active members', and both insisted 'upon a training in directive ideas as part of the militant qualification'. See H. G. Wells, *Experiment in Autobiography: Discoveries and Conclusions of a Very Ordinary Brain (Since 1866) Volume II* (London: Faber and Faber, 1969), pp. 662–3.

16 Wells, *A Modern Utopia*, p. 96.

17 Ibid., p. 100.

18 Ibid., p. 244.

19 *Athenaeum*, 29 April 1905, p. 519.

20 H. G. Wells, *First and Last Things: A Confession of Faith and Rule of Life* (London: Watts and Co. Ltd, 1929), p. 21.

21 Norman and Jean MacKenzie, *The Time Traveller: The Life of H. G. Wells* (London: Weidenfeld and Nicholson, 1974), p. 298.

22 Wells, *Experiment in Autobiography*, p. 666.

23 H. G. Wells, *The War That Will End War* (London: Frank and Cecil Palmer, 1914), p. 9.

24 Ibid., p. 11.

25 Ibid., p. 37.

26 Ibid., pp. 55–6.

27 Ibid., pp. 57–8.

28 Ibid., p. 58.

29 Ibid., p. 47.

30 Ibid., p. 52.

31 Ibid., p. 59.

32 Ibid., p. 60.

33 Ibid., p. 94.

34 H. G. Wells, *The Peace of the World* (London: Daily Chronicle, 1916), p. 12.

35 Ibid., p. 91.

36 Ibid., p. 148.

37 Ibid., p. 113.

38 Ibid., p. 123.

39 H. G. Wells, *What Is Coming? A Forecast of Things after the War* (London: Cassell and Company Ltd, 1916), p. 22.

40 *English Review*, April 1917, pp. 382–3.

41 *Times Literary Supplement*, 22 February 1917, p. 89.

42 H. G. Wells, *War and the Future: Italy, France and Britain at War* (London: Cassell and Company Ltd, 1917), p. 28.

43 Ibid., pp. 27–8.

44 Ibid., p. 177.

45 Ibid., pp. 275–7.

46 Ibid., p. 287.

47 Ibid., p. 211.

48 Ibid., p. 215.
49 Ibid., p. 224.
50 Ibid., p. 297.
51 David C. Smith, *H. G. Wells: Desperately Mortal* (New Haven: Yale University Press, 1986), p. 231.
52 Richard M. Gamble, *The War for Righteousness: Progressive Christianity, the Great War, and the Rise of the Messianic Nation* (Washington: ISI Books, 2003), pp. 163–6.
53 'Mr Wells Describes "Renascant Religion"', *New York Times*, 13 May 1917.
54 E. W. Stead, 'A World Theocracy', *Review of Reviews*, July 1917, p. 69.
55 *Athenaeum*, July 1917, p. 345.
56 William Archer, *God and Mr Wells* (London: Watts and Co., 1917).
57 L. E. Binns, *Mr Wells' Invisible King: A Criticism* (New York: The MacMillan Company, 1919).
58 H. G. Wells, *God the Invisible King* (London: Cassell and Company Ltd, 1917), p. v.
59 Ibid., pp. vi–vii.
60 Ibid., pp. 6–8.
61 Ibid., p. xiii.
62 Ibid., p. 2.
63 Ibid., pp. 25–8.
64 Ibid., p. 87.
65 Ibid., pp. 47–8.
66 Ibid., p. 64.
67 Ibid., p. 67.
68 Ibid., pp. 80–1.
69 Ibid., p. 67.
70 Ibid., pp. 77–8.
71 Ibid., p. 115.
72 Ibid., p. 120.
73 Ibid., p. 121.
74 Ibid., p. 125.
75 Ibid., p. 129.
76 Ibid., p. 144.
77 Ibid., p. 185.
78 Ibid., p. 186.
79 Ibid., p. 188.
80 Ibid., p. 199.
81 Ibid., pp. 205–6.
82 H. G. Wells, *The Research Magnificent* (London: MacMillan and Co. Ltd, 1915), p. 394.
83 *English Review*, November 1915, p. 438.
84 Samuel Hynes, *A War Imagined: The First World War and English Culture* (New York: Atheneum, 1990), pp. 22–4.
85 *Athenaeum*, June 1915, p. 506.
86 H. G. Wells, *Boon, The Mind of the Race, The Wild Asses of the Devil, and The Last Trump* (London: T. Fisher Unwin Ltd, 1915), p. 334.
87 Ibid., p. 339.
88 *Times Literary Supplement*, 21 September 1916, p. 451.
89 MacKenzie, *The Time Traveller*, p. 311.
90 H. G. Wells, *Mr Britling Sees It Through* (London: MacMillan and Co. Ltd, 1916), p. 197.

91 Ibid., p. 344.
92 Ibid., p. 351.
93 Ibid., p. 395.
94 Ibid., p. 427.
95 Ibid., p. 432.
96 The *North American Review*, vol. 204, no. 733 (1916), pp. 939–41.
97 The *North American Review*, vol. 206, no. 744 (1917), pp. 786–92.
98 H. G. Wells, *The Soul of a Bishop* (New York: The MacMillan Company, 1917), p. 26.
99 Ibid., p. 26.
100 Ibid., p. 73.
101 Ibid., p. 74.
102 Ibid., p. 129.
103 Ibid., p. 185.
104 Ibid., p. 218.
105 Ibid., p. 220.
106 *Review of Reviews*, November 1917, p. 389.
107 *Times Literary Supplement*, 13 September 1917, p. 438.
108 H. G. Wells, *Joan and Peter* (Bath: Cadric Chivers Ltd, 1974), p. 318.
109 Ibid., p. 194.
110 *Saturday Review of Politics, Literature, Science and Art*, 5 October 1918, p. 917.
111 *Athenaeum*, October 1918, p. 438.
112 Ibid., p. 291.
113 Ibid., pp. 325–6.
114 Ibid., p. 350.
115 Ibid., pp. 355–8.
116 Ibid., p. 395.
117 Ibid., p. 398.
118 *English Review*, July 1919, p. 95.
119 H. G. Wells, *The Undying Fire: A Contemporary Novel* (London: Cassell and Company Ltd, 1919), p. 23.
120 Ibid., p. 151.
121 Ibid., p. 162.
122 Ibid., p. 167.
123 Ibid., p. 198.
124 Ibid., p. 228.
125 Ibid., p. 246.
126 H. G. Wells, *In The Fourth Year: Anticipations of a World Peace* (London: Chatto and Windus, 1918), pp. 111–12.
127 Ibid., p. 154.
128 Ibid., pp. 155–6.
129 H. G. Wells, *Russia in the Shadows* (New York: George H. Doran Company, 1921), p. 17.
130 Ibid., p. 18.
131 Ibid., p. 179.
132 *English Review*, July 1921, p. 79.
133 H. G. Wells, *The Salvaging of Civilisation* (London: Cassel and Company Ltd, 1921), p. 10.
134 Ibid., p. 80.
135 Ibid., p. 101.

136 Ibid., p. 102.
137 Ibid., p. 107.
138 Ibid., p. 110.
139 Ibid., p. 135.
140 The *Observer*, 29 August, p. 13.
141 H. G. Wells, *The Outline of History: Being a Plain History of Life and Mankind* (London: The Waverly Book Company Ltd, 1920), p. 85.
142 Ibid., p. 208.
143 *Times Literary Supplement*, 23 September 1920, p. 612.
144 Ibid., p. 436.
145 Ibid., p. 483.
146 Ibid., pp. 560–1.
147 Ibid., p. 578.
148 Ibid., p. 590.
149 Ibid., p. 608.
150 *Athenaeum*, November 1920, p. 690.
151 *English Review*, December 1922, p. 578.
152 See Philip Coupland 'H. G. Wells's "Liberal Fascism"' in Bloom, Harold ed., *H. G. Wells* (Chelsea House Publishers, 2005).

Conclusion

1 T. E. Lawrence, *Seven Pillars of Wisdom: A Triumph* (London: Penguin Books, 2000), p. 23.
2 Bertrand Russell, *Principles of Social Reconstruction* (London: Unwin Books, 1971), pp. 168–70.
3 Patrick Pearse in Seán Farrell Moran, *Patrick Pearse and the Politics of Redemption: The Mind of the Easter Rising, 1916* (Washington, DC: Catholic University of America Press, 1994), p. 152.
4 Victor Turner, *The Ritual Process. Structure and Anti Structure* (New York: Aldine de Gruyter, 1997), p. 95.
5 Ibid., p. 96.
6 See Anthony F. C. Wallace, *Revitalizations and Mazeways: Essays on Cultural Change, Volume 1* (Lincoln: University of Nebraska Press, 2003), p. 170.

Bibliography

Journals and periodicals cited

Athenaeum

Blast

Colliers Magazine

Economic Journal

Egoist

English Review

Little Review

Manchester Guardian

The New Age

New York Times

North American Review

Observer

Outlook

Pall Mall Gazette

Review of Reviews

Saturday Review of Politics, Literature, Science and Art

Sociological Review

The *Times*

Times Literary Supplement

The *Tyro*

Works cited and consulted

Anderson, Benedict, *Imagined Communities: Reflections on the Origins and Spread of Nationalism*, Revised Edition (London: Verso, 2002).

Archer, William, *God and Mr Wells* (London: Watts and Co., 1917).

Ardis, Ann J., *Modernism and Cultural Conflict, 1880–1922* (Cambridge: Cambridge University Press, 2002).

Batchelor, John, *H. G. Wells* (Cambridge: Cambridge University Press, 1985).

Baudelaire, Charles (translated by James McGowan), *The Flowers of Evil* (Oxford: Oxford University Press, 1993).

— (translated by P. E. Charvet), *Selected Writings on Art and Literature* (London: Penguin, 2006).

Bauman, Zygmunt, *Modernity and Ambivalence* (Cambridge: Polity Press, 1991).

Benjamin, Walter (translated by Harry Zorn), *Illuminations* (London: Pimlico, 1999).

Bergonzi, Bernard, *Heroes Twilight: A Study in the Literature of the Great War,* Third Edition (Manchester: Carcanet Press Ltd, 1996).

Berman, Marshall, *All that is Solid Melts into Air. The Experience of Modernity* (London: Verso, 1982).

Biddiss, Michael D., *The Age of the Masses: Ideas and Society in Europe Since 1870* (London: Penguin Books, 1977).

Binns, L. E., *Mr Wells' Invisible King: A Criticism* (New York: The MacMillan Company, 1919).

Bradbury, Malcolm and McFarlane, James (eds), *Modernism. A Guide to European Literature 1890-1930* (London: Penguin Books, 1991).

Bridgewater, Patrick, *Nietzsche in Anglosaxony: A Study of Nietzsche's Impact on English and American Literature* (Leicester: Leicester University Press, 1972).

Brome, Vincent, *H. G. Wells: A Biography* (Thirsk: House of Straus Ltd, 2001).

Brooker, Peter and Thacker, Andrew, *The Oxford Critical and Cultural History of Modernist Magazines: Volume I: Britain and Ireland 1880-1955* (Oxford: Oxford University Press, 2009).

Brown, Ivor, *Old and Young* (London: Bodley Head, 1971).

Buitenhuis, Peter, *The Great War of Words: Literature as Propaganda 1914-18 and After* (London: B. T. Batsford Ltd, 1989).

Burger, Thomas, *Max Weber's Theory of Concept Formation: History, Laws, and Ideal Types* (Durham: Duke University Press, 1976).

Calinescu, Matei, *Five Faces of Modernity: Modernism, Avant-Garde, Decadence, Kitsch, Postmodernism* (Durham: Duke University Press, 1987).

Carey, John, *Intellectuals and the Masses: Pride and Prejudice among the Literary Intelligentsia 1880-1939* (London: Faber and Faber, 1992).

Carpenter, L. P., *G.D.H. Cole: An Intellectual Biography* (Cambridge: University Press, 1973).

Childs, Peter, *Modernism* (London: Routledge, 2000).

Cole, G. D. H., *Labour in Wartime* (London: G. Bell and Sons, Ltd, 1915).

—, *The World of Labour: A Discussion of the Present and Future of Trade Unionism* (London: G. Bell and Sons, Ltd, 1917).

Collini, Stefan, *Absent Minds: Intellectuals in Britain* (Oxford: Oxford University Press, 2006).

Corbett, David Peter, "'Grief With a Yard Wide Grin': War and Wyndham Lewis's Tyros' in Corbett, ed., *Wyndham Lewis and the Art of Modern War* (Cambridge: Cambridge University Press, 1988).

Coren, Michael, *The Invisible Man: The Life and Liberties of H. G. Wells* (London: Bloomsbury Publishing Ltd, 1993).

Coupland, Philip, 'H. G. Wells' "Liberal Fascism"', *Journal of Contemporary History,* vol. 35, no. 4 (2000).

Csengeri, Karen (ed.) T. E. Hulme, *The Collected Writings of T. E. Hulme* (Oxford: Clarendon Press, 1994).

Dangerfield, George, *The Strange Death of Liberal England* (New York: Capricorn Books, 1961).

DeGroot, Gerard J., *Blighty: British Society in the Era of the Great War* (London: Longman, 1996).

Dickson, Lovat, *H. G. Wells: His Turbulent Life and Times* (London: MacMillan, 1971).

Dorril, Stephen, *Blackshirt: Sir Oswald Mosley and British Fascism* (London: Penguin Books, 2006).

Edwards, Paul, *Wyndham Lewis: Painter and Writer* (New Haven: Yale University Press, 2000).

Eksteins, Modris, *Rites of Spring: The Great War and the Birth of the Modern Age* (London: Papermac, 2000).

Ferguson, Niall, *The Pity of War* (London: Penguin, 1999).

Ferguson, Robert, *The Short Sharp Life of T. E. Hulme* (London: Allen Lane, 2002).

Ferro, Marc (translated by Nicole Stone), *The Great War, 1914-1918* (London: Routledge, 2002).

Field, Frank, *British and French Writers of the First World War: Comparative Studies in Cultural History* (Cambridge: Cambridge University Press, 1991).

Foot, Michael, *H. G. The History of Mr Wells* (London: Black Swan, 1996).

Ford, Boris (ed.), *The New Pelican Guide to English Literature: 7. From James to Eliot* (Middlesex: Penguin, 1983).

Foshay, Toby, *Wyndham Lewis and the Avant-Garde: The Politics of the Intellect* (Montreal: McGill-Queen's University Press).

Fussell, Paul, *The Great War and Modern Memory* (Oxford: Oxford University Press, 2000).

Gamble, Richard M., *The War for Righteousness: Progressive Christianity, the Great War, and the Rise of the Messianic Nation* (Wilmington: ISI Books, 2003).

Gąsiorek, Andrzej, *Wyndham Lewis and Modernism* (Tavistock: Northcote House Publishers Ltd, 2004).

Gay, Peter, *The Cultivation of Hatred: The Bourgeois Experience from Victoria to Freud* (London: W. W. Norton and Company, 1994).

—, *Modernism. The Lure of Heresy from Baudelaire to Beckett and Beyond* (London: William Heinemann, 2007).

Gennep, Arthur van, *The Rites of Passage* (London: Routledge, 1960).

Geoff Gilbert, 'Shell-Shock, Anti-Semitism, and the Agency of the Avant-Garde', in Corbett, ed., *Wyndham Lewis and the Art of Modern War* (Cambridge: Cambridge University Press, 1988).

Gerth, Hans and Mills, C. Wright (eds), Max Weber, *From Max Weber: Essays in Sociology* (London: Routledge, 2004).

Giddens, Anthony, *Modernity and Self-Identity. Self and Society in the Late Modern Age* (Stanford: Stanford University Press, 1991).

Glass, S. T., *The Responsible Society: Ten Ideas of the English Guild Socialist* (London: Longman, 1966).

Görtschacher, Wolfgang, *Little Magazine Profiles: The Little Magazines in Great Britain 1939–1993* (Salzburg: University of Salzburg, 1993).

Griffin, Roger, *The Nature of Fascism* (London: Routledge, 1993).

—, *Fascism* (Oxford: Oxford University Press, 1995).

—, *Modernism and Fascism: The Sense of a Beginning under Mussolini and Hitler* (Basingstoke: Palgrave, 2007).

Hamilton, Ian, *The Little Magazines: A Study of Six Editors* (London: Weidenfeld and Nicolson, 1976).

Hardegen, Christine, 'Actors and Spectators in the Theatre of War: Wyndham Lewis's First World War Art and Literature', in Corbett, ed., *Wyndham Lewis and the Art of Modern War* (Cambridge: Cambridge University Press, 1988).

Harvey, David, *The Condition of Postmodernity: An Enquiry into the Origins of Cultural Change* (Oxford: Blackwell, 1990).

Hobsbawm, Eric, *The Age of Revolution: Europe 1789–1848* (London: Abacus, 1962).

—, *The Age of Empire, 1875–1914* (London: Abacus, 1994).

Hobsbawm, Eric and Ranger, Terence (eds), *The Invention of Tradition* (Cambridge: Cambridge University Press, 1992).

Hobson, S. G., *Pilgrim to the Left: Memoirs of a Modern Revolutionist* (London: Edward Arnold and Co., 1938).

Hoffman, Frederick J., Allen, Charles and Ulrich, Carolyn F., *The Little Magazine: A History and a Bibliography* (Princeton: Princeton University Press, 1946).

Hughes, H. Stuart, *History as Art and as Science. Twin Vistas on the Past* (Chicago: The University of Chicago Press, 1975).

—, *Consciousness and Society: The Reformation of European Social Thought 1890–1930* (Brighton: The Harvester Press, 1979).

Hulme, T. E., 'Translator's Preface', in Georges Sorel, *Reflections on Violence* (London: Allan and Unwin, 1916).

—, *Selected Writings* (Manchester: Carcanet, 1998).

Hutchinson, Frances and Burkitt, Brian, *The Political Economy of Social Credit and Guild Socialism* (Charlbury: John Carpenter Publishing, 2005).

Hynes, Samuel, *Edwardian Occasions: Essays on English Writing in the Early Twentieth Century* (London: Routledge and Kegan Paul, 1972).

—, *A War Imagined: The First World War and English Culture* (New York: Atheneum, 1990).

Jackson, Holbrook, *The Eighteen Nineties: A Review of Art and Ideas at the Close of the Nineteenth Century* (Franklin: Tantallon Press, 2002).

Jackson, Paul, '"Union or Death!": Gavrilo Princip, Young Bosnia and the Role of "Sacred Time" in the Dynamics of Nationalist Terrorism', *Totalitarian Movements and Political Religions*, vol. 7, no. 1 (2006).

—, '"The Exquisite Moment": May Sinclair's Vision of a New Spiritual Reality Forged through War', in Paul Jackson *Minerva: Women and War*, vol. 1, no. 2 (2007).

Jameson, Frederick, *Fables of Aggression: Wyndham Lewis, the Modernist as Fascist* (Berkeley: University of California Press, 1979).

Joll, James, *The Origins of the First World War*, Second Edition (London: Longman, 1992).

Jones, Ernest, 'War and Individual Psychology', *The Sociological Review*, vol. 8, no. 3 (July 1916).

Keegan, John, *The First World War* (London: Pimlico, 1999).

Kermode, Frank, *The Sense of an Ending: Studies in the Theory of Fiction* (Oxford: Oxford University Press, 2000).

Kern, Steven, *The Culture of Time and Space, 1880–1918* (Cambridge: Harvard University Press, 2000).

Lawrence, T. E., *Seven Pillars of Wisdom: A Triumph* (London: Penguin Books, 2000).

Leed, Eric J., *No Man's Land: Combat and Identity in World War I* (New York: Cambridge University Press, 1981).

Levenson, Michael H., *A Genealogy of Modernism: A Study of English Literary Doctrine 1908–1922* (Cambridge: Cambridge University Press, 1986).

Levenson, Michael (ed.), *The Cambridge Companion to Modernism* (Cambridge: Cambridge University Press, 1999).

Lewis, Wyndham, *Hitler* (London: Chatto and Windus, 1931).

—, *Rude Assignment: A Narrative of my Career Up-to-date* (London: Hutchinson, 1950).

—, *Blasting and Bombardiering: An Autobiography (1914–1926)* (London: John Calder, 1982).

—, *The Caliph's Design: Architects! Where is Your Vortex?* (Santa Barbara: Black Sparrow Press, 1986).

—, *Tarr: The 1918 Version* (Santa Rosa: Black Sparrow Press, 1990).

Linehan, Thomas, *British Fascism, 1918–1939: Parties, Ideology and Culture* (Manchester: Manchester University Press, 2000).

—, *Communism in Britain, 1920–39: From the Cradle to the Grave* (Manchester: Manchester University Press, 2007).

Lipsey, Roger, *Coomaraswamy 3: His Life and Works* (New Jersey: Princeton University Press, 1977).

MacKenzie, Norman and Jean, *The Time Traveller: The Life of H. G. Wells* (London: Weidenfeld and Nicholson, 1974).

Maeztu, Ramiro de, *Authority, Liberty and Function in the Light of the War* (London: George Allen and Unwin, 1916).

Martin, Wallace, *The New Age Under Orage: Chapters in English Cultural History* (Manchester: Manchester University Press, 1967).

Marwick, Arthur, *The Deluge: British Society and the First World War* (London: MacMillan, 1975).

Masterman, C. F. G., *The Condition of England* (London: The Shenval Press, 1960).

Moran, Seán Farrell, *Patrick Pearse and the Politics of Redemption: The Mind of the Easter Rising, 1916* (Washington: Catholic University of America Press, 1994).

Morris, William, *News from Nowhere and Other Writings* (London: Penguin, 1998).

Morrison, Mark S., *The Public Face of Modernism: Little Magazines, Audiences and Reception 1905–1920* (Madison: University of Wisconsin Press, 2001).

Mosse, George L., *The Culture of Western Europe: The Nineteenth and Twentieth Centuries, an Introduction* (London: John Murray, 1963).

—, *Fallen Soldiers. Reshaping the Memory of the World Wars* (Oxford: Oxford University Press, 1990).

Muir, Edwin, *An Autobiography* (Edinburgh: Cannongate Classics, 2000).

Munton, Alan, 'Wyndham Lewis: From Proudhon to Hitler (and back): The Strange Political Journey of Wyndham Lewis', *E-rea*, vol. 4, no. 2 (2006).

Murray, Brian, *H. G. Wells* (New York: Continuum, 1990).

Nichols, Peter, *Modernisms: A Literary Guide* (Basingstoke: MacMillan, 1995).

Nietzsche, Friedrich (translated by R. J. Hollingdale), *Thus Spoke Zarathustra: A Book for Everyone and No One* (London: Penguin, 1969).

— (translated by Marion Faber), *Beyond Good and Evil* (Oxford: Oxford University Press, 1998).

— (translated by Douglas Smith), *The Birth Of Tragedy* (Oxford: Oxford University Press, 2000).

Normand, Tom, 'Wyndham Lewis, the Anti-War Artist', in Corbett, ed., *Wyndham Lewis and the Art of Modern War* (Cambridge: Cambridge University Press, 1988).

O'Keeffe, Paul, *Some Sort of Genius: A Life of Wyndham Lewis* (London: Pimlico, 2001).

Orage, A. R., *Friedrich Nietzsche, the Dionysian Spirit of the Age* (London: no publisher, 1906).

—, *Consciousness: Animal, Human and Superhuman* (London: no publisher, 1907).

—, *An Alphabet of Economics* (London: T. Fisher Unwin, Ltd, 1917).

Orage, A. R. (ed.) and Hobson, S. G., *National Guilds: An Inquiry into the Wage System and the Way Out* (London: G. Bell and Sons, Ltd, 1914).

Osborne, Peter, *The Politics of Time: Modernity and the Avant-Garde* (London: Verso, 1995).

—, *Philosophy in Cultural Theory* (London: Routledge, 2000).

Partington, John S., 'The Death of the Static: H. G. Wells and the Kinetic Utopia', *Journal of Utopian Studies*, vol. 11, no. 2 (2000).

—, 'The Time Machine and A Modern Utopia: The Static and Kinetic Utopias of the Early H. G. Wells', *Journal of Utopian Studies*, vol. 13, no. 1 (2002).

—, 'H. G. Wells's Eugenic Thinking of the 1930s and 1940s', *Journal of Utopian Studies*, vol. 14, no. 1 (2003).

Peart-Binns, John S., *Maurice B. Reckitt: A Life* (Basingstoke: Bowerdean and Marshall Pickering, 1988).

Penty, A. J., *The Restoration of the Gild System* (London: Swan Sonnenschein and Co., Ltd, 1906).

—, *Old Worlds for New: A Study of the Post-Industrial State* (London: George Allen and Unwin, Ltd, 1917).

Peppis, Paul, '"Surrounded by a Multitude of Other Blasts": Vorticism and the Great War', *Modernism/Modernity*, vol. 4, no. 2 (1997).

Pick, Daniel, *Faces of Degeneration: A European Disorder, c.1848–c.1918* (Cambridge: Cambridge University Press, 1989).

—, *War Machine: The Rationalisation of Slaughter in the Modern Age* (London: Yale University Press, 1993).

Por, Odon, *Fascism* (London: Labour Publishing Company, 1923).

—, *Guilds and Co-operatives in Italy* (London: Labour Publishing Company, 1923).

Reckitt, Maurice B. and Bechhofer, C. E., *The Meaning of National Guilds* (London: Cecil Palmer and Hayward, 1918).

Redman, Tim, *Ezra Pound and Italian Fascism* (Cambridge: Cambridge University Press, 1991).

Robb, George, *British Culture and the First World War* (Basingstoke: Palgrave, 2002).

Romein, Jan (translated by Arnold J. Pomerands), *The Watershed of Two Eras: Europe in 1900* (Middletown: Wesleyan University Press, 1978).

Roshwald, Aveil and Stites, Richard (eds), *European Culture in the Great War: The Arts, Entertainment and Propaganda, 1914–1918* (Cambridge: Cambridge University Press, 2002).

Russell, Bertrand, *Principles of Social Reconstruction* (London: Unwin Books, 1971).

Schleifer, Ronald, *Modernism and Time. The Logic of Abundance in Literature, Science, and Culture* (Cambridge: Cambridge University Press, 2000).

Scholes, Robert and Wulfman, Clifford, *Modernism in the Magazines: An Introduction* (New Haven: Yale University Press, 2010).

Schusterman, Richard, 'Remembering Hulme: A Neglected Philosopher-Critic-Poet', *Journal of the History of Ideas*, vol. 46, no. 4 (1985).

Searle, Geoffrey R., *A New England? Peace and War, 1886–1918* (Oxford: Clarendon Press, 2004).

Sherry, Vincent, *The Great War and the Language of Modernism* (Oxford: Oxford University Press, 2003).

Smith, David C., *H. G. Wells: Desperately Mortal* (New Haven: Yale University Press, 1986).

Steel, Tom, *Alfred Orage and the Leeds Art Club 1893–1923* (Mitcham: The Orage Press, 2009).

Steven, Martin, *The Price of Pity: Poetry, History and Myth in the Great War* (London: Leo Cooper, 1996).

Stevenson, David, *1914–1918: The History of the First World War* (London: Penguin, 2005).

Stone, Dan, *Breeding Superman: Nietzsche, Race and Eugenics in Edwardian and Interwar Britain* (Liverpool: Liverpool University Press, 2002).

Stone, Norman, *Europe Transformed 1878–1919* (London: Fontana Press, 1985).

Stromberg, Roland, *Realism, Naturalism, and Symbolism: Modes of Thought and Expression in Europe, 1848–1914* (London: MacMillan, 1968).

—, *Redemption by War: The Intellectuals and 1914* (Kansas: Regents Press of Kansas, 1982).

Summerfield, Henry, *That Myriad-Minded Man: A Biography of George William Russell 'A.E.'* (Gerrards Cross: Colin Smythe, 1975).

Surette, Leon, *Pound in Purgatory: From Economic Radicalism to Anti-Semitism* (Urbana: University of Illinois Press, 1999).

Susser, Leslie, 'Right Wings over Britain: T. E. Hulme and the Intellectual Revolt against Democracy', in Sternhell, Z. (ed.), *The Intellectual Revolt Against Liberal Democracy, 1870–1945* (Jerusalem: Israel Academy of Sciences and Humanities, 1996).

Taylor, Gary, *Orage and The New Age* (Sheffield: Sheffield Hallam University Press, 2000).

Thatcher, David S., *Nietzsche in England, 1890–1914* (Toronto: University of Toronto Press, 1970).

Thurlow, Richard, 'The Return of Jeremiah: The Rejected Knowledge of Sir Oswald Mosley in the 1930s', in Lunn, K. and Thurlow, R. eds., *British Fascism: Essays on the Radical Right in Inter-War Britain* (Oxford: Billig and Sons, Ltd, 1980).

—, *Fascism in Britain: From Oswald Mosley's Blackshirts to the National Front* (London: I. B. Tauris, 1998).

Tickner, Lisa, 'The Popular Culture of Kermesse: Lewis, Painting, and Performance 1912–13', *Modernism/modernity*, vol. 4, no. 2 (1997).

Tönnies, Ferdinand (translated by Charles P. Loomis), *Community and Society (Gemeinschaft und Gesellschaft)* (New York: Dover, 2002).

Turner, Victor, *The Ritual Process. Structure and Anti-Structure* (New York: Aldine de Gruyter, 1997).

Villis, Tom, *Reaction and the Avant-Garde: The Revolt Against Liberal Democracy in Early Twentieth-Century Britain* (London: Tauris Academic Studies, 2006).

Wallace, Anthony F. C., *Revitalizations and Mazeways: Essays on Cultural Change, Volume 1* (Lincoln: University of Nebraska Press, 2003).

Warger, W. Warren, *H. G. Wells and the World State* (New Haven: Yale University Press, 1961).

Welch, Louise, *Orage with Gurdjieff in America* (London: Routledge, 1982).

Wells, H. G., *Anticipations of the Reaction of Mechanical and Scientific Progress upon Human Life and Thought* (London: Chapman and Hall, 1914).

—, *The War That Will End War* (London: Frank and Cecil Palmer, 1914).

—, *Boon, The Mind of the Race, The Wild Asses of the Devil, and the Last Trump* (London: T. Fisher Unwin Ltd, 1915).

—, *The Research Magnificent* (London: MacMillan and Co. Ltd, 1915).

—, *Mr Britling Sees it Through* (London: MacMillan and Co. Ltd, 1916).

—, *The Peace of the World* (London: Daily Chronicle, 1916).

—, *What Is Coming? A Forecast of Things After the War* (London: Cassell and Company Ltd, 1916).

—, *The Elements of Reconstruction* (London: Nisbet and Co. Ltd, 1917).

—, *God the Invisible King* (London: Cassell and Company Ltd, 1917).

—, *The Soul of a Bishop* (New York: The MacMillan Company, 1917).

—, *War and the Future: Italy, France and Britain at War* (London: Cassell and Company Ltd, 1917).

—, *In The Fourth Year: Anticipations of a World Peace* (London: Chatto and Windus, 1918).

—, *The Undying Fire: A Contemporary Novel* (London: Cassell and Company Ltd, 1919).

—, *The Outline of History: Being a Plain History of Life and Mankind* (London: The Waverly Book Company Ltd, 1920).

—, *Russia in the Shadows* (New York: George H. Doran Company, 1921).

—, *The Salvaging of Civilisation* (London: Cassel and Company Ltd, 1921).

—, *First and Last Things: A Confession of Faith and Rule of Life* (London: Watts and Co. Ltd, 1929).

—, *Experiment in Autobiography: Discoveries and Conclusions of a Very Ordinary Brain (Since 1866) Volume II* (London: Faber and Faber, 1969).

—, *Joan and Peter* (Bath: Cadric Chivers Ltd, 1974).

—, *A Modern Utopia* (London: Penguin Books Ltd, 2005).

—, *Tono-Bungay* (London: Penguin Classics, 2005).

—, *The Time Machine* (London: Penguin, 2006).

Wilkinson, Alan, *The Church of England and the First World War* (London: SCM Press Ltd, 1996).

Williams, Louise Blakeney, *Modernism and the Ideology of History: Literature, Politics, and the Past* (Cambridge: Cambridge University Press, 2002).

Williams, Raymond, *Culture and Society: Coleridge to Orwell* (London: The Hogarth Press, 1982).

Wilson, Trevor, *The Myriad Faces of War: Britain and the Great War, 1914–1918* (Cambridge: Polity, 1986).

Winter, Jay, *Sites of Memory, Sites of Mourning: The Great War in European Cultural History* (Cambridge: Cambridge University Press, 2000).

Winter, J. M., *The Great War and the British People,* Second Edition (Basingstoke: Palgrave, 2003).

Wohl, Robert, *The Generation of 1914* (London: Weidenfeld and Nicolson, 1980).

—, 'Heart of Darkness: Modernism and Its Historians', *The Journal of Modern History,* vol. 74, no. 3 (September 2002).

Wright, Anthony W., 'Guild Socialism Revisited', *Journal of Contemporary History,* vol. 9, no. 1 (1974).

Index

Lightning Source UK Ltd.
Milton Keynes UK
UKOW04n0827260914

239223UK00007B/108/P